M000223481

DEMOCRACIES DIVIDED

DEMOCRACIES DIVIDED

The Global Challenge of
Political Polarization

Edited by
Thomas Carothers
Andrew O'Donohue

BROOKINGS INSTITUTION PRESS
Washington, D.C.

Copyright © 2019
THE BROOKINGS INSTITUTION
1775 Massachusetts Avenue, N.W.,
Washington, D.C. 20036
www.brookings.edu

All rights reserved. No part of this publication may be reproduced or transmitted in any form or by any means without permission in writing from the Brookings Institution Press.

The Brookings Institution is a private nonprofit organization devoted to research, education, and publication on important issues of domestic and foreign policy. Its principal purpose is to bring the highest quality independent research and analysis to bear on current and emerging policy problems. Interpretations or conclusions in Brookings publications should be understood to be solely those of the authors.

Library of Congress Cataloging-in-Publication data are available.
ISBN 978-0-8157-3721-6 (paperback : alk. paper)
ISBN 978-0-8157-3722-3 (ebook)

9 8 7 6 5 4 3 2 1

Typeset in Adobe Jensen Pro

Composition by Elliott Beard

Contents

PART III
Elite Polarization in Relatively Homogenous Societies

PART IV
Staying Clear?

PART V
Conclusion

DEMOCRACIES DIVIDED

Introduction

THOMAS CAROTHERS
ANDREW O'DONOHUE

At the end of the twentieth century, many political observers assumed that the coming decades would be a time of democratic triumph, with the remarkable democratic wave of the 1980s and 1990s coming to full fruition. Instead, democratic stagnation and setbacks have marked the first two decades of this century to such an extent that today, talk of a global democratic crisis is widespread. New and old democracies alike are confronting a daunting array of internal and external challenges, from the crumbling of public support for long-established political parties and the swelling popularity of illiberal politicians to the growing assertiveness and influence of authoritarian powers and ideas across borders. Recent developments in democracies around the world make clear that political polarization—manifested in increasingly harsh divides between opposing political camps and diminishing shared political ground—is a crucial part of this troubling picture.

Political polarization, particularly in the United States, tends to be studied as a unique national pathology. Yet as this volume demonstrates, it is a widespread phenomenon, with common negative consequences for democracy across diverse national contexts. It routinely weakens respect for democratic norms, corrodes basic legislative processes, undermines the nonpartisan stature of the judiciary, and fuels public disaffection with political parties. It exacerbates intolerance and discrimination, diminishes societal trust, and increases violence throughout the society. Moreover, it reinforces and entrenches itself, dragging countries into a downward spiral of anger and division for which there are no easy remedies.

A quick global tour highlights how pervasive polarization is among democracies today and how serious its effects frequently are. After a period of generally low political polarization in Latin America during the 1990s, high levels of divisive partisanship are damaging various Latin American democracies. Venezuela was for decades one of the most stable democracies in the region, but an intense, irreconcilable split between the governing forces of the left and the opposition has torn the society apart. Bolivian politics have undergone a profound change in the past decade, as the collapse of many traditional parties has reconfigured political competition around a deep cleavage based on ethnicity and culture. Colombia has become bitterly divided over the 2016 Peace Accord between the government and the Revolutionary Armed Forces of Colombia. With the 2018 election of President Jair Bolsonaro, a far-right populist who ran a stridently polarizing campaign, Brazil may have entered a phase of serious polarization. Latin America specialist Steven Levitsky argues that Chile, El Salvador, Mexico, and Peru also show signs of growing polarization.[1]

South and Southeast Asia exhibit multiple serious cases of political polarization. Under the leadership of Prime Minister Narendra Modi, India has experienced increasingly polarized conflict between a sociopolitical vision rooted in Hindu nationalism and a more secular and pluralist alternative. During the past two decades, neighboring Bangladesh has descended into harsh polarization between two staunchly opposed political camps. Before the 2006 and 2014 military coups, Thailand's democracy was wracked by a profound fissure between two competing sides, popularly known as the "yellow shirts" and "red shirts," that were split by social class, region, and other identity markers. Although Indonesia has enjoyed a generally positive democratizing run since the fall of strongman President Suharto in 1998, recent elections have been marked by an upsurge in divisive and exclusivist Islamist rhetoric.

In the Middle East, some of the political forces and energy released in the 2011 Arab Spring have resulted in bitterly polarized polities. Egypt's brief episode of open multiparty competition after the fall of President Hosni Mubarak in 2011 descended into profound and violent polarization between Islamist political forces and their opponents. The eruption of protests against Syrian president Bashar al-Assad in 2011 triggered a hellish descent into civil war. Despite hopes that the rise of the Islamist Justice and Development Party in Turkey might usher in a period of inclusive democracy, Turkish politics have instead become a domain of intense division, anger, and conflict between the ruling party and its opponents. Competitive party politics in Iraq, Israel, Lebanon, and Palestine have also been marked by significant levels of polarization.

Various sub-Saharan African countries have lived for decades with intense polarization, sometimes within democratic frameworks and sometimes within authoritarian or semiauthoritarian systems. An example of the former is Kenya, where a political system dominated off and on by contending tribal groups erupted into serious electoral violence in 2007. The country has lived since then with a precarious political settlement between two deeply divided sides. Burundi, Cameroon, Uganda, and Zimbabwe all exemplify the latter pattern. An especially serious case is Côte d'Ivoire, where divisions along religious and regional lines over the issue of Ivorian national identity have been mobilized in two civil wars.[2]

Rising polarization is not just a developing world story. Decades-old patterns of relatively consensual competition in Europe between center-right and center-left parties are giving way to greater political polarization as populist forces challenge traditional political actors and norms. Poland, for example, has surprised many political observers by moving from what looked like a relatively smooth process of democratic consolidation into severe polarization. Escalating tensions there between a right-wing populist party and the antagonized opposition camp pose a serious threat to the independence of the Polish judiciary and other vital democratic institutions. In France, a multiparty system long characterized by alternation of power between moderate forces on the left and right dissolved in the presidential elections of 2017, which resulted in a polarizing contest between a new centrist formation, En Marche, and the right-wing National Front (as of 2018, National Rally). In Great Britain, the 2016 referendum on whether the nation should leave the European Union opened up a startlingly deep divide between "Remainers" and "Leavers" and threw the country into what has become protracted political conflict and dysfunction. Other European democracies have also witnessed serious polarization recently as a result of rising populist forces, as in Greece and Hungary, or have long been mired in communal divisions, as in Belgium and Bosnia and Herzegovina.

In North America as well, rising levels of partisanship and polarization along left-right lines have unsettled democracies long known for their relative political stability. In Canada, particularly since the reconsolidation of the country's party system in 2004, the parties have grown further apart ideologically, and partisan animosities have ramped up throughout the society. The United States is suffering to an even greater extent from a widening political and social divide that has grown acute in recent years. For many American political observers, polarization underlies many of the maladies afflicting U.S. democracy, from institutional gridlock to diminished sociocultural trust. In the words of former U.S. senator Jeff Flake, "Tribalism is ruining us. It is tearing our country apart. It is no way for sane adults to act."[3]

To be sure, polarization is not everywhere in the democratic world. In East Asia, Japan has avoided severe polarization, whether as a result of certain sociocultural traditions, electoral rules, or the structure of the party landscape. In Latin America, Ecuador's president, Lenín Moreno, has made notable strides to rebuild consensus and temper political divisions that his predecessor aggravated. In the Middle East, Tunisia stands out as a case in which competitive electoral politics have not devolved into irreconcilable divisions. In Europe, some countries, like Ireland, Norway, and Portugal, show few signs of growing polarization. Yet the relative scarcity of positive cases attests to how widespread and consequential political polarization in democracies has become globally.

Analytic Complexities

At first view, political polarization appears to be a relatively straightforward concept: a country's political life is polarized to the extent that competing political forces diverge in their ideas and actions and lack any significant common ground. Nonetheless, upon closer examination it presents significant analytic complexities. One important puzzle concerns the line between positive and negative levels of polarization. A certain amount of polarization in a democratic system is normal given that parties compete hard with each other, seek to build their own loyal constituencies, and frequently distinguish themselves by having distinctive programmatic agendas. Especially in new and emerging democracies that are trying to build stable party systems, some degree of polarization may be useful. As Noam Lupu argues:

> Party polarization may strengthen party brands and clarify voters' choices. . . . Presented with a clear set of choices among parties, citizens may also form stronger party attachments. In developing democracies—where democratic competition and party attachments are nascent—clear choices and stronger party attachments may bolster electoral stability.[4]

However, when polarization reaches a certain degree of intensity, it can corrode democratic systems in the ways described above. Some ideological difference between competing parties is normal, but when does the breadth or depth of the divide become harmful? Partisan loyalties and differing programmatic visions among voters can help stabilize a party system, but when are these loyalties so unchanging and visions so antithetical that they undermine democracy? Not only is any easily identifiable measuring stick for differentiating helpful from harmful polarization elusive, but also the answer will surely depend upon the national context.[5] In Great Britain, for example, the polarization in the 1980s between Thatcherite conservatism and the opposing Labour camp did not tear down the walls of British democracy. Yet that same degree of ideological distance and societal division might well have provoked violent conflict in a society with weaker institutions and a less-established tradition of democratic pluralism.

Another complexity is that polarization can exist at different levels. Political scientists distinguish between elite polarization and mass polarization, an intuitively clear distinction.[6] The parameters of these categories, however, are difficult to define. Elite polarization usually refers to polarization among formal political actors—political parties and politicians—or institutions populated by these actors, such as legislatures. Yet the boundaries of this elite category are fluid. Some analysts persuasively note that the label of elite should include organizations that advocate or lobby for political agendas, as well as prominent media figures—such as talk radio hosts in the United States—or other opinion makers who influence political life.[7] Some such organizations and individuals are identifiably elite, but others may be grassroots-based or grassroots-oriented, and thus fall more ambiguously within this category. Here, too, different national contexts will have different conceptions of what is considered the domain of elite polarization.

The category of mass polarization, also referred to sometimes as societal polarization, similarly presents definitional issues.[8] Some analysts distinguish the politically informed and engaged public from the less informed and less engaged public.[9] Intense polarization might occur among politically informed citizens of a country, while large numbers of less engaged citizens might well remain mostly unaffected by such divisions. Looked at with a focus on engaged citizens, the country could be said to suffer from considerable societal polarization, yet the society as a whole might not appear to be all that polarized. National differences in the potential meaning of key terms such as the "informed" or "engaged" public are vast here as well, and a single concept of mass polarization would stretch uneasily across varied contexts.

A Focus on Severe Polarization

The chapters in this volume investigate and assess when and how polarization becomes a negative force in democracies, with a special focus on the phenomenon of *severe polarization*. To help define what constitutes severe polarization (as opposed to lesser though still potentially harmful polarization), this study draws upon the path-breaking recent work on comparative polarization by Jennifer McCoy and Murat Somer.[10] These authors define severe, or what they also call "pernicious," polarization as "a process whereby the normal multiplicity of differences in the society increasingly align along a single dimension, cross-cutting differences become reinforcing, and people increasingly perceive and describe politics and society in terms of 'us' versus 'them.'"[11] In this definition, "the key feature of polarization is not necessarily ideological or social distance, which most conventional definitions emphasize. Rather, it is how the process of polarization simplifies the normal complexity of politics and social relations. *Polarization does so by aligning otherwise unrelated divisions, emasculating cross-cutting cleavages, and dividing society and politics into two separate, opposing, and unyielding blocks* [emphasis added]."[12] In a related article with Tahmina Rahman, they note that in cases of severe polarization, "distance between groups moves beyond principled issue-based differences to a *social identity* [emphasis added]."[13]

This definition pinpoints the key feature of the sort of polarization gripping many democracies today: a single cleavage dominating pluralistic political life, overriding other cleavages, effacing countervailing links among political and societal actors, and creating a powerful dynamic of irreconcilable opposition between camps that question or even deny each other's legitimacy. This definition, however, does not provide a straightforward empirical basis for distinguishing between severe and nonsevere cases of polarization. It is difficult, for example, to assess and measure the extent to which cross-cutting cleavages have weakened.

To help reach these judgments about when polarization has become rooted in social identities and become severe, this volume uses three criteria that are part of or follow from McCoy and Somer's definition. These criteria provide useful observable indicators for determining whether polarization is severe. First, severe polarization *fuses elite and mass polarization*, creating large opposing blocks that comprise both elites and nonelites. Thus, acrimonious rivalries within the political elite alone do not constitute severe polarization. A crucial component of this first criterion is that severe polarization has a *strong affective dimension* at the mass level. That is, the opposing camps differ rancorously not just in their specific political opinions but more broadly in their sociocultural outlooks, to the extent that individuals dislike those on the other side and feel they cannot peacefully coexist with them on a personal level in friendships or marriages.

Second, severe polarization is structured around a *binary division*, meaning that a country has become split into two large camps that dominate political life. Each camp need not fall under a single party banner and may instead consist of multiple parties, united by little more than their opposition to the other side. Crucially, however, countries where a small extremist party or group emerges yet remains at the edges of political life, deeply at odds with the mainstream, are not severely polarized by this volume's definition. In Germany, for example, the divide between the right-wing populist Alternative for Germany party and the traditional German parties represented in the Bundestag is wide yet does not make up a binary division dominating political life. Of course, polarization at the edges may develop over time into binary polarization. If German politics for example were to evolve as Polish politics have, with the right-wing populist party winning a growing share of the vote, and electoral contests revolving primarily around the divide between that party on the one hand and its opponents on the other, then the country likely would be on a trajectory toward severe polarization.

Finally, being rooted in clashing social identities, severe polarization tends to be *sustained*, lasting beyond a specific polarizing event and usually beyond the rule of a specific polarizing leader. For instance, even though Venezuelan president Hugo Chávez was for years the driver of polarization in his country, the core *chavista* versus *anti-chavista* divide persisted after his death, having become deeply entrenched within Venezuelan society not just politically but socioculturally. When leaders rule in a divisive fashion that splits the society between their supporters and detractors, but does not foster or draw upon an identity-based cleavage, the polarization they create may fade not long after their departure from power. Thus, for example, Indonesia and Taiwan experienced polarizing leadership under President Abdurrahman Wahid (1999–2001) and President Chen Shuibian (2000–08), respectively. But after those leaders left the scene, the degree of divisiveness in political life diminished notably.[14] A crucial question with which this volume grapples is whether severely polarized countries—in which divisions are entrenched at the societal level and show few signs of abating—can sustain functional democracies over the long term.

Case Studies and Questions

The authors in this volume examine nine case studies: Bangladesh, Brazil, Colombia, India, Indonesia, Kenya, Poland, Turkey, and the United States. All are countries that meet or recently have met the minimum criteria for "electoral democracy."[15] In their geographic diversity, these cases span the multiregional landscape of polarization. They are experiencing varied degrees of polarization, including both clear cases of severe polarization and contexts that are marked by a significant political fissure but do not meet the abovementioned three criteria for severe polarization. They also exhibit significant variation in their political institutions, societal makeup, and levels of economic development, thus providing a strong foundation for comparative analysis of the roots and drivers of polarization.

Each case study examines four main issues and related questions:

Roots: What is the basis of polarization in the country? When did polarization emerge, and why? What are the key differences between the opposing sides?

Trajectory: How has polarization changed over time in terms of its intensity, dividing lines, and sociopolitical manifestations? What factors— such as political leadership, conjunctural political events, political system design, economic performance, and changes in the media and information space—have influenced the trajectory of polarization? Is polarization confined to the elite level, or has it spread more widely in the society?

Consequences: What are the political and societal effects of polarization? How is it affecting the functioning of the political system—for example, with respect to legislative processes, policymaking, and the integrity of democratic institutions? What kinds of social tensions and conflicts is it producing?

Remedial actions: What efforts have been made to reduce polarization? From which parts of society have these efforts originated—from groups and persons operating within the polarized political system, or outside of it? Have they had any noticeable success?

To provide an analytic framework for the volume as a whole, the case studies have been divided into four categories, two containing cases that meet this volume's definition of severe polarization and two containing cases that do not. Part I examines the turbulent experiences of two countries—Turkey and Kenya—gripped by severe polarization that has contributed to the breakdown of democratic institutions, whether currently or in the recent past. In the Turkish case, Senem Aydın-Düzgit explores how the deep cleavage between secularists and Islamists has made Turkey one of the most polarized nations in the world. Despite hopes of mutual accommodation during the early 2000s, the political leadership of Recep Tayyip Erdoğan proved deeply divisive, as his government increasingly utilized polarizing and ultimately authoritarian tactics. Particularly remarkable is how rapidly polarization has eroded public discourse, divided Turkish society, and undermined democracy. In the Kenyan case, Gilbert Khadiagala explores why the country's politics have become so intensely polarized between two ethnic groups—the Kikuyu and Luo—that prior to Kenyan independence did not have a history of conflict. His analysis highlights how elite entrepreneurs, political centralization, and economic inequalities have amplified ethnic divisions, causing the degradation or collapse of democratic institutions at various points since Kenya's independence. Troublingly, remedial actions such as political decentralization and international intervention have been unable to tame polarization and at times have been counterproductive.

Part II turns to the cases of the United States, India, and Poland, also countries beset by severe polarization, but where the degradation of institutions has not resulted in a full democratic breakdown. The United States, as Thomas Carothers highlights, is in crucial respects a unique case. The current polarization first emerged more at the societal level than at the elite level and then seeped into the political parties and national political life over the span of several decades. Furthermore, whereas in most other highly polarized countries a single identity-based cleavage involving religion, race, or ideology divides the society, in the United States all three of these divisions compound one another. Niranjan Sahoo's chapter on India underscores that while many cleavages exist within the world's largest democracy, Hindu nationalism is the one dividing issue that can pose an existential threat to Indian democracy. He argues that skilled but divisive leadership within the Hindu nationalist camp, coupled with the failings of the secular Congress Party, have caused polarization to escalate markedly since the 1980s. In the Polish case, Joanna Fomina traces how a populist and nationalist party has risen to power by raising highly contentious issues related to Polish national identity. The result has been asymmetrical polarization, in which the populist camp is cohesive and mobilized but its opponents are fragmented and reactive. Political tensions have fueled intolerance and undermined democratic accountability, as well as disrupting Polish foreign policy.

In the other cases, polarization does not qualify as severe based on this volume's definition, because it has not become rooted in contrasting social identities and remains largely confined to the elite level. Nevertheless, intense conflict among political elites is causing worrisome political and societal consequences. Part III examines the cases of Colombia and Bangladesh, in which polarization has become intense at the elite level but has not deeply divided these societies along racial, religious, or ideological lines in recent years. In Colombia, Andreas Feldmann shows that polarization has flared up over one particular but powerfully important issue: the 2016 Peace Accord negotiated with the country's largest rebel group. Rivalries within the political elite, rather than clear ideological differences, have been the primary driver of this polarization. Bangladesh, Naomi Hossain writes, poses a puzzle: partisan conflict there is bitter and intense, but it does not appear to be strongly rooted in any substantial programmatic or identity difference between the opposing sides. Rather, it is primarily a naked competition for political power, in a context where the victor is subject to few checks and balances, that has fueled political acrimony. Efforts to mitigate polarization, such as the military's intervention and creation of a nonparty caretaker government, have arguably exacerbated the problem.

Finally, the chapters in Part IV look at two countries that have stayed clear of severe polarization despite increasingly contentious electoral competition in recent years and sociopolitical features that might incline them toward such an outcome. In Indonesia, Eve Warburton explores how certain sociopolitical shifts, including a gradual Islamization of the society, created an environment ripe for populist figures employing exclusivist Islamist rhetoric. Although polarization remains relatively shallow and limited to periods surrounding elections, deepening political divisions have nonetheless contributed to a worrisome decline in democracy. The incumbent government has increasingly used illiberal tactics against its political opponents, and relatively secular leaders have chosen to accommodate majoritarian agendas rather than defending pluralism. In the Brazilian case, Umberto Mignozzetti and Matias Spektor explore why—despite recent political upheaval and a societal tableau vulnerable to polarization—levels of ideological and partisan polarization remain surprisingly low. They argue that paradoxically, institutional arrangements facilitating undemocratic, oligarchic politics have tempered polarization but also fueled the rise of the populist Jair Bolsonaro, whose victory in the 2018 presidential election may have set Brazil on a path of rising polarization.

The concluding chapter distills some cross-cutting findings and conclusions from the case studies as well as from the experiences of other divided democracies. Behind the diversity of the countries examined herein lie both some striking similarities, and revealing particularities, in patterns of polarization. Overall, a sobering picture emerges. Polarization roots itself with equal tenacity in multiple types of social identities, including ones built around religion, ethnicity, and ideology. Given the fact that a turn toward identity politics is a powerful trend across the democratic world—for reasons that political analysts are only starting to probe—the seeds of still wider and deeper polarization are continuing to spread. Additional global trends are fueling the pervasive rise of polarization, like the growth of social media and its tendency to magnify extreme sociopolitical views and to make it easier for citizens to live within separated information bubbles. The negative effects of severe polarization are often profound, not just for the functioning of core political institutions, but for societal cohesion generally. Remedial actions to limit or contain the phenomenon remain tentative at best in most polarized countries, often bouncing off entrenched processes of mutual division and delegitimization.

The authors and editors of this volume hope that the analysis contained herein will help political actors and observers across the democratic world to better understand the challenge that polarization presents to democracy globally and to find more effective ways to respond to it.

NOTES

1. Steven Levitsky, "Latin America's Shifting Politics: Democratic Survival and Weakness," *Journal of Democracy* 29, no. 4 (2018): 102–13.

2. Adrienne LeBas, "Can Polarization Be Positive? Conflict and Institutional Development in Africa," *American Behavioral Scientist* 62, no. 1 (2018): 59–74.

3. Thomas L. Friedman, "The American Civil War, Part II," *New York Times*, October 2, 2018 (www.nytimes.com/2018/10/02/opinion/the-american-civil-war-part-ii.html).

4. Noam Lupu, "Party Polarization and Mass Partisanship: A Comparative Perspective," *Political Behavior* 37, no. 2 (2015): 332.

5. LeBas, for instance, highlights the balance of forces between political camps and the absence of a history of formal group exclusion as two key factors that determine whether the overall impact of polarization is positive or negative. See LeBas, "Can Polarization Be Positive?"

6. See, for instance, Matthew Levendusky, *The Partisan Sort: How Liberals Became Democrats and Conservatives Became Republicans* (Chicago: The University of Chicago Press, 2009).

7. David Karol, "Party Activists, Interest Groups, and Polarization in American Politics," in *American Gridlock: The Sources, Character, and Impact of Political Polarization*, eds. James A. Thurber and Antoine Yoshinaka (New York: Cambridge University Press, 2015), 68–85.

8. For a definition of societal polarization, see Jennifer McCoy, Thamina Rahman, and Murat Somer, "Polarization and the Global Crisis of Democracy: Common Patterns, Dynamics, and Pernicious Consequences for Democratic Polities," *American Behavioral Scientist* 62, no. 1 (2018): 20–21.

9. In the U.S. context, see Alan I. Abramowitz, *The Disappearing Center: Engaged Citizens, Polarization, and American Democracy* (New Haven, CT: Yale University Press, 2010).

10. Most notably, McCoy and Somer have made excellent recent contributions as the editors of two special editions of academic journals on the subject of political polarization. See Jennifer McCoy and Murat Somer, eds., "Polarization and Democracy: A Janus-Faced Relationship with Pernicious Consequences," Special Issue, *American Behavioral Scientist* 62, no. 1 (2018); Jennifer McCoy and Murat Somer, eds., "Polarizing Polities: A Global Threat to Democracy," Special Issue, *The ANNALS of the American Academy of Political and Social Science* 681, no. 1 (2019).

11. Murat Somer and Jennifer McCoy, "Déjà Vu? Polarization and Endangered Democracies in the 21st Century," *American Behavioral Scientist* 62, no. 1 (2018): 2.

12. Ibid., 3.

13. McCoy, Rahman, and Somer, "Polarization and the Global Crisis of Democracy," 19.

14. Dan Slater and Aries A. Arugay, "Polarizing Figures: Executive Power and Institutional Conflict in Asian Democracies," *American Behavioral Scientist* 62, no. 1 (2018): 92–106.

15. Following Larry Diamond (1999), we employ a minimalist definition of electoral democracy as "a civilian, constitutional system in which the legislative and chief executive offices are filled through regular, competitive, multiparty elections with universal suffrage." See Larry Diamond, *Developing Democracy: Toward Consolidation* (Baltimore: Johns Hopkins University Press, 1999), 7–10.

Part I

SEVERE POLARIZATION AND DEMOCRATIC BREAKDOWN

ONE

The Islamist-Secularist Divide and Turkey's Descent into Severe Polarization

SENEM AYDIN-DÜZGIT

O n multiple different measures of polarization, Turkey today is one of the most polarized nations in the world.[1] Deep ideological and policy-based disagreements divide its political leaders and parties; Turkish society, too, is starkly polarized on the grounds of both ideology and social distance.[2] This chapter focuses on the bases and manifestations of polarization in Turkey, the main reasons behind its increase, and its ramifications for the future of democracy and governance in the country.

The current dominant cleavage between secularists and Islamists has its roots in a series of reforms intended to secularize and modernize the country after the foundation of the Turkish Republic in 1923. These reforms created a deep division within Turkish society, but until the beginning of the twenty-first century, the secularist elite dominated key state institutions such as the military, allowing it to repress conservative groups and thus keep conflict over the soul of Turkey from coming into the open. Since 2002, however, the remarkable electoral success of Recep Tayyip Erdoğan and his Justice and Development Party (Adalet ve Kalkınma Partisi; AKP) has brought the Islamist-secularist divide to the fore.

Despite the AKP's initial moderation, several developments, including the collapse of the European Union (EU) accession process, the success of polarization as an electoral strategy, and undemocratic threats from the secularist state establishment, pushed the AKP toward increasingly populist, divisive rhetoric and politics, beginning with the 2007 general elections. As the AKP's dominance has grown since the late 2000s, its own authoritarian behavior has largely driven further polarization. The problem of constant electioneering, the rise of majoritarianism, an erosion of democratic institutions, and a polarized and unfree media landscape have further deepened Turkey's divisions. Although the Islamist-secularist cleavage remains the most salient divide in Turkish politics today, the AKP has inflamed other divisions, particularly between Turkish and Kurdish nationalists, to play the opposition parties against one another.

The consequences of these developments are as clear as they are worrisome. Polarization has eroded fact-based public debate, facilitated a dramatic retrenchment of democracy, undermined the legitimacy of public institutions, divided civil society, and hurt social cohesion. Given that Turkey's political elites cannot even agree that such polarization exists, this problem is unlikely to abate, and no substantial efforts have been made to address it.

Roots

The origins of Turkey's current polarization lie in the foundational reforms of the 1920s that sought to remove religion from public life and thus fomented a political and cultural divide between secularist and Islamist camps. After the collapse of the Ottoman Empire following the end of World War I, the founder of modern Turkey, Mustafa Kemal Atatürk, enacted a series of sweeping top-down reforms to transform the nation along Western, secularist lines: he abolished the caliphate, replaced sharia courts with a secular civil code, and placed all religious institutions under state control to monitor and strictly limit the role that religion would play in public life.

These radical reforms deeply polarized Turkish society and fomented a values-based *kulturkampf* (cultural struggle). As Şerif Mardin's "center-periphery thesis" argues, since the establishment of the modern Turkish Republic in 1923, the modernizing and westernizing reforms undertaken by the Republican elite ("the center") in both the political and cultural domains have been resisted by a significant segment of Turkish society ("the periphery").[3] On one side are those close to the center, "whose lifestyles are shaped on the basis of an image of the good society with science and human rationality at its core, which we may loosely refer to as a 'Secular Image of Good Society.'"[4] On the other side are those close to the periphery, "whose lifestyles are based on the core values of tradition and religion (mainly Sunni Islam), which may best be referred to as a 'Conservative Image of Good Society.'"[5]

Across the rest of the 20th century, the secularist elite used its control of key state institutions such as the military and judiciary to repress its conservative opponents and thus suppress the symptoms of this divide. On the whole, the center dominated, and those who subscribed to the conservative image of good society were kept on the sidelines. Although the strict secularism of the Kemalist elite managed to exclude Islam from political life, religion remained a powerful force in the formation of individual and communal identities in the country. Turkey's top-down modernization thus succeeded in restructuring the country's political institutions but failed to ensure that Turkish society accepted the process of secularization. Instead, Islam remained a powerful symbolic force in the everyday life of Turkish people and in the way in which they define themselves as Muslims.[6] In the first two decades of the 21st century, this divide sharpened and deepened, becoming the basis of the harsh polarization that afflicts Turkey today. The following section examines the process by which polarization intensified and the key drivers of this process.

Three other notable divides also have existed in modern Turkey, but they have either faded over time or been exploited to exacerbate the dominant divide between secularists and Islamists. First, between 1960 and 1980, Turkey witnessed the rise of a left-wing labor movement and a nationalist right that defined itself as anticommunist. Societal and political polarization between the nationalist right and the far left increased in the 1970s, resulting in widespread civil violence that culminated in the military coup of September 12, 1980. The 1980 coup radically changed the Turkish social and political landscape. The military regime abandoned the strict secularism of the early republic to increase its popular support and opened up the liberalizing economy and the domestic market to Islamic capital.

These changes helped strengthen Islamic movements within the state and civil society and contributed to the rise of Islamic identity as a strong political force in the 1990s. The nationalist-religious (Turkish-Islamic) ideology of the military regime led it to conduct a massive crackdown on the Turkish left, exceeding by far its suppression of the nationalist right. The military's neoliberal agenda also further marginalized the Turkish labor movement as a political force.

In the second half of the 20th century, two additional fault lines in Turkish politics and society—namely, an ethnic cleavage between Turkish and Kurdish identity and a sectarian divide between Sunnis and Alevis—intensified. To win the Kurds' support during Turkey's war of independence and in the early years of the republic, Atatürk originally appealed to a common Ottoman or pan-Islamic identity to create a multicultural sense of solidarity. Yet the vacuum left by the removal of Islamic elements in state ideology soon started to be filled with an emphasis on ethnic Turkishness, signifying a policy shift from Ottomanism to Turkification. This shift soon helped alienate the Kurds but did not immediately lead to the emergence of an ethnic or national Kurdish identity, mainly because of the regional, feudal, and religious divides among the Kurds themselves.

Such an identity, however, began to emerge in the 1950s and developed in the following decades, as modernization and urbanization led to high rates of Kurdish migration to industrialized cities. The traditional establishment perceived Kurdish demands for recognition of this identity as threats to the territorial integrity of the state and met them with hostility, especially after the 1980 coup. Similar to its role in the rise of political Islam, the 1980 coup also played an important role in the rise of nationalism, deepening the ethnic cleavage between Turkish and Kurdish identity. This divide erupted into conflict in 1984, when the Kurdistan Workers' Party (Partiye Karkeren Kurdistan; PKK), a terrorist-guerrilla organization, launched a violent secessionist campaign in the southeast. The late 1980s and 1990s were marked by the escalation of the PKK's conflict with the Turkish military and the ensuing rise in the number of casualties, alongside gross human rights abuses and the forced displacement of a large number of Kurds from the southeast to western cities.

The third and final fault line is the one between Sunnis and Alevis. The Alevi faith is a distinct sect of Islam, which differs from the Sunni sect in terms of both theology and religious practice. It is estimated that Alevis constitute roughly 10 to 20 percent of the Turkish population.[7] The roots of the Sunni-Alevi divide also go back to the early years of the Turkish Republic, when the Republican project sought to construct a national identity that was not only Turkish but also Sunni Muslim, and had no room for minority sects of the dominant religion. Alevis almost uniformly attach themselves to the secularist camp in the prevailing cultural divide of the country, translating into support for center-left political parties and currently the main opposition Republican People's Party (Cumhuriyet Halk Partisi; CHP). Although historical animosities between these two sects have been largely contained in the Republican era, the divide has grown stronger following key traumatic events, the most notable of which were the 1978 Maraş and 1993 Sivas massacres of Alevi citizens, which are still vivid in Alevis's collective memory.

Trajectory

The rise of the intense polarization of Turkish politics and society between secularists and Islamists started in the late 1990s and early 2000s. Those years saw the political rise of the AKP under the skillful and charismatic leadership of Recep Tayyip Erdoğan. The party emerged as a splinter of the Islamist Virtue Party (Fazilet Partisi; FP), which the Turkish Constitutional Court had banned in 2001 on the grounds that it had engaged in antisecular activities. The AKP's core constituency was conservative segments of society, though it also attracted some liberals and Kurds as it mounted a fundamental challenge to the dominant position of the secularist elite. The party first came to power in the November 2002 elections, following a major economic crisis in 2001 that wiped out almost all of the established parties of the center from the political scene.

Between 2002 and 2006, the AKP pushed for EU accession, a policy goal that united many Islamists, liberals, Kurds, Alevis, and secularists. The party's coming to power coincided with the growing prospect of EU accession for Turkey (which was officially declared an EU candidate country in 1999) as well as a strong economic recovery program led by the International Monetary Fund. Immediately upon coming to power, the party successfully promoted EU accession and its democratic reform agenda to widen its support base toward the center, to preserve its core voter base by promising expanded religious freedoms, and to guarantee its survival in the face of the secularist state establishment in the judiciary and the military. Democratic reforms went hand in hand with the growth of the Turkish economy and the country's rising profile in foreign policy. The rise of the AKP was generally viewed favorably in the West, where its record of demo-cratic reforms was considered as a possible model for other Middle Eastern countries to emulate. Turkish official rhetoric matched this discourse by frequently pointing at the significance of the Turkish "model" in underlin-ing the need for democracy in the wider region.

From the mid-2000s onward, however, the AKP adopted increasingly polarizing rhetoric and policies that led first to the stagnation and later to the regression of Turkish democracy. Several distinct causes prompted it to foster political and societal polarization through the populist rhetoric of then-Prime Minister Erdoğan, starting with the 2007 general elections. First, the partial freeze of EU accession negotiations in December 2006 significantly dampened hopes of Turkish membership and thus eliminated a significant factor that had induced the AKP's moderation. Second, this polarizing rhetoric was highly effective, particularly given the AKP's domi-nant status in the political party system and a weak and divided opposition. The party capitalized tremendously on feelings of "victimhood" among the peripheral masses, which felt alienated and discriminated against by the former secularist state establishment in the center as embodied in the military, judiciary, and state bureaucracy. The success of this discourse in the 2007 elections encouraged it to use similar rhetoric in the following general, local, and presidential elections, as well as in two constitutional referenda.[8] A key element of this populist polarizing rhetoric has been an "us" versus "them" divide, referring respectively to the "people," constitut-ing the public will and represented at the political level by Erdoğan through his leadership of the AKP, mainly as opposed to the corrupt "Republican elite," which represents the "establishment" embodied in the main opposi-tion party, the CHP. This populist view of the "people" vs. the "elite," where the party and its leader are represented as "the voice" of the genuine "will of the people" as opposed to that of the "elite" identified with the opposition, has encouraged a binary worldview across society.

Finally, a serious and often undemocratic threat from the secularist establishment contributed to the AKP's polarizing turn. At the societal level, secularist pushback took the form of mass "Republican" rallies in 2007, grouped around secular masses who felt threatened by the rise of the AKP. Meanwhile, at the political level, secularists within the military high command issued a memorandum seeking to prevent the AKP from winning the presidency, while judicial interventions aimed to prevent Erdoğan from becoming the president in 2007 and to close down the AKP in 2008. Because of the relational nature of polarization, this secularist resistance and attack—often expressed in the binary dichotomy of the "secular" and "progressive" "us" against the "religious" and "backward" "them"—provided fertile ground for the AKP's polarizing rhetoric to flourish and resonate in the broader society.

Starting with the 2010 constitutional referendum, the AKP's efforts to consolidate its power over state institutions and crack down on the opposition have been a primary driver of polarization. To free itself from the threat posed by the secularist state apparatus, the party changed the Turkish Constitution through a referendum in September 2010. The twenty-six constitutional amendments covered a variety of issues, ranging from the granting of positive discrimination to women to the creation of an ombudsman office and from the right to information to the reform of the judicial system. Most of the controversy, however, focused on two amendments that concerned the composition of the Constitutional Court and the High Council of Judges and Public Prosecutors, the latter of which determines the career paths of judges and prosecutors through appointments, transfers, promotions, reprimands, and other mechanisms. At the time, the AKP was still closely allied with the Gülen movement, an Islamist group founded by the Turkish imam Fetullah Gülen and referred to since 2016 by the Turkish state as the Fethullahist Terrorist Organization (FETÖ), which encouraged students in its schools to pursue careers in the state bureaucracy.[9] The introduced amendments ultimately paved the way for the then progovernment Gülenist cadres to rapidly infiltrate the judiciary and then launch sham trials against secularist military officials, leading to massive purges in the military. Feeling politically more secure after the 2007 elections and the 2010 constitutional referendum, the party could rely less on the EU and its democratization agenda. The EU's credibility of conditionality had been waning in the face of rising opposition within Europe to

Turkish accession, which made it easier for the AKP to increasingly violate democratic principles and weaken fundamental freedoms in the country.

The AKP's repression of the political opposition further intensified polarization in the aftermath of two notable events, the Gezi Park protests of June 2013 and the failed coup attempt of July 15, 2016. The Gezi Park protests, which began as a protest against an urban development plan for Taksim Gezi Park in Istanbul, quickly spiraled into mass nationwide protests against the government, resulting in police brutality and the death of five protestors. The protests increased the government's sense of insecurity and led to further measures curtailing democratic space for opposition, further deepening the divide between the two camps. In addition, the failed coup attempt of July 15, 2016, not only enabled the government to further curb fundamental freedoms, but also heightened the insecurities of oppositional segments in society, who witnessed the violence and mobilization of progovernment masses in reaction to the coup attempt and feared that this might turn against them in the future.[10] The aftermath of the coup attempt was marked by an extended state of emergency that lasted for almost two years, and led to massive purges in all state institutions as well as severe curtailments of fundamental rights and freedoms in the country.

It was within this context that the campaign on the April 2017 constitutional referendum on the introduction of the executive presidential system was fought. The electorate was left to decide the future of the country's political regime in an extremely polarized environment and with restricted information provided by overwhelmingly dominant progovernment media outlets. Yet even with governmental pressure and heavily deployed resources, the result was a close call, with 51.41 percent of the electorate voting in favor and 48.59 percent against the constitutional changes. The AKP and Erdoğan soon moved to hold elections so that the new regime could be implemented, and the presidential and parliamentary elections both took place on the same day in June 2018. Wary of its declining popularity in the face of the economic downturn affecting Turkey at the time, the AKP entered the elections in an electoral alliance with the ultranationalist right-wing Nationalist Action Party (Milliyetçi Hareket Partisi; MHP), which proved crucial in electing Erdoğan to the presidency and in helping the new coalition secure a majority in parliament. Under the new executive presidential system, political power is now highly centralized in the office of the presidency at the expense of the parliament, with minimal regard for checks and balances. This centralization of power has provided fertile ground for polarization to flourish. With Erdoğan now wielding more formal and informal power than ever, polarization has become increasingly personalized and defined by support for or hatred of the president.[11] Most recently, the informal AKP-MHP coalition stoked polarization along these lines during the March 2019 local elections, in which it based its campaign largely on the personalistic cult of Erdoğan and publicly demonized opposition candidates on the grounds that they were affiliated with terrorist organizations.

Additional Cleavages

Although the Islamist-secularist *kulturkampf* employed by the AKP is the strongest basis of polarization in Turkey, the AKP has skillfully stoked ethnic and sectarian polarization to play opposition parties against one another and maintain its majority in parliament. Polarization along the Islamist-secularist axis refers mostly to the rift between the governing AKP and the main opposition CHP and to some extent, the pro-Kurdish Peoples' Democratic Party (Halkların Demokratik Partisi; HDP). Since 2015, however, the AKP has deepened the Kurdish-Turkish cleavage to win support from the ultranationalist and anti-Kurdish MHP, and has sharpened the divide between the AKP/MHP and the pro-Kurdish HDP.

Although the MHP is an opposition party like the CHP and HDP, its base and the party itself stand closer to the AKP, and starting in 2018, it entered an alliance with the AKP in parliament. The affinity between the two parties was seen most recently in the June 2018 elections, in which votes shifted from the AKP to the MHP and the two parties formed a de facto coalition in its aftermath. Yet between 2002 and 2015, the AKP and MHP had been staunch political opponents, as the former sought to expand freedoms for Turkey's Kurdish population and to negotiate with the PKK. The official view on the Kurdish issue had shifted in 1999, following the capture of PKK leader Abdullah Öcalan and the emergence of Turkish prospects for EU membership, and had led to significant reforms intended to improve the lives of Kurds in the country in the initial years of the 2000s. Nonetheless, violence reemerged in 2004 and continued on and off, with brief interludes in 2009 and 2012–13 as the two sides conducted peace negotiations. The peace process ultimately broke down in the wake of the June 2015 general elections, in which the success of the pro-Kurdish HDP deprived the AKP of a parliamentary majority for the first time since 2002. Subsequently, President Erdoğan realized that peace negotiations with the PKK were benefitting the HDP more than his own party and moved instead to court the ultranationalist vote.

By escalating the conflict with the PKK since 2015, the AKP has stoked ethnic cleavages and polarization in order to diminish support for the pro-Kurdish HDP and to win the backing of the MHP. According to various studies, this history of conflict and violence has already fostered a political and social environment of "mutual negative feelings and high levels of mistrust between the Kurds and the Turks."[12] After the peace process collapsed in 2015, the government chose to demonize the HDP by persistently equating it with the PKK and by jailing its leader along with numerous party representatives, further deepening the political and societal divide on this front. As observed both before and after the June 2018 presidential elections, the AKP's discourse now places the HDP and the CHP firmly together on the opposite pole in its rhetoric, branding both as pro-Kurdish and proterrorist political parties. Meanwhile, the AKP's anti-Kurdish turn has aligned the party more closely with the MHP base and allowed it to maintain a parliamentary majority through its alliance with the MHP.

The Sunni-Alevi cleavage is less intense than the former two divides but has become one part of the partisan polarization between the AKP/MHP and CHP. Studies have found that negative perceptions of Alevis are widely prevalent across Turkish society.[13] Moreover, the AKP's pro-Sunni policies aimed at Islamizing Turkish politics and society have further contributed to Alevis's growing anxiety and alienation, their almost undivided support for the secularist CHP, and the deepening rift between the two sides.

The Current State of Polarization

The most comprehensive and recent study of polarization in Turkey has found that "the level of political polarization in Turkey has reached a level that should alarm even optimists."[14] A majority of the Turkish public also seems to acknowledge this claim, as 62 percent of the population is reported to believe that the country is deeply polarized.[15]

Overall, polarization in contemporary Turkey has been driven by elites. Although strong ethnic, sectarian, and value-based cleavages have long divided Turkish society, the populist discourse and governance of the ruling party and its leader, as well as earlier undemocratic maneuvers by the secularist opposition, have played key roles in cultivating these largely identity-based societal divisions and locating them firmly in distinct partisan identifications throughout society.

Turkish polarization extends from the level of political parties to that of the general society, where citizens regularly assess key political issues by reference to their partisan affiliations. Crucially, citizens who support different political parties frequently hold vastly different opinions on the basic facts of recent political history and the legitimate structure of government. For instance, while 81 percent of AKP supporters believe that the Gezi protests of June 2013 were engineered by foreign powers intent on weakening the AKP, 85 percent of those who support the CHP believe that they were peaceful protests undertaken in reaction to government policies.[16] Similarly, while 84 percent of AKP supporters regard the new presidential system introduced in 2017 as good for the future of the country, this figure drops to 5 percent and 22 percent for CHP and HDP supporters, respectively.[17] Polarization is also visible in the way in which individuals' partisan affiliations determine their trust in public institutions. For instance, both AKP and MHP supporters display high rates of support for all state institutions, but for CHP and HDP supporters these figures are dramatically reversed.[18]

Where polarization is extreme, it "extends into other aspects of social relations," affecting interpersonal relationships across society.[19] Societal polarization often is evident in the way in which partisan identities translate into people's preferences in everyday practices. For instance, the abovementioned study on political polarization found that 74 percent of the Turkish public rejects the idea of doing business with someone who votes for the party from which they feel most distant, 79 percent would not want their daughters to marry someone who supports that party, 70 percent would not wish to see them as neighbors, and 68 percent are against their children playing with their peers from families supporting that party.[20] The same study also found "signs of perceived moral superiority," with 90 percent of the respondents expressing that the supporters of their chosen political party are "honorable," 80 percent claiming that the supporters of the most distant political party are "arrogant," and 85 percent stating that supporters of the most distant party pose a "threat to the country."[21]

The polarization between political parties and across society thus rests on the articulation of key sociopolitical, ethnic, and sectarian identities along partisan lines. AKP and MHP supporters cluster around Turkishness, nationalism, conservative values, and religiosity (Sunni Islam); CHP supporters define themselves mainly with reference to secularism, the principles of Atatürk, and the Alevi faith; and Kurdishness seems to be the main defining trait for HDP supporters.[22] On a more positive note, when taken out of the partisan context, the social distance between individuals seems to decline. For instance, a recent report on social cohesion in Turkey has found that 76 percent of the population does not have a problem with having a neighbor from a different ethnic group, and 79 percent of the population would accept a neighbor from a different sectarian background (Sunni/Alevi). Similarly, 67 percent of the public does not mind their children making friends with their peers from families that hold different political views.[23] Although these numbers are far from ideal for a cohesive society, they nonetheless indicate that Turkey's identity-based cleavages are polarizing instruments mainly when framed in partisan terms and less so outside a partisan context. This evidence suggests that developments in the political realm between political actors in terms of discourses and policies are the main catalyst for polarization in Turkish society.

Elite views on polarization provide little hope for change at this level. A recent study found considerable polarization across the spectrum of the Turkish elite concerning the existence of polarization in Turkey, a disparity that overlaps with the bipolar partisan divide between the government (defined broadly as the AKP and MHP) and opposition.[24] Whereas progovernment elites publicly deny the existence of polarization in the country, the opposition considers polarization to be a fundamental problem that must be urgently addressed. Progovernment elites claim either that polarization has never existed in the country, or that it has always been present but has declined, implying that there is no current cause for concern. They also argue that foreign enemies intent on harming Turkey, as well as the

AKP's domestic opponents, have stirred up debate regarding polarization to weaken the government. Conversely, opposition elites who publicly acknowledge the existence and salience of polarization in the country base their justificatory narratives on their personal perceptions of exclusion, othering, and "living in parallel worlds" on cultural, religious, ethnic, and sectarian grounds. Overwhelmingly, they perceive that the government has been forcing existing societal divides into a bipolar polarization that is driving the two camps of society ever further apart.

The same study also found that those in the progovernment camp who deny the existence of polarization claim that four factors have prevented it: essentialist traits of Turkish society, such as its assumed hospitality; an essentialist reading of Turkish history, referencing a mythic Ottoman imperial past characterized by harmony; a reductionist assumed continuity and comparison with the more recent past; and the assumed societal diversity lying behind the AKP's electoral support. In this view, polarization, to the extent that it exists, is the work of enemies who want to destabilize the government and the country. Attributing polarization to the actions of these underdefined (and apparently uncontrollable) internal and external enemies prevents the possibility of meaningful dialogue that grapples with the role of political processes, instruments, and agency. In stark contrast with such accounts, those who publicly acknowledge the presence of polarization in Turkey stress the significance of the "political" in fostering or easing polarization through careful management of the country's key cleavages.

This gap in itself implies that, in the absence of a radical change in political constellations, the currently reported high rates of polarization in Turkey can only be expected to remain as they are, at best, in the near future. Yet the prevailing mode of denial in the progovernment camp also runs the risk of sustaining precisely the type of governance and the policies that contribute to polarization, as well as increasing perceptions of vulnerability among those who feel excluded and marginalized. Such an impasse would lead to even higher levels of polarization, which in turn would make it all the more difficult to attain the minimal societal will to live together that is required for Turkey to become an electoral democracy once more.

Additional Drivers

Although the populist rhetoric of the AKP and its leader is a critical driver of polarization, other institutional factors have also exacerbated political divisions. The constant electioneering mode that has taken hold of Turkish politics, majoritarianism as a mode of governance and the concomitant erosion of democratic institutions, and increased partisanship in the media landscape have all contributed to polarization—and polarization in turn intensifies these factors, creating a vicious downward spiral marked by heightened antagonism and democratic backsliding.[25]

Turkey has been in a constant electioneering mode since 2014, with presidential and local elections in 2014, two general elections in 2015, a referendum on the introduction of a presidential system in 2017, presidential and parliamentary elections in 2018, local elections in March 2019, and a rerun of the Istanbul mayoral election in June 2019. While some of these elections (e.g., the March 2019 local elections) were scheduled, regular elections, others (i.e., the 2017 referendum and 2018 presidential elections) were necessitated by regime change and one (i.e., the November 2015 general elections) was a rerun of a previous election in which the AKP had lost its majority in parliament. This constant electioneering has fueled the intensity of political debates and stark divisions across partisan lines.

The deterioration of the rule of law and the rise of majoritarian governance methods under AKP rule also have contributed to polarization. Majoritarianism has marginalized the opposition in governance and overall political discourse, and restricted the democratic space for opposition and independent forces. In 2018, for the first time in nearly two decades, Freedom House's "Freedom in the World" assessment downgraded Turkey's status from "Partly Free" to "Not Free."[26] World Bank governance indicators likewise show that the rule of law in Turkey has declined rapidly since 2014.[27] Marginalization of the opposition has contributed to the growing polarization between the AKP and opposition parties, mostly the CHP and HDP, at both the political and societal levels. Those who feel increasingly excluded and vulnerable as a result of the majoritarian governance style and repression are locked into a perpetual support for the opposition regardless of the policy issues in question. They also become more attentive to negative events and information from progovernment circles, thereby bolstering both their in-group cohesiveness and their hostility toward the other group. The institutional decay that accompanies the erosion of democracy also has fueled political polarization by degrading trust, especially among the opposition, in moderating public institutions such as the judiciary.

Along with these political factors, the Turkish media landscape favors the rise of polarization. Since the late 1990s, the state of Turkish media has resembled a "polarized pluralist model" characterized by "high media integration into party politics (or political parallelism) and state intervention, along with low media commercialization and journalistic professionalism."[28] The AKP has intensified this situation. After the 2007 general elections, the AKP took important steps to tame and weaken the former mainstream media, and established its own progovernment media bloc by encouraging and facilitating media ownership by businesses that are close to the party.[29] As of March 2019, progovernment businesses dominate the conventional media landscape, with only a few exceptional outlets associated with the opposition. Thus, in addition to partisanship, Turkey also suffers from an "unfree press," ranking 163rd out of 198 places in Freedom House's 2017 press freedom list.[30] This context fosters a climate in which partisanship trumps fact-based debate, as citizens are drawn to receiving political news from media sources that align with their own thinking.

The polarizing nature of the media landscape, also referred to as the "echo chamber effect," extends from conventional media to new social media platforms such as Facebook and Twitter. The government crackdown on traditional media has led to a rise of social media platforms as an alternative source of information in a country where approximately half of all households have access to the internet. Yet research also has shown that on social media platforms, as in conventional media use, people prefer to hear views similar to their own, leading different political party supporters to inhabit different worlds that seldom overlap or interact.[31] Furthermore, social media has made it easier for the government to track down and suppress opposition, which also helps to fuel polarization. Thousands of people have been put on trial or even persecuted on the basis of the statements that they posted on Facebook and Twitter.

Consequences

Polarization is having dire consequences for Turkish democracy and society. First of all, in a polarized political environment, people pay less attention to facts and more to the people and political parties that advocate certain policy positions from given perceived identity clusters. In other words, *what* is being said matters far less than *who* is saying it. For instance, in a recent experimental study that asked respondents to provide their views on certain statements related to Turkish politics, the study participants changed their views when they were told that some of the statements came from President Erdoğan.[32] This polarized political context inhibits rational, fact-based public debate on key issues of Turkish domestic and foreign policy. It also has a crucial impact on electoral contests, where people's voting behavior hinges on their emotional or identity-based attachment to the parties and their leaders, rather than the evidence on the ground and the parties' policy positions. This dynamic leads to an almost predetermined voting composition that is reflected in parliament, where intraparty vote shifts between the blocs are almost nonexistent and prospects for change in power constellations are limited.

Second, as democratic backsliding deepens polarization, polarization in turn strengthens democratic regress, creating a vicious cycle that is difficult to break. Because of polarization, AKP supporters in particular "tolerate . . . the party's illiberal policies and overlook its involvements in state capture and corruption."[33] The uneven playing field for the opposition is hardly a matter of concern for the AKP electorate. A context shaped by zero-sum considerations diminishes prospects for cooperation and compromise.[34] Furthermore, polarization helps to suppress intraparty opposition or criticisms within the governing party. AKP leaders underscore the perceived need to stick together in the face of common enemies and threats, such as the old Republican elite, and during election periods they frequently remind the electorate of the secularists' past misdeeds, particularly their restrictions on the public expression of Islam, such as the ban on wearing headscarves in public institutions. The vicious cycle of polarization also extends to the media landscape. The current Turkish media environment, already conducive to polarization, further perpetuates distinct echo chambers in which polarized individuals turn to media sources that support their partisan attachments. In such an environment, it is difficult to create a public space where diverse voices can be heard.

Third, polarization is eroding public institutions, most notably the parliament and the judiciary. Even before the presidential system took effect with the June 2018 elections, the utility of the Turkish parliament had greatly diminished. With the help of political allies such as the MHP, the AKP passed bills unilaterally without seeking the opposition's support and vetoed almost every bill proposed by opposition parties. This lack of cross-party cooperation and approval for legislation damaged the legitimacy of the legislature. Full partisan control over the judiciary has curtailed any prospect of judicial independence. It is thus not surprising that public trust in the Turkish courts has declined considerably in the past decade, from 67 percent in 2007 to 45 percent in 2016, ranking Turkey ten percentage points behind the average trust levels in the judiciary across the member states of the Organisation for Economic Co-operation and Development (OECD).[35] A similar picture is visible concerning the office of the presidency. In the new presidential system, the office of the president holds an extraordinary amount of political power with minimal checks and balances. The phrase "he is not my president" is commonly heard in a society where Erdoğan's election to the presidency was by a close 52 percent in a highly polarized context. The public legitimacy of political decisions likely will be contested further as the exercise of political power becomes even more firmly located and centralized in the office of the presidency.

Fourth, polarization is shaping Turkish civil society. With a few exceptions, Turkish civil society organizations (CSOs) are divided along partisan lines, in line with the familiar identity cleavages discussed above. Cooperation is rare, and the norm is to push for the rights of one's own. To some extent, this trend existed before the recent polarization, yet the government has aggravated this situation by favoring like-minded CSOs, instrumentalizing them for political purposes, and repressing CSOs that are perceived to voice oppositional views.[36]

Finally, polarization is undermining societal cohesion. At this point, few values are keeping Turkish society together. Partisan polarization may not translate into intense societal conflict in people's everyday lives, but the few commonalities that bind citizens from different political persuasions together seem to be negative attitudes toward the West and toward

Syrian migrants.[37] Levels of social trust are low in general and only relatively strong within the identity clusters around the polarized divide.[38] World Values Surveys show that Turkey ranks at the bottom of all OECD countries in terms of levels of interpersonal trust, with only 12 percent of the population expressing trust in others.[39]

Remedial Actions

Currently, neither the Turkish elite nor Turkish society as a whole has made substantial efforts to reduce the levels of polarization in the country. There were some promising developments at the elite level before the June 2018 presidential and parliamentary elections, but these produced only limited results. The anti-AKP electoral alliance formed between the CHP, the nationalist İYİ Party (or Good Party, founded by discontented former MHP members before the 2018 elections), and the pro-Islamist Felicity Party (Saadet Partisi; SP) initially appeared to be a potential step toward overcoming polarization, as it encompassed a broad base of secular Republicans, nationalists, and Islamists who all favored a return to parliamentary democracy. However, following the alliance's poor performance in both the parliamentary elections and the presidential race, it soon was said that they had failed because of their proximity to the CHP, and the alliance dissipated almost immediately after the elections. The 2018 election results also suggested that despite elite-level efforts to draw support away from the pro-government bloc, nationalist and Islamist voters did not leave their home base. Similarly, despite the government crackdown (including the imprisonment of its leader), the beleaguered HDP managed to pass the 10 percent electoral threshold required to enter parliament, partly thanks to CHP voters in the west of Turkey who did not wish to see the HDP seats taken over by the AKP in the event that the HDP failed to pass the electoral threshold. Nonetheless, this effort, which could be interpreted as a movement toward normalcy on the Kurdish-Turkish cleavage, soon fell victim to the polarizing tactics of government representatives, who struck back at this challenge to their authority by branding the CHP and its support base as terrorists alongside the HDP.

In the March 2019 local elections, the opposition fared significantly better by forming strategic alliances in key urban centers and ultimately winning the three largest cities in the country, including Istanbul and the capital, Ankara. The opposition's mayoral candidate in Istanbul, Ekrem İmamoğlu, quickly became popular and well-known across the country for his inclusive and tolerant discourse. By declaring the Istanbul vote invalid on highly contested legal grounds and deciding to rerun the election, the Supreme Election Council, which until then was perceived as a relatively impartial institution, dealt a severe blow to its credibility in the eyes of the opposition. On a more positive note, İmamoğlu's landslide victory in the rerun has shown growing public discontent with the ruling elite's polarizing policies and discourse.

In recent years, Turkish academia and the think-tank community have shown greater interest in the study of polarization, focusing mainly on its root causes and manifestations. For instance, the German Marshall Fund and Istanbul Bilgi University conducted the first extensive survey on polarization in Turkey in 2017, while the Istanbul Policy Center undertook an extensive project on polarization by bringing together different stakeholders from the government, CSOs, and the media to discuss the issue and propose solutions. Nonetheless, the dramatic divide among Turkish elites concerning the mere existence of polarization hinders potential spillovers from these realms from affecting the political parties, where the root of the problem mainly lies.

NOTES

1. Alban Lauka, Jennifer McCoy, and Rengin B. Firat, "Mass Partisan Polarization: Measuring a Relational Concept," *American Behavioral Scientist* 62, no.1 (2018): 107–26.

2. E. Fuat Keyman, "The AK Party: Dominant Party, New Turkey and Polarization," *Insight Turkey* 16, no. 2 (Spring 2014): 19–31; and Emre Erdoğan and Pınar Uyan Semerci, *Fanusta Diyaloglar: Türkiye'de Kutuplaşmanın Boyutları* [Dialogues in a bell jar: Dimensions of polarization in Turkey] (Istanbul: Bilgi University Press, 2018).

3. Şerif Mardin, "Center-Periphery Relations: A Key to Turkish Politics?," *Daedalus* 102, no. 1 (Winter 1973): 169–90.

4. Ersin Kalaycıoğlu, "*Kulturkampf* in Turkey: The Constitutional Referendum of 12 September 2010," *South European Society and Politics* 17, no. 1 (2012): 7.

5. Ibid.

6. Senem Aydın and E. Fuat Keyman, "European Integration and the Transformation of Turkish Democracy," *EU–Turkey Working Papers* 2 (Brussels: Centre for European Policy Studies, August 2004), 6.

7. The exact numbers are unknown, since Alevis mostly live in urban centers and are reluctant to publicly acknowledge their identity. See Ali Çarkoğlu and Nazlı Çağın Bilgili, "A Precarious Relationship: The Alevi Minority, the Turkish State and the EU," *South European Society and Politics* 16, no. 2 (2011): 353.

8. Kalaycıoğlu, "*Kulturkampf* in Turkey"; E. Özlem Atikcan and Kerem Öge, "Referendum Campaigns in Polarized Societies: The Case of Turkey," *Turkish Studies* 13, no. 3 (2012): 449–70; Senem Aydın-Düzgit, "No Crisis, No Change: The Third AKP Victory in the June 2011 Parliamentary Elections in Turkey," *South European Society and Politics* 17, no. 2 (2012): 329–46; Şakir Dinçşahin, "A Symptomatic Analysis of the Justice and Development Party's Populism in Turkey: 2007–2010," *Government and Opposition* 47, no. 4 (2012): 618–40; Özge Kemahlıoğlu, "Winds of Change? The June 2015 Parliamentary Election in Turkey," *South European Society and Politics* 20, no. 4 (2015): 445–64; Sabri Sayarı, "Back to a Predominant Party System," *South European Society and Politics* 21, no. 2 (2016): 263–80; and Berk Esen and Şebnem Gümüşçü, "A Small Yes for Presidentialism: The Turkish Constitutional Referendum of April 2017," *South European Society and Politics* 22, no. 3 (2017): 303–26.

9. Scott T. Fitzgerald, "Conceptualizing and Understanding the Gülen Movement," *Sociology Compass* 11, no. 3 (2017).

10. Ayşe Betül Çelik, Evren Balta, and Murat Paker, "Yeni Türkiye'nin Yurttaşları: 15 Temmuz Darbe Girişimi Sonrası Siyasi Tutumlar, Değerler ve Duygular" [Citizens of the new Turkey: Political attitudes, values, and emotions in the aftermath of the July 15 coup attempt], KONDA Report (Istanbul: KONDA Research and Consultancy, May 2017), 73–74.

11. Murat Somer, "Turkey: The Slippery Slope from Reformist to Revolutionary Polarization and Democratic Breakdown," *The ANNALS of the American Academy of Political and Social Science* 681, no. 1 (2019): 42–61.

12. Ayşe Betül Çelik, Rezarta Bilali, and Yeshim Iqbal, "Patterns of 'Othering' in Turkey: A Study of Ethnic, Ideological, and Sectarian Polarisation," *South European Society and Politics* 22, no. 2 (2017): 220.

13. Ibid.

14. Emre Erdoğan, "Turkey: Divided We Stand," German Marshall Fund of the United States, April 12, 2016 (www.gmfus.org/publications/turkey-divided-we-stand).

15. Özge Özdemir, "Muhafazakar Kesim Kutuplaşmaya Nasıl Bakıyor?" [How do the conservative segments view polarization?], *BBC Türkçe*, January 27, 2017 (www.bbc.com/turkce/haberler-turkiye-38667730).

16. Erdoğan and Uyan Semerci, *Fanusta Diyaloglar*, 120.

17. Ibid., 122.

18. Ibid., 110–11.

19. Jennifer McCoy, Tahmina Rahman, and Murat Somer, "Polarization and the Global Crisis of Democracy: Common Patterns, Dynamics, and Pernicious Consequences for Democratic Politics," *American Behavioral Scientist* 62, no. 1 (2018): 20.

20. Erdoğan and Uyan Semerci, *Fanusta Diyaloglar*, 64.

21. Ibid., 64–65.

22. Ibid., 73–75.

23. Ayşen Ataseven and Çağla Bakış, "Türkiye'de Sosyal Uyum" [Social cohesion in Turkey], Istanbul Policy Center Report, Sabancı University, June 2018, p. 25.

24. Senem Aydın-Düzgit and Evren Balta, "When Elites Polarize Over Polarization: Framing the Polarization Debate in Turkey," *New Perspectives on Turkey* 60, no. 1 (2019): 153–76.

25. On the "built-in, perverse dynamics of an 'authoritarian spiral of polarizing-cum-transformative politics,'" see Somer, "Turkey: The Slippery Slope."

26. Freedom House, "Freedom in the World 2018" (https://freedomhouse.org/report/freedom-world/2018/turkey).

27. World Bank, "Worldwide Governance Indicators" (http://info.worldbank.org/governance/wgi/#home).

28. Uğur Cevdet Panayırcı, Emre İşeri, and Eser Şekercioğlu, "Political Agency of News Outlets in a Polarized Media System: Framing the Corruption Probe in Turkey," *European Journal of Communication* 31, no. 5 (2016): 552.

29. Burak Özçetin and Banu Baybars-Hawks, "Framing the Russian Aircraft Crisis: News Discourse in Turkey's Polarized Media Environment," *Uluslararası İlişkiler* 15, no. 57 (2018): 39.

30. Freedom House, "Freedom of the Press 2017" (https://freedomhouse.org/report/freedom-press/2017/turkey).

31. Erdoğan and Uyan Semerci, *Fanusta Diyaloglar*, 93–102.

32. "Prof. Yılmaz Esmer: Soğan 3 Lira Değil 5 Lira Bile Olsa Seçmen Oyunu Değiştirmez" [Prof. Yılmaz Esmer: Even if onions are not 3 lira but 5 lira, it does not change the constituent's vote], *Habertürk*, July 1, 2018 (www.haberturk.com/prof-yilmaz-esmer-secim-sonuclarini-ve-gundemi-degerlendirdi-2039566).

33. McCoy, Rahman, and Somer, "Polarization and the Global Crisis of Democracy," 32.

34. Ibid., 25.

35. Organisation for Economic Co-operation and Development (OECD), "Country Fact Sheet: Turkey," Government at a Glance 2015 (www.oecd.org/gov/Turkey.pdf), 1; and OECD, "Country Fact Sheet: Turkey," Government at a Glance 2017 (www.oecd.org/gov/gov-at-a-glance-2017-turkey.pdf), 4.

36. "Trends in Turkish Civil Society," Center for American Progress, July 2017 (www.americanprogress.org/issues/security/reports/2017/07/10/435475/trends-turkish-civil-society/).

37. Erdoğan and Uyan Semerci, *Fanusta Diyaloglar*, 131–42.

38. Ataseven and Bakış, "Türkiye'de Sosyal Uyum," 27.

39. OECD, "Society at a Glance 2016: OECD Social Indicators" (Paris: OECD, 2016), 130. See also the World Values Survey, "Online Data Analysis," (www.worldvaluessurvey.org/WVSOnline.jsp).

TWO

Persistent Ethnic Polarization in Kenya

GILBERT M. KHADIAGALA

lthough the momentum for democratization globally in the 1990s promised the building of participatory and representative institutions that would mitigate polarization, the resurgence of new and old political fissures has raised profound questions about the solidity of these processes. In Africa, where democratization has barely taken root, regional and ethnic cleavages have resurfaced to cast a shadow on the prospect of creating sustainable democracies. Kenya is one of the few countries in Africa that is polarized between two dominant ethnic groups—the Kikuyu and Luo. In its geographic, regional, and ethnic dimensions, this polarization has shaped the course of postcolonial politics. This chapter suggests that polarization trends in Kenya are the result of the incompleteness of nation-building and integration, and that over time, these cleavages have prevented the emergence of solid institutions of governance in Kenya. For this reason, polarization has occasioned a stalemate at both the political and societal levels over Kenya's future.

The first section identifies ethnolinguistic and geographical differences as the basis of Kenya's ethnic cleavages and then highlights how three factors—elite entrepreneurship, political centralization, and economic inequalities in a context of patronage politics—have exacerbated polarization between two important groups, the Kikuyu and Luo. Appreciating the roots of the Kikuyu-Luo divide is critical to comprehending how ethnic conflicts have manifested themselves at critical junctures in Kenya's postcolonial history. The second section delineates these moments, starting with independence in 1963. Although the nationalist movement against British rule initially produced a Kikuyu-Luo alliance, political centralization and the weakness of checks and balances led to severe fragmentation between the two groups. Between 1963 and 1978, under the rule of President Jomo Kenyatta, the Kikuyu dominated Kenya's economy and politics, engendering resentment from the Luo and other ethnic groups. In turn, Kenyatta's successor, Daniel Arap Moi, wielded the immense power of the presidency to advance his own ethnic group, the Kalenjin, and effectively marginalized the Kikuyu and Luo. Although Kenya returned to multiparty elections in 1991, political pluralism brought back the old patterns of mobilization along the Kikuyu-Luo divide. In the context of ethnic-based political alliances, pluralism has heightened polarization by increasing the stakes around competition for power and resources. Since the first decade of the twenty-first century, the changing configuration of ethnic alliances has reinforced the primary Kikuyu-Luo fissure, resulting in both bouts of electoral violence and inklings of institutional change. The concluding sections examine the consequences of political polarization and possible remedial actions, pointing to the difficulties of building meaningful institutions in the prevailing climate of polarization.

Roots

In Kenya, linguistic and geographical differences between the Kikuyu and Luo form the underlying basis for ethnic polarization, and a combination of elite entrepreneurship, political centralization, and inequalities exacerbated by patronage politics has compounded this divide. Rather than serving as a flexible mode of social identity, ethnicity has evolved as a rigid tool that is employed in political mobilization, the organization of public life, and the allocation of resources. Elites on both sides of the political divide are creatures and captives of ethnicity, benefiting from but also trapped by this polarizing cleavage.

Kenya has a population of about 50 million people divided into forty-two ethnic groups. The major ethnic conflicts have involved the Kikuyu and Luo, who represent 18 percent and 11 percent of the total population, respectively. The Kikuyu's numerical strength is bolstered by their ability to rally ethnic groups with similar linguistic and cultural affinities that reside in central Kenya, particularly the Embu and Meru. These groups have sided with the Kikuyu in all major political contests. The Luo, by contrast, have often mobilized ethnic groups primarily from the western and coastal regions, but cultural and linguistic differences have prevented them from creating a solid block to counter that of the Kikuyu. With the exception of the twenty-four years under President Daniel Arap Moi (1978–2002), all of Kenya's presidents have been Kikuyu: Jomo Kenyatta (1963–78), Mwai Kibaki (2003–13), and Uhuru Kenyatta (since 2013). The Luo, led by the prominent father-and-son pair Jaramogi Oginga Odinga and Raila Odinga, have, with few exceptions, contested the perceived Kikuyu political and economic hegemony. Moi's presidency further intensified the polarization by elevating the Kalenjin, an assortment of ethnic groups from the Rift Valley that share similar linguistic and cultural characteristics, into formidable power brokers between the Kikuyu and Luo. A significant number of Kikuyu migrants also live in the Rift Valley and coastal regions, a fact that has led to violent conflicts over land between them and indigenous groups.

Although ethnicity typically manifests itself in some measure of cultural distinctiveness, the ethnic stereotypes at the heart of the Kikuyu-Luo divide have no deep cultural or historical roots. The Kikuyu belong to the Bantu linguistic group, while the Luo are part of the Nilotic group; these groups are differentiated by language and some traditional attributes such as circumcision rites, but the latter are not as important in modern times. The Kikuyu and adjacent groups live in the Mount Kenya/central region, while the Luo predominantly live around Lake Victoria in the western region. Ethnicity in Kenya primarily reflects established linguistic, geographical, and regional boundaries, which were reinforced by colonial and postcolonial governments. Before the creation of the modern Kenyan state, the two groups did not have any significant interactions because they occupy geographically distinct parts of Kenya. Urbanization has brought the two together in major cities, but the majority of the Kikuyu and Luo are peasant farmers in their respective regions. In primarily peasant societies with marked geographical distances, ethnic stereotypes prevail because people have limited opportunities for interactions and intermingling. These stereotypes become severe, as in the case of the Kikuyu-Luo divide, when elite entrepreneurs highlight linguistic and cultural differences and when successive generations are socialized into believing these stereotypes.[1]

Three factors in particular have intensified the Kikuyu-Luo divide and turned political competition into a polarizing struggle for power and resources. First, elite entrepreneurs have stoked ethnic divisions to consolidate their bases of electoral support. In neopatrimonial systems where power is largely personalized, the mobilization of ethnicity increases the chances of ascending to power. Even in the era of multiparty politics, political organizations have remained personalistic machines that rally support in their distinctive geographical and regional domains. Leaders of the two communities have opportunistically used ethnic appeals in order to win elections and gain access to scarce resources, making conflict almost inevitable. Jomo Kenyatta and Oginga Odinga joined forces in the nationalist movement, the Kenya African National Union (KANU), which won independence in 1963, but this alliance collapsed in the mid-1960s, starting the acrimonious polarization that became a permanent feature of national politics.[2]

Second, Kenya emerged as a highly centralized state with substantial resources in the hands of the executive presidency, fueling incessant competition for central power. The Kenyatta government initially supported the centralization of power in order to bolster nationalism and stem the disintegrative tide of ethnic political coalescence, but over time the centralized state became a magnet for convulsive ethnic competition. Because of this centralization, Luo grievances have revolved around the perception that the Kikuyu have tried to deny them the presidency in both the one-party and multiparty periods. In effect, the centralization around the presidency meant that the struggle for power and access to key resources gradually became defined in zero-sum contexts of ethnicity and region.[3]

Third, particularly given the importance of patronage politics, the politicization of ethnicity builds on and exacerbates horizontal economic inequalities between the Kikuyu and Luo. These are economic and social inequalities based primarily on ethnic and cultural differences.[4] In Kenya, the Luo complain about systemic discrimination by the Kikuyu, who had advanced remarkably during the colonial period because of their proximity to the colonial state. In contrast, the remoteness of the Luo from the colonial center diminished their chances of making an economic head start. These economic asymmetries have persisted in the postcolonial period because the Luo have never won control of Kenya's presidency and thus have been denied the spoils of state patronage. Use of the state as an instrument of material acquisition has meant that power holders who benefit from the unequal structures of access attempt to exclude their opponents, creating a zero-sum conflict for resources that has fomented ethnic tensions. Some critics of Jomo Kenyatta have pointed out that he laid the foundation for ethnic polarization by sacrificing the nationalist ethos of self-sacrifice, unity, and inclusion on the altar of wealth acquisition, selfishness, and exclusion.[5] In the postcolonial period, horizontal inequities have remained a source of contestation, as the Luo and neighboring groups in western regions of Kenya have protested their marginalization by the central government. Coastal communities have made similar complaints of systemic political marginalization by successive Kenyan governments.[6]

Ethnic mobilization based on competition for power and resources has at times coincided with ideological divergences, but these differences have never been profound or deep-seated. During the Cold War in the 1960s, Kenyatta was perceived as a pro-Western leader sympathetic to capitalist policies, whereas Odinga favored left-leaning policies, including land redistribution to those marginalized by the colonial government. On land, Kenyatta was a proponent of gradual "willing buyer, willing seller" policies that would not disrupt agricultural production. In the mid-1960s, whereas Kenyatta strongly supported a centralized and unitary state, Odinga campaigned for a decentralized system that would grant neglected regions more autonomy and a greater share of state resources.[7] In the early 2000s, Raila Odinga, like his father, advocated for policies that would reduce inequities and corruption, problems that he identified with the Kikuyu leadership. However, such ideological differences primarily reflect ethnic competition, rather than serving as an independent driver of polarization in themselves. In the 1960s, the right-left divide merely concealed the ethnic scramble for power between Kenyatta and Odinga; in recent years, both Kikuyu and Luo leaders have not made any pretenses to ideology.

Trajectory

As in most of Africa, ethnic polarization in Kenya is a creature of the postcolonial state, which meshed different cultural and linguistic groups into arbitrarily drawn territories. By imposing indelible group identities upon individuals, colonial laws created modern ethnic groups that subsequent postcolonial governments have sought to unite through state- and nation-building. Since independence, these processes have entailed efforts to manage ethnic and regional diversities, create state institutions with a national reach and outlook, and mobilize new national symbols to minimize ethnicity. The endurance of ethnic polarization, in large measure, symbolizes the failure of state- and nation-building initiatives. As one of Kenya's leading economists poignantly remarked in March 2016: "Kenya has never been a more distant idea than it is now at the beginning of the 21st Century. Nationalism is dead, replaced by sub-nationalism. The tribe has eaten the nation."[8]

The struggle for independence allowed the emergence of a nationalist movement, KANU, led by Kikuyu and Luo leaders. In the early to mid-1960s, Kenyatta and Odinga had a brief moment of mutual understanding. From the late 1970s into the 1990s, with these two ethnic groups out of power, the Kalenjin arose as a national counterweight to the Kikuyu and Luo, but political mismanagement, corruption, and repression prevented Kenya's leaders from consolidating this opportunity to ease ethnic polarization. These problems led, at least in part, to the pressures for political pluralism in the 1990s. In the era of multiparty politics, the Kikuyu-Luo cleavage surfaced afresh, marked by the scrambling of old and new political alliances, electoral violence, and a deterioration in national discourse on the future of Kenya.

The Promises and Pitfalls of KANU Nationalism, 1963 to 1978

Political polarization in the period immediately after independence pivoted around a combination of ideological clashes between Kenyatta and Odinga and contestation over economic policies that would redress ethnic economic inequalities. Within the dominant party, KANU, these differences came to a head in the mid-1960s when Odinga broke with Kenyatta to create the Kenya People's Union (KPU), a predominantly Luo party. KPU's "socialist orientation," however, concealed a raft of populist policies on land reforms and socioeconomic redistribution.

Even during the halcyon days of the Kikuyu-Luo alliance (1963–66), it was clear that ethnic identities would be a primary basis of political mobilization. Ethnicity became salient because political mobilization revolved almost exclusively around the geographical and regional distinctions that coincided with ethnic groups. In those days, KANU under Kenyatta and Odinga competed against what was popularly known as the alliance of "small tribes," which consisted of the Kalenjin, Kamba, Kisii, Luhya, and *Mijikenda* (coastal people), organized under the Kenya African Democratic Union (KADU). KANU supported a unitary government with power centered in Nairobi, whereas KADU campaigned for political decentralization along regional lines to prevent Kikuyu-Luo dominance.

Soon, however, a vicious ethnic rift occurred within KANU, based mainly on competing visions regarding land redistribution, socioeconomic reforms, and Kenya's future direction. Harping on land grievances in central Kenya and the Rift Valley, Odinga challenged Kenyatta's free-market-based land reforms. Odinga further charged that the Kenyatta family and its allies had taken prime land at the expense of the public. The conflict worsened in 1966 when Kenyatta removed Odinga from the vice presidency and induced the opposition KADU leaders to join KANU.[9]

The immense power of the Kenyan presidency—coupled with the weakness of checks and balances in the newly independent nation—allowed polarization to escalate rapidly, as Kenyatta violently repressed Odinga's supporters. Odinga was forced to form a new party, the KPU, which had a populist inclination. As the two leaders appropriated competing notions of the nationalist narrative, they retreated into their ethnic enclaves to rally political support. From then on, the Kenyatta-Odinga conflict took on decidedly ethnic undertones, with the Luo depicted as "lazy," "anti-Kenya," and "friends of the Soviet Union," while the Luo labelled the Kikuyu as "capitalist thieves," "power hungry," and "land grabbers." Some of these stereotypes have prevailed as dominant narratives in framing ethnic polarization between them.[10] After a violent confrontation in October 1969 between Kenyatta and Odinga supporters in Kisumu, the major city on Lake Victoria, Kenyatta proscribed the KPU and detained Odinga, along with his key supporters. This confrontation marked a major juncture in the rift between the two and effectively ended the postindependence experiment with multiparty politics. From that point on, Kenyatta was able to consolidate KANU's rule by exploiting the specter of the "hordes from the lake" and "beasts from the west" as powerful mobilization symbols.[11]

KANU's consolidation helped to entrench the Kikuyu as the dominant group in Kenya's economy and bureaucracy, further fueling Luo ethnic resentments of the Kikuyu. The Kenyatta state took advantage of the significant sinecures opened up by the departure of colonial authorities to promote the interests of the Kikuyu and kindred groups in the Mount Kenya region, who became dependable allies. Although the government often made rhetorical references to nation-building and equitable development, the distribution of national resources skewed heavily toward central Kenya. Between 1963 and 1978, Kenya's prosperity reflected the economic and political imprint of the Kikuyu elite through ethnic patronage.[12] The Kenyatta government created elaborate patronage networks, which allowed the centralized state to incorporate key regional leaders in the government and the economy in exchange for support. These networks served as both the carrots for inclusion and the sticks for exclusion, providing the state with tools to guarantee loyalty from Kenyatta's allies and to punish recalcitrant ethnic groups. But these networks also laid the foundations for widespread corruption and looting of public resources to reward Kenyatta's followers. In the mid-1970s, before he died in office, Kenyatta tried to make some political overtures toward Odinga, but opposition from the dominant Kikuyu faction that was angling to succeed him prevented him from fully reaching out to his erstwhile opponent.[13]

The Rise of the Kalenjin: The Moi Era (I), 1978 to 1991

Between 1978 and 1991, authoritarian one-party rule under President Moi temporarily suspended ethnic polarization between the Kikuyu and Luo, but only because Moi sought to secure the power of his own ethnic group, the Kalenjin. For Moi to erode Kikuyu dominance, he had to rally around Kalenjin identity. In subsequent years, the mobilization of the Kalenjin coincided with land grievances that the Kalenjin had against Kikuyu settlers in the Rift Valley, igniting ethnic violence that continues to scar the region.

As Kenyatta's vice president, Moi's succession to power in 1978 was not a smooth transition. Although a faction of Kikuyu elites tried to prevent Moi from ascending to the presidency, this bid failed. Because he came from a minority group and did not have strong nationalist credentials, Moi originally appealed for national unity in attempts to build a broad national support base. However, a combination of political and economic challenges led Moi to consolidate power around the Kalenjin elite. An attempted coup d'état in 1982, led by junior Luo officers in the Kenya Air Force, tilted Moi toward political repression and centralization of power. The coup attempt gave Moi the opportunity to purge the bureaucracy and security services of perceived opponents, including many Kikuyu, and to create new patronage networks. The Luo, already marginalized by the Kenyatta government, faced more repression as their leaders, including Raila Odinga, were accused of masterminding the coup plot and jailed.[14] In addition, the Kenyan economy deteriorated in the 1980s, whittling down the sources of patronage and forcing Moi to consolidate economic and political power around the Kalenjin.

In trying to dismantle the Kikuyu stranglehold on the economy, Moi faced formidable challenges. To dislodge the Kikuyu middle class and establish a Kalenjin-dominated economy, Moi initiated a massive transfer of resources from the Kikuyu to the Kalenjin. However, the Kalenjin who took over most of the commercial enterprises lacked the skills to sustain them. Thus, when the Moi state failed to create a viable Kalenjin-controlled economy, it resorted to supporting a predatory class preoccupied with the systematic looting of state resources. Under Moi, therefore, corruption and the hollowing-out of state institutions worsened. During the Kenyatta period, the entrepreneurial capacity of the Kikuyu middle classes gave them some autonomy from the state, but the Kalenjin economic actors staked their fortunes more closely to the Moi government. As a result, the state's redistributive policies led to increased brutality and violence to secure resources for the Kalenjin.[15]

Under Moi, the destruction of national institutions further undermined the search for a collective ethos and national identity. Moi's failure to create encompassing institutions that would overcome the Kikuyu-Luo divide deprived the Kalenjin of the chance to develop an alternative power center that could rally nation-building efforts. The combination of political repression and worsening economic conditions spurred the growth of

movements for political change, which arose in the late 1980s. These domestic movements coincided with pressures from international donors that
forced Moi to legalize opposition parties in 1991.

Pluralism as an Antidote to Polarization? The Moi Era (II), 1991 to 2002

Although the onset of pluralism promised to broaden the spectrum of
political voices, elite competition has been dominated by grand alliances
and coalitions that have not overcome the Kikuyu-Luo cleavage. As democratization raised the stakes of electoral competition, elites from various ethnic groups coalesced on either side of the existing divide to secure
advantages. Thus, political pluralism exacerbated polarization, resulting in
electoral violence and further weakening national institutions. The start
of multiparty competition ushered in a period of realignment between the
Kikuyu and Luo in their effort to defeat the Moi government. A first coalition (1991–92) failed to dislodge Moi from power, though a second one
(2002–03) succeeded.

Civil society organizations and political parties proliferated following
the introduction of a multiparty system in 1991, but the vistas for mobilization beyond the Kikuyu-Luo divide were ephemeral. The breakthrough
of the early 1990s provided breathing spaces for ethnic elites to create new
but still ethnically-based political parties. Civil society organizations op-
timistically intended to carve out a distinctive role in the polarized space
of Kenyan politics, but they soon lapsed into ethnic and sectarian politics.
Furthermore, the Moi government used the multiparty system as a vehicle
to reorganize itself and reclaim its declining legitimacy.[16]

In the first phase of crafting a new national coalition, the Kikuyu and
Luo rallied other ethnic groups under the umbrella of the Forum for the
Restoration of Democracy (FORD) to defeat Moi's KANU. These attempts, however, quickly unraveled as ethnic tensions and leadership squabbles resumed. Moi also resorted to violence and the large-scale evictions of
mainly Kikuyu landowners from the Rift Valley. In the 1997 elections, the
violent mobilization of Kalenjin identity resulted in the evictions of "outsiders" from the Rift Valley, in a precursor to the 2007–08 electoral violence.
The combination of a divided opposition and state-sponsored violence enabled Moi to win the 1992 and 1997 elections with slim majorities.[17]

Another vital moment in the ethnic jostling for power occurred in the aftermath of the 1997 elections when Moi forged an alliance with Raila Odinga, the new Luo leader. This alliance, in turn, sparked a counter-alliance led by a Kikuyu, Mwai Kibaki. But in the lead-up to the 2002 elections, the Kalenjin-Luo coalition collapsed after Odinga joined the National Rainbow Coalition (NARC) led by Kibaki, constituting the second phase in the search for a Kikuyu-Luo political coalition. In the unity pact, Kibaki and Odinga agreed on a pre-election power-sharing arrangement that would cement their relationship after the December 2002 elections. For the first time since the early 1960s, prominent Kikuyu and Luo leaders were working together to create a coalition that downplayed ethnic differences. The NARC enabled Kibaki to win the December 2002 elections with an overwhelming majority.[18]

Back to Polarization: The Kibaki Years, 2003 to 2007

The interethnic coalition led by the Kikuyu and Luo demonstrated the possibilities of inclusive politics that would rise above ethnicity. This coalition, however, collapsed in acrimony amid the resurgence of ethnic mobilization, contests over constitutional reforms, and disagreements on socioeconomic policies. These differences fueled postelection violence in 2007–08, resulting in an externally mediated power-sharing agreement. As with previous moments of interethnic coalition-building, this agreement provided only a temporary respite from the polarization.

Barely a year into the NARC government's tenure, conflict over the allocation of power and resources brought the Kikuyu-Luo divide back to the fore. Claiming that Kibaki had ignored the pre-election power-sharing agreement, Odinga pulled out of the NARC government in 2003. These events resurrected the traditional pattern of ethnic mobilization along the Kikuyu-Luo fault line. More importantly, the NARC's collapse developed into a battle that crystallized around the constitutional reforms that had started in the late 1990s. Odinga alleged that Kibaki and the Kikuyu elites were trying to water down key provisions regarding the reduction of presidential powers and political decentralization. After several drafts throughout 2003 and 2004, Kenya held a referendum on the new constitution in 2005.[19]

In the lead-up to the referendum, severe polarization gripped the country as Kikuyu government supporters battled on the airwaves, social media, and other forums against Odinga's supporters. Kibaki lost the highly divisive referendum, exacerbating the disarray in the government. Odinga's supporters subsequently organized a new political movement, the Orange Democratic Movement (ODM), to compete in the 2007 elections. A new entrant into ODM was William Ruto, who was rising as the new Kalenjin leader following Moi's retirement. Responding to ODM, Kibaki rallied political parties from the Mount Kenya heartland.[20]

The polarization that marked the campaigns for the December 2007 elections mirrored the previous referendum contest with its prominent ethnic stereotyping, hate speech, and demonization. Odinga built on the energy of the referendum victory by crafting a platform that blamed Kibaki for the impasse in constitutional reforms, rampant corruption, and the economic marginalization of non-Kikuyu. Kibaki, by contrast, touted Kenya's economic progress since 2003 and castigated Odinga for downplaying these achievements to garner votes. As the most competitive and contentious election in Kenya's history, the 2007 presidential race ended in violence as Odinga's supporters, claiming to have been denied victory by Kibaki, rose up in arms in the Rift Valley, the Luo region, and Nairobi. Alongside the security forces, government supporters retaliated by targeting mostly Luo residents in Nairobi and the Rift Valley. Cumulatively, the postelection violence led to 1,500 deaths and the displacement of more than 600,000 people. Peace was restored when the African Union led a mediation initiative that resulted in the formation of a Government of National Unity (GNU) in February 2008.[21]

The postelection violence brought the Kikuyu-Luo divide to its ultimate dénouement. Virulent ethnic mobilization—born of years of zero-sum mentalities, grievances stemming from horizontal inequities, and political marginalization—had produced a combustible context in which violence seemed inevitable. High levels of youth unemployment, the historical discontent around land ownership in the Rift Valley, and worsening poverty and frustration across Kenya fueled the violence. Most of the foot soldiers in the electoral violence were armed ethnic militias funded by politicians and business leaders from opposing sides. David Ndii has blamed the Kibaki government for inflaming the Kikuyu-Luo divide between 2003 and 2008:

Kibaki tore up the political covenant [with Odinga], tribalized the government and went back to the post-independence doctrine of wealth above all else. The Kibaki administration's belligerence and political thuggery brought the country to the brink of civil war. Ironically, Kibaki ended up with exactly the same cohabitation in his second term that he had refused to honor in the first.[22]

Regrouping through Power Sharing, 2008 to 2013

International actors rescued Kenya from collapse, furnishing a new moment of national regeneration through power sharing. The GNU temporarily eased Kikuyu-Luo polarization and enabled the passage of a new constitution in August 2010, with provisions for political decentralization and equitable sharing of resources. Yet despite these positive steps, the tenuous Kikuyu-Luo alliance that dominated the GNU quickly began to fray and was eclipsed by a Kikuyu and Kalenjin alliance after a split between Odinga and Ruto, the Kalenjin leader. The International Criminal Court's (ICC) indictment of key alliance leaders Uhuru Kenyatta and William Ruto over their involvement in the postelection violence solidified this arrangement. Since the 2013 elections, the Kikuyu-Kalenjin coalition has taken the center stage in Kenya's unending ethnic politics.

Though disparaged by both Kibaki and Odinga, the GNU took significant steps toward reducing ethnic polarization by establishing multiple commissions to address long-standing questions of ethnicity, inequalities, and regional imbalances that had retarded national cohesion and contributed to violence. In the face of international pressure, the Kenyan government also established a commission to investigate the circumstances that led to the 2007 postelection violence. Equally vital, after intense negotiations over constitutional reforms, the political parties compromised on a new constitution, which was approved through a referendum in 2010. Among its key provisions are a bill of rights, devolution of power and resources to county governments, ethical leadership, and safeguards to prevent ethnic conflicts. Odinga lost the campaign to introduce a parliamentary system of government that would have strengthened the power of parliament at the expense of the executive. As a result, a strong presidency continues to coexist uneasily with decentralized structures.[23]

However, the fragmentation within Odinga's party following the split with Ruto and the Kalenjin overshadowed the GNU's constitutional achievements. Although Ruto had supported Odinga in the 2007 elections, he felt marginalized in the GNU and opted to pursue an independent line. After the GNU failed to agree on local measures to deal with international crimes committed in the 2007 postelection period, the ICC launched investigations into Ruto and Kenyatta, as well as their close allies. Subsequently, the ICC indicted Ruto for leading the killings of Kikuyu as well as Kenyatta for his involvement in Kikuyu retaliatory violence. On the eve of the 2013 elections, Kenyatta and Ruto found common cause in a new Jubilee Alliance that competed against Odinga's alliance, ending the five-year Kikuyu-Luo power-sharing coalition. As their primary campaign platform, Kenyatta and Ruto rallied against the ICC's interference in Kenyan politics and decried Odinga's alleged support for the ICC.[24]

The Kikuyu-Kalenjin Alliance and the Changing Forms of Ethnic Realignments, 2013 to the Present

The alliance between the Kikuyu and Kalenjin since 2013 has intensified Kenya's ethnic polarization rather than mitigating the traditional Kikuyu-Luo cleavage. The enduring trend is the Kikuyu's determination to deny victory to their old Luo nemesis, symbolized by Odinga. The Kalenjin, with a large voter base in the Rift Valley, have emerged as a formidable ethnic bloc to further frustrate Luo efforts to gain power.

The new Kikuyu-Kalenjin alliance has inflamed ethnic divisions by threatening to shut the Luo and their allies out of power over the long term. To be sure, the Jubilee Alliance continues to be a "negative" coalition, molded by leaders who once mobilized their ethnic groups in violence against one another. Yet Jubilee has created an almost unbeatable alliance based on the large numbers of Rift Valley and central Kenya voters, to the disadvantage of the Luo and their allies. Some Kenyan analysts have described this phenomenon as the "tyranny of numbers," in which the numerical superiority of the populous Kikuyu and Kalenjin allows them to defeat any combination of opposition coalitions.[25] Furthermore, after defeating the opposition in the 2013 elections, Kenyatta and Ruto hinted that Jubilee would guarantee rotation in power between the Kikuyu and Kalenjin.

Under this scenario, after Kenyatta completes his two presidential terms in 2022, he would then be succeeded by Ruto, the current deputy president, for ten years before a new set of leaders emerges from the two ethnic groups. Facing a numerically dominant Kikuyu-Kalenjin coalition, opposition parties now appear to have the unenviable choice of either joining the winning coalition or remaining on the political periphery.

Crucially, the formal institutional changes enacted in 2010 have done little to change the informal practices of corruption and patronage that fuel ethnic polarization, supported by the lingering legacies of the centralized state. Although the new constitution has created decentralized institutions, there are still profound debates about how much resources the central government can devolve to these entities. Governors have battled to wrest fiscal power from the central government, but these efforts remain inconclusive and are not immune from the dominant ethnic divisions. The central government has been able to divide governors through promises of more resources for their regions at the expense of opposition governors.[26] In addition, Jubilee controls the majority in parliament, which makes resource allocation decisions that are often skewed against the minority opposition parties. Through the office of the presidency the central government also retains significant control of large but opaque security and military budgetary allocations, which are often diverted for political patronage. As a result of the persistence of strong presidential powers, the sources of corruption and patronage have remained unchanged.

Invariably, presidential elections continue to be contentious and divisive, as the major ethnic blocks vie for resources to feed their patronage networks. Thus, as in the 1960s and 1970s, groups that are aligned with the Jubilee government look to the center for resources because the decentralized structures are still underresourced. More worrisome, the patronage networks built on massive corruption at the center have reemerged, particularly as Jubilee elites scramble for resources to reward their followers and win elections. In the absence of efforts to strengthen Kenya's decentralized institutions, the "tyranny of numbers," erected solidly on ethnicity, may signal a future marked by profound instability, marginalization, and the reversal of the gains made through constitutional reforms.

The conduct of the 2017 elections suggested that the Jubilee government's authoritarian practices will continue to aggravate the resentment of the Luo and their allies, encourage repeated violence, and undermine efforts to reduce polarization. Though capable of comfortably securing a majority, the Jubilee government failed to invest in credible and transparent electoral systems, leading to the Supreme Court's nullification of the August 2017 presidential elections. Kenya has a history of electoral mismanagement that combines incompetence and the willful manipulation of electoral institutions by those in power. Although the nullification was broadly hailed as marking the maturation of judicial independence in Kenya, Odinga and his allies boycotted the rerun elections in October 2017, claiming that the electoral commission was not prepared for a free election. In the aftermath, violence broke out in opposition regions between security forces and protestors, and some of Odinga's supporters made veiled threats of secession as the way to redress marginalization. Proponents of secession cited Kenya's many years of rule by two ethnic groups, with consistent patterns of rigged elections, economic marginalization, and extrajudicial killings.[27] In March 2018, as Kenya teetered on the brink of a fresh cycle of violence, Kenyatta and Odinga agreed on a political truce and the formation of a framework, the Building Bridges Initiative, to work out long-term measures to reduce ethnic tensions between the Kikuyu and Luo. The two leaders negotiated the truce without consulting their followers, underscoring the fluidity and personalization of political agreements.

The March 2018 agreement lowered political temperatures and heralded another effort to find meaningful reconciliation between the two groups, but, as an essentially elite-based compromise, it will not yield fundamental outcomes to reverse the course of ethnic divisions. For Kenyatta, the agreement ended the tumultuous events sparked by the 2017 elections and enhanced his legitimacy and legacy as a national leader, particularly since he will not be competing in the 2022 elections. Moreover, Kenyatta gave Odinga a face-saving concession, one that allowed Odinga to remain a significant player in Kenyan politics but left the opposition out of the government. Yet the Building Bridges Initiative has no true legal standing and has no specific deadlines to reach an agreement; the government is not required to implement any recommendations that the initiative produces. Besides, if the initiative drags on for a few more years, its usefulness will diminish as Kenya enters another electioneering period. Odinga realized that brinkmanship and threats of secession were creating the conditions for the state to use more force against his followers. By reaching out to Kenyatta, Odinga was able to reclaim national stature in the wake of his followers' futile attempts to have him declared as the "people's president." To the Ruto camp of the Jubilee coalition, the truce has raised misgivings because of fears that Kenyatta may be preparing to reconcile with the Luo and abandon the Kalenjin. Beginning in early 2019, Ruto started to reach out to Kikuyu leaders who were disgruntled with the Kenyatta-Odinga alliance. Thus, even though the Building Bridges Initiative was a welcome reprieve from the tensions surrounding the 2017 elections, it has produced new ethnic polarization between the Luo and Kalenjin as Odinga and Ruto jostle to win over Kenyatta's Kikuyu supporters in the lead-up to the 2022 elections.

Why Has Polarization Persisted for More Than Five Decades?

The persistence of ethnic polarization is attributable to four factors: (1) the failure to create a modern state with shared national values; (2) the generational reproduction of ethnic cleavages, despite the growth of a cosmopolitan middle class; (3) the inability of Kikuyu and Luo leaders to reach a broad consensus about how to resolve their differences; and (4) the absence of moderate countervailing power centers to smooth over the Kikuyu-Luo fissure.

To begin, the objective of nationhood that Jomo Kenyatta and Oginga Odinga envisaged for Kenya in the 1950s and 1960s has failed in large measure to take firm root, despite some progress in creating a middle class that could anchor a national identity. The Kenyan middle class has grown over the years largely because of the government's substantial investments in education, rural infrastructure, and services, as well as the middle class's own ability to seize economic and professional opportunities within East Africa and globally. Unlike its neighbors, Kenya has a relatively more globally competitive human resource base because of its educated population. But because of lingering attachments to ethnic identities, this middle class has not translated its social power into genuine national movements for reordering politics in the direction of national values and institutions. Voting figures for presidential candidates in Kikuyu and Luo regions reveal the reality that votes are cast on a strictly ethnic basis. These voting patterns reinforce the political salience of ethnicity and ensure that competing candidates cannot reach out to areas inhabited by opposing groups.

Second, even though Kenya's middle class has grown dramatically, this socioeconomic change has not reduced the role of ethnic identity in politics. Several analysts claim that the rise of the middle class and processes of generational change are crucial in lessening the salience of ethnic identities. By this logic, new generations are supposedly more predisposed to jettison primordial identities in exchange for new cosmopolitan ones. In Kenya, the new generations have not lived up to this expectation. In routine social interactions, the middle classes show evidence of cosmopolitanism, but during political contests, they lapse back into their ethnic identities. Moreover, with the prevalence of new technologies and media, the new generations have found highly effective tools to promote ethnic hatreds. Since the 2005 constitutional referendum, social media has inflamed ethnic passions and violence. Similarly, the vernacular radio stations, which came into being in the 1990s with the relaxation of media controls, have played a role in propagating hate speech and disseminating inflammatory statements.[28]

Equally vital, generational change has not produced leaders with new national political identities; instead, the rising generation has reproduced the cleavages that have undermined nation-building. For the most part, the recent Odinga-Kenyatta political rivalry symbolizes the continuity of ethnic polarization that has marked Kenyan politics since the 1960s. Even though both leaders speak of themselves as the "new generation," they have not departed from the divisiveness that their fathers established in previous years. Since the introduction of political pluralism, Kikuyu and Luo leaders have not sufficiently seized the opportunities to build trust and create durable national institutions. For instance, by reverting back to ethnic mobilization, Kikuyu and Luo elites squandered the momentum for national coalescence in the early 1990s produced by the legalization of political parties. Similarly, in the early 2000s, the formation of the NARC alliance indicated that the Kikuyu and Luo could downplay their differences and lead a national coalition for change. Yet the collapse of the coalition dealt a severe blow to efforts to resurrect national institutions after twenty-four years of Moi's misrule. The 2007 electoral violence jolted the elites toward working together, but this episode was not sufficient to alter the trajectory of ethnic animosities. As a result, despite momentary coalitions, the bitter rivalries at the elite level have expanded to encompass the Kikuyu and Luo populations more broadly, hardening societal cleavages and creating further barriers to reconciliation.

Finally, from the 1960s to the present, the absence of moderate power centers (composed either of coalitions of small ethnic groups or social movements with programs that rise above ethnicity) has further hampered steps to mitigate polarization. In the 1960s, KADU tried to marshal small ethnic groups to counter Kikuyu-Luo hegemony, but this effort was short-lived because its leaders joined Kenyatta in the formative confrontation with Odinga. In the early 1990s, numerous parties tried to organize on an ideological and nonethnic basis, but most of them folded because they could not compete with the dominant ethnic alliances, demonstrating the challenges of political mobilization outside the established frames of ethnicity. To a large extent, the prevalence of patronage networks impairs the evolution of strong countervailing movements or parties. Without the resources or the numbers to be effective competitors, small groups bandwagon on the Kikuyu and Luo movements to obtain the advantages of patronage. As a key feature of power centralization, patronage has depended on presidential efforts to build regional power centers through the dispensing of economic resources; these power centers, which effectively are ethnic and regional, provide political support for the ruling elites. The culture of patronage, in turn, creates additional ethnic divisions across Kenya because access to resources hinges on alignments with the ethnic group or coalitions in power. More vitally, because both dominant groups are able to rally small ethnic groups for the ends that drive polarization, it has been difficult to craft national encompassing political coalitions that can overcome the extant cleavages and strengthen national institutions.

Consequences

Ethnic polarization has given rise to institutional paralysis, fueled electoral violence, exacerbated horizontal inequalities, and frustrated the search for consensus about building solid institutions of citizenship and identity. The profound impact of polarization on institutional development is apparent in the exclusion of large portions of Kenyans from employment in the public service, which in turn has weakened professionalism. Since the 1960s, there has been no meritocracy in recruitment for the civil service and state-owned institutions, as the ethnic groups that control the presidency have used recruitment to reward their followers. Moi purged the civil service of Kikuyu professionals and replaced them with the Kalenjin; in the current era, hiring in public institutions is divided between the Kikuyu and the Kalenjin.

In addition, ethnic polarization weakens the integrity and independence of multiple institutions such as the electoral commission, anticorruption bodies, the national treasury, and the security services because they are continually forced to do the bidding of the elites in power rather than serve national interests. With respect to electoral institutions, ethnic maneuvering has undercut the search for neutral rules of competition because none of the competing sides has a stake in accountable and transparent electoral rules. Thus, elections routinely fall victim to the ethnic divide. In the aftermath of the 2017 elections, Kenya's electoral commission sunk into disarray and confusion as its leaders blamed each other for the fiasco at the polls. Similarly, Kenya has failed to erect sound anticorruption institutions because the patronage system that undergirds ethnic polarization thrives on the plunder and abuse of state resources. Widespread complaints about the resurgence of grand corruption schemes under Kenyatta and Ruto stem from the fact that the Kikuyu-Kalenjin alliance has created a large number of claimants, who are needed to sustain the patronage networks. Polarization has also affected parliament because the majority of its members belong to the Jubilee party; in the fragmented political environment, they cannot criticize the executive. In essence, polarization prevents parliamentary bipartisanship.

Polarization also has affected the decentralized institutions created by the 2010 constitution. Although the framers of Kenya's new constitution envisioned decentralization as the key to development, political stability, and national integration, the continued existence of a strong central government with enormous resources has guaranteed that ethnic elites will remain focused on winning the presidency rather than strengthening other Kenyan political institutions. Kibaki and Kenyatta campaigned to retain a strong center because the executive, alongside the legislature, would play a large role in distributing resources to the decentralized institutions. But as parliament is paralyzed by polarization, the executive naturally exercises more control over resource distribution. In the current context, Kenya's governors have tried to organize and obtain more resources for their counties from the central government, but these efforts are not coherent or cohesive because these leaders are also captive to the polarizing dynamics of the Kikuyu-Luo divide. For this reason, ethnicity has impeded the maturation of decentralized institutions.

Remedial Actions

The actors and institutions that have sought to address polarization are animated by the conviction that the exclusive framing of politics has had deleterious effects on Kenya's emergence as a modern nation-state, and that Kenya will continue to underperform in all respects if it cannot manage its ethnic conflagrations. By this logic, the perennial relapse into ethnic politics has prevented genuine and urgent debates about how to address the pressing issues of inequality, poverty, and social marginalization that threaten the Kikuyu and Luo elites in equal measure. The search for solutions has involved national actors, civil society, parliament, and international donors.

In the aftermath of the 2007 elections, the GNU created a National Cohesion and Integration Commission (NCIC) with the mandate to find solutions to ethnic intolerance, hate speech, skewed hiring practices in public institutions, and long-standing grievances. The rationale behind the commission was that any plan to manage ethnicity would depend on conscious efforts to craft strategies for ethnic harmony and understanding. Through national conversations and campaigns, the NCIC has raised awareness about the scourge of ethnicity and advocated for lasting solutions that address economic inequality and provide opportunities for all. Since its formation, however, the NCIC has struggled to become an effective institution in the face of underfunding and limited relevance outside Nairobi. The local press may give enthusiastic coverage of its national campaigns to foster harmony and reduce polarization, but its recommendations are not taken seriously. The cycle of electoral violence since the 1990s has also jumpstarted broad civil society efforts to support reconciliation and peacebuilding initiatives in local communities, particularly in the Rift Valley and in informal urban settlements throughout Kenya. Although these initiatives are important in building peace in the affected communities, they often are too localized to have an impact on national politics.

A wide array of Kenyan civil society organizations that straddle ethnic divisions have campaigned for the deescalation of ethnic competition. Most of these organizations are led by professional, religious, and civic actors who played critical roles in previous efforts for constitutional reform. Organizations such the Kenya Human Rights Commission, the Catholic Justice and Peace Commission, and the National Council of Churches of Kenya are active in national integration debates. Overall, these civil society organizations have had a mixed record in reducing polarization. On the positive side, most are part of the broad mobilization to inject more voices into Kenyan political debates. National mobilization campaigns by these organizations have been pivotal in the constitutional breakthroughs that have been made since the 1990s. Furthermore, civil society organizations are critical sites for the socialization of a large number of leaders who have assumed major positions in government and parliament. Many expected that these leaders would help shift the style and substance of national politics away from ethnic polarization. On the negative side, these organizations have been unable to create national constituencies for effective change, in part because they are elite- and urban-based and, more critically, because they are torn by the centrifugal forces of ethnicity, particularly during elections. Kenyan civil society groups are likely to work together when there are national emergencies such as electoral violence or terrorist attacks, but once these crises diminish, individual organizations revert to their primordial identities. In this regard, civil society mirrors the Janus-faced malaise of Kenya's middle class: it is cosmopolitan and progressive in everyday life, but it polarizes along ethnic lines during elections.

In parliament, the Kenya Young Parliamentarians Association has led an initiative to mobilize across parties and ethnicities to find common positions on national issues. This caucus reached out to young legislators in the county assemblies across the country. In the long run, these efforts could galvanize national coalitions beyond ethnicity, but at present they are confined largely to lobbying for more resources for youth programs. Besides, there are limits to such organizational efforts because the young legislators belong to polarized political coalitions that sponsored them as candidates.

Finally, donor interventions since the 1990s have supported the democratization process, civic engagement in politics, and broad institutional reforms. After the electoral violence in 2007–08, international donors advocated for overhauling the Kenyan constitution to introduce decentralization as a proposed cure for ethnic convulsions. But these interventions have not made a significant impact on reducing polarization, largely because durable solutions to ethnic fragmentation need to be negotiated locally. In addition, most donors stepped back from pushing for additional political reforms following the backlash from the Kalenjin and Kikuyu elites over the ICC's alleged excessive interference in domestic politics. At the same time, donors have also inadvertently abetted polarization, such as by supporting dysfunctional electoral management and anticorruption bodies, a form of aid that provides only the illusion of deep political change.

Kenya's prospects for managing its political polarization are bleak because the constituencies that are fighting polarization have yet to gain national traction, relevance, and respect. It seems that the sixty years of Kenya's statehood have not been able to generate alternative movements and institutions that can break the stalemate of polarization.

NOTES

1. Dina Ligaga, "Ethnic Stereotypes and the Ideological Manifestations of Ethnicity in Kenyan Cyber Communities," *Africa Insight* 39, no. 1 (2009): 72–85.

2. Joel Barkan, ed., *Beyond Capitalism vs. Socialism in Kenya and Tanzania* (Boulder, CO: Lynne Rienner, 1994); and Robert Bates, *Beyond the Miracle of the Market: The Political Economy of Agrarian Development in Kenya* (Cambridge, UK: Cambridge University Press, 1989).

3. Peter Anyang' Nyong'o, "State and Society in Kenya: The Disintegration of the Nationalist Coalition and the Rise of Presidential Authoritarianism," *African Affairs* 88, no. 351 (1989): 229–51; and Albert Gordon Omulo and John James William, "A Survey of the Influence of 'Ethnicity' in African Governance, with Special Reference to its Impact in Kenya vis-à-vis the Luo Community," *African Identities* 16, no. 1 (2018): 87–102.

4. Frances Stewart, "Horizontal Inequalities: A Neglected Dimension of Development," QEH Working Paper Series no. 81 (Oxford: Queen Elizabeth House, Oxford University, 2002).

5. David Ndii, "Kenya Is a Cruel Marriage, It's Time We Talk Divorce," *Daily Nation* (Nairobi), March 26, 2016 (www.nation.co.ke/oped/opinion/Kenya-is-a-cruel-marriage--it-s-time-we-talk-divorce/440808-3134132-154vra2/index.html); and Alphonse Shiundu, "The Untold Story of the Kenyattas' Wealth," *The Standard* (Nairobi), January 29, 2017 (www.standardmedia.co.ke/article/2001227584/the-untold-story-of-the-kenyattas-wealth).

6. Arne Bigsten, Damiano Kulundu Manda, Germano Mwabu, and Anthony Wambugu, "Incomes, Inequality, and Poverty in Kenya: A Long-Term Perspective," in *Growth and Poverty in Sub-Saharan Africa*, eds. Channing Arndt, Andy McKay, and Finn Tarp (Oxford: Oxford University Press, 2016), 343–69.

7. William Attwood, *The Reds and Blacks: A Personal Adventure* (New York: Harper and Row, 1967); and Colin Leys, *Underdevelopment in Kenya: The Political Economy of Neo-Colonialism* (London: Heinemann, 1975).

8. Ndii, "Kenya Is a Cruel Marriage."

9. Nicholas Nyangira, "Ethnicity, Class, and Politics in Kenya," in *The Political Economy of Kenya*, ed. Michael Schatzberg (New York: Praeger, 1987), 15–32.

10. Frank Mbaya Asirigwa, Furaha Chai, and Nabea Wendo, "Ethnic Stereotyping on Facebook during the 2013 Political Elections in Kenya: An Analysis of Linguistic Features of Facebook Posts and Comments," *IOSR Journal of Humanities and Social Sciences* 21, no. 12 (2016): 22–32.

11. E. S. Atieno-Odhiambo, "Democracy and the Ideology of Order in Kenya," in Schatzberg, *The Political Economy of Kenya*, 177–202.

12. Goran Hyden, "Capital Accumulation, Resource Distribution, and Governance in Kenya: The Role of the Economy of Affection," in Schatzberg, *The Political Economy of Kenya*, 117–36.

13. David Throup and Charles Hornsby, *Multi-Party Politics in Kenya: The Kenyatta and Moi States and the Triumph of the System in the 1992 Election* (Oxford: James Currey, 1998).

14. Charles Hornsby, *Kenya: A History since Independence* (London: I. B. Tauris, 2012).

15. Jacqueline M. Klopp, "Pilfering the Public: The Problem of Land Grabbing in Contemporary Kenya," *Africa Today* 47, no. 1 (2000): 7–26; and E. S. Atieno-Odhiambo, "Hegemonic Enterprises and Instrumentalities of Survival: Ethnicity and Democracy in Kenya," *African Studies* 61, no. 2 (2002): 223–49.

16. Jeffrey S. Steeves, "Re-Democratisation in Kenya: 'Unbounded Politics' and the Political Trajectory towards National Elections," *Journal of Commonwealth & Comparative Politics* 35, no. 3 (1997): 27–52; and Stephen Ndegwa, "The Incomplete Transition: The Constitutional and Electoral Context in Kenya," *Africa Today* 45, no. 2 (1998): 193–211.

17. Colin Kahl, "Population Growth, Environmental Degradation, and State-Sponsored Violence: The Case of Kenya, 1991–93," *International Security* 23, no. 2 (1998): 80–119.

18. Joel D. Barkan, "Kenya after Moi," *Foreign Affairs* 83, no. 1 (2004): 87–100.

19. David M. Anderson, "Briefing: Kenya's Elections 2002: The Dawning of a New Era?" *African Affairs* 102, no. 407 (2003): 331–42.

20. Sebastian Elischer, "Ethnic Coalitions of Convenience and Commitment: Political Parties and Party Systems in Kenya," Working Paper no. 68 (Hamburg: German Institute of Global and Area Studies, February 2008); and Gabrielle Lynch, "The Fruits of Perception: 'Ethnic Politics' and the Case of Kenya's Constitutional Referendum," *African Studies* 65, no. 2 (2006): 233–70.

21. Clark Gibson and James Long, "The Presidential and Parliamentary Elections in Kenya, December 2007," *Electoral Studies* 28, no. 3 (2009): 497–502; and Daniel Branch and Nic Cheeseman, "Democratization, Sequencing, and State Failure in Africa: Lessons from Kenya," *African Affairs* 108, no. 430 (2009): 1–26.

22. Ndii, "Kenya Is a Cruel Marriage."

23. Karuti Kanyinga and James Long, "The Political Economy of Reforms in Kenya: The Post-2007 Election Violence and a New Constitution," *African Studies Review* 55, no. 1 (2012): 31–51; and Jill Cotrell and Yash Ghai, "Constitution Making and Democratization in Kenya (2000–2005)," *Democratization* 14, no. 1 (2007): 1–25.

24. Sabine Hohn, "New Start or False Start? The ICC and Electoral Violence in Kenya," *Development and Change* 45, no. 3 (2014): 565–88; and Susanne Mueller, "Kenya and the International Criminal Court (ICC): Politics, the Election, and the Law," *Journal of Eastern African Studies* 8, no. 1 (2014): 25–42.

25. Justin Willis, Nic Cheeseman, and Gabrielle Lynch, "Kenya 2017: The Interim Elections?," SciencesPo Centre for International Studies, Paris, July 2017; and Rafiq Raji, "Ethnic Politics and the 2017 Elections in Kenya," NTU-SBF Centre for African Studies, Singapore, 2018.

26. Nic Cheeseman, Gabriella Lynch, and Justin Willis, "Decentralisation in Kenya: The Governance of Governors," *Journal of Modern African Studies* 54, no. 1 (2016): 1–35.

27. John Burke, "Kenya Election: Government Accused of 'Genocide' against Ethnic Minorities," *The Guardian*, October 27, 2017 (www.theguardian.com/world/2017/oct/27/kenya-election-less-than-half-of-those-eligible-thought-to-have-voted); and John Mukum Mbaku, "Foresight Africa Viewpoint: Elections in Africa in 2018: Lessons from Kenya's 2017 Electoral Experiences," *Africa in Focus* (blog), Brookings Institution, February 1, 2018 (www.brookings.edu/blog/africa-in-focus/2018/02/01/foresight-africa-viewpoint-elections-in-africa-in-2018-lessons-from-kenyas-2017-electoral-experiences/).

28. Ligaga, "Ethnic Stereotypes;" and Mbaya Asirigwa, Chai, and Wendo, "Ethnic Stereotyping on Facebook."

Part II

SEVERE POLARIZATION AND DEMOCRATIC STRESS

THREE

The Long Path of Polarization in the United States

THOMAS CAROTHERS

The United States is in the grips of severe polarization. The country's two main political parties are deeply at odds ideologically and locked in almost continuous combat. Partisan rancor hobbles the U.S. Congress and many state legislatures, and is spreading into the judiciary and other law enforcement institutions, as well as into many domains once fully outside the boundaries of partisan politics, like the national census and official responses to natural disasters. The current president, Donald Trump, governs in a purposely polarizing fashion, continuously stoking his political base with divisive stances and comments, while harshly confronting and alienating those he does not count as supporters. Polarization has spread widely in American society, fueling divisions, anger, and conflict among ordinary citizens to a startling degree.

This chapter argues that contemporary U.S. polarization has its roots in the dramatic sociocultural changes that swept through U.S. society in the 1960s and 1970s, creating a deep divide between two dominant visions for the country, one progressive and the other conservative. This conflict within the society gradually translated into the political domain, as activists pushed the Democratic and Republican parties to become more ideologically defined and programmatic. Political and societal polarization became mutually reinforcing, while a number of additional factors, such as the design of U.S. political institutions and changes in the media landscape, accelerated the country's slide into severe polarization. Polarization has intensified to the point that it is a major factor behind the main democratic shortcomings bedeviling the United States, from institutional gridlock and the degradation of checks and balances to the loss of public faith in election administration, political parties, and the political establishment more generally. Efforts to address and potentially alleviate the polarization, such as initiatives to foster civic dialogue and reform the electoral system, are multiplying in response to the growing seriousness of the problem. Yet thus far they have not gained enough traction to alter the trend. In the thick of a poisonous polarizing fog, the United States struggles to see a future in which its divisions heal rather than continue to deepen.

Roots

The roots of contemporary U.S. polarization are diverse and deep. Divisions between white and black Americans and the long and difficult struggle for racial equality run throughout American history. Since its founding, the United States has also grappled with profound differences over the role and powers of the federal government, whether along the axis of states' rights versus federal power, bigger government versus smaller government philosophies, or rural versus urban perspectives. Religious differences, especially concerning the appropriate role of religion in politics, have been another source of division, whether between Protestants and non-Protestants, revivalists and traditionalists, or simply more religious and less religious Americans.

The conflicting conservative and progressive visions that today underlie U.S. political and societal polarization crystallized in the 1960s. In that decade, a wave of cultural and political change hit the United States, unsettling the relatively stable postwar consensus that had unified American society around the shared goals of postwar renovation, rapid economic growth, and defense of the "free world" against Soviet-led communism. This wave of change had many elements, but at its core it was a set of new impulses and ideas challenging established authority, social traditions, traditional morality, and entrenched sociocultural hierarchies.[1] It took form in disruptive change in numerous areas of U.S. society, including civil rights movements for African Americans and other minority groups, the women's rights movement, the environmental movement, the start of a push for gay rights, a new emphasis on youth culture, and challenges to traditional religious values. It also entailed a surging revolution in popular culture that included the arrival of new musical styles such as rock 'n' roll; the spread of a new television-centered entertainment culture; the liberalization of sexual mores, including changing attitudes toward marriage and the rise of divorce; as well as changes in hairstyles, dress, and many elements of personal comportment. Two distinct overarching societal visions emerged in response to this wave of change. One was progressive, embracing these many different changes and seeing them as vital steps toward a more just, free, and equitable society. The other was conservative, resisting these changes and regarding them as troubling developments that portended a decline in order, virtue, and civility.

Many other Western democracies experienced some of the same pressures for change in those years, but they did not divide as much into two fiercely opposed visions, neither going as headlong into radical social change as did the United States, nor experiencing as strong a conservative counter-reaction. This wave of sociocultural change was particularly polarizing in the United States because it activated or built upon three deep cleavages in American society, cleavages that were not as present in most other Western democracies. First, it brought to the fore the struggle for racial equality and the profound racial divide in U.S. society, both in political life and throughout the society more generally. Second, every area of social change raised the question of the appropriate role of the government, whether as a facilitator of progressive change or as a bulwark of conservative resistance to change, or in simple terms, whether small government or big government was desirable. Third, many of the areas of change, such as the drive to legalize abortion, increase access to birth control, and limit the place of prayer in schools, brought religion directly into political debates and decisions. The higher levels of religiosity in the United States (especially compared to most other Western democracies) lent unusually significant force to the conservative outlook. These three societal cleavages—racial, ideological, and religious—aligned along the axis of the overarching progressive-conservative division, forming an "iron triangle" of U.S. polarization that continues to this day.

Trajectory

Many Americans did not fully embrace either the progressive or conservative outlooks that began to harden in the 1960s and 1970s. They held moderate views that hovered between the two sides or that drew eclectically from one or both of them. Yet these clashing visions, driven by social and political activists on both sides, took root and became the poles of a sociocultural spectrum that increasingly defined American life. Soon this sociocultural divide began crossing over into political life and transforming the two main U.S. political parties. The spectrum became weighted around the ends rather than the middle, both in political life and in the society more broadly. Within the space of a generation and a half, the U.S. political landscape had experienced dramatic changes that reshaped not only the two political parties that dominated national politics, but also the ways in which ordinary Americans thought of and identified themselves as a part of the political system.

The Advent of the Culture Wars: The 1960s and 1970s

As multiple waves of change swept through American life over the course of the 1960s, the battles of what came to be called "the culture wars" roiled U.S. society on many fronts. The most critical and harshly fought of these domains was the movement for political and civil rights for African Americans, a crucible of sociocultural transformation that affected all Americans. At the same time, other issues also came to the forefront of political life. The push for women's rights became a major domain of contention and change. A strong conservative reaction against the feminist movement gained force in the 1970s, coalescing around the successful struggle to defeat the Equal Rights Amendment to the U.S. Constitution. Divisive arguments and campaigns proliferated over abortion, prayer in schools, drug laws, criminal justice reforms, and air and water pollution, and the term "family values" became a rallying cry for conservative activists who claimed that progressive activists were destroying the traditional values of American family life.

Clashing responses to the Vietnam War were also an arena of enormous contention between the two sides. The opposition to the war, manifested in mass protests and a broad antiwar coalition, was a profound public questioning of governmental authority and wisdom in a domain—foreign policy—that traditionally had been the purview of elite decision-makers. Through their vocal opposition to U.S. involvement in Vietnam, antiwar protestors challenged the entire scope of U.S. foreign policy in the postwar era—in particular, its focus on containing the spread of communism by projecting U.S. military power overseas. The fight became not just about conflicting assessments of the value of the war effort, but about competing views of patriotism and loyalty to the country.

The Watergate scandal of the early 1970s was of similar consequence, the domestic parallel to the national divide over Vietnam. As President Richard Nixon and members of his inner circle faced multiple charges of conducting clandestine and often illegal activities against their perceived political enemies, the progressive and conservative communities clashed over opposing views of governmental legitimacy. The progressive outlook maintained that it was fundamentally necessary to question governmental authority, not least to check potential abuses of power such as those exposed in the Watergate investigation, while the conservative outlook continued to embrace governmental prerogative, at least until late in the crisis. Nixon's resignation in August 1974, and his subsequent pardoning by President Gerald Ford a month later, did little to heal the deep rifts that the Watergate scandal had exposed in the domestic political scene.

As the culture wars raged across these many different issue areas, activist groups largely aligned into two broader camps that consistently opposed each other's views. Over time, progressivism or liberalism on the one hand and conservativism on the other became increasingly all-encompassing outlooks—not merely points of view about a certain set of political choices, but sociocultural identities with wide-ranging views regarding how life should be lived and how the country should be organized.

The Polarization of American Politics: The 1960s and 1970s

This growing polarization of society steadily fostered a growing polar-ization of politics. Both of the major U.S. political parties had long been relatively heterogeneous, catch-all parties, characterized by considerable ideological diversity and relatively low levels of central control over state and local party institutions. But as society became more divided between clashing sociocultural visions, activists on both sides pushed to have po-litical parties to embrace their causes and embody their emergent identi-ties. By the end of the 1970s, the Republican and Democratic parties had become more ideologically defined and programmatic, with greater levels of central control over policy positions. As the parties made their ideologi-cal orientation more explicit, voters used these cues to "sort" into the par-ties, aligning their ideological beliefs and partisan identification.[2]

THE REPUBLICAN PARTY Prior to the 1960s, the Republican Party had contained both very conservative elements, often tied to conservative reli-gious groups, and moderately conservative, even somewhat liberal figures. Yet in the later part of the 1950s, a hardline conservative movement that was dissatisfied with the comparatively moderate Republicanism of Presi-dent Dwight Eisenhower stepped up to actively resist the new progressive trends in America. As the 1960s unfolded, Republicans found themselves embroiled in an ideological struggle over the soul of their party.[3] In 1964, the "movement conservatives" successfully pushed for the nomination of a hardline conservative, Arizona senator Barry Goldwater, as the Repub-lican presidential candidate, narrowly defeating the more moderate New York governor Nelson Rockefeller in the party primaries. However, Presi-dent Lyndon Johnson's crushing defeat of Goldwater set back these forces within the party. The nomination in 1968 of Richard Nixon represented a compromise between the more moderate, business-oriented parts of the party and the movement conservatives. Nixon was a business lawyer and a practical negotiator known to and comfortable with business elites. Yet during his time as vice president to President Dwight Eisenhower, he had played the role of angry, confrontational conservative in contrast to Eisen-hower's moderate stance. Throughout 1968, he campaigned for president on a law-and-order platform that had sharply divisive racial overtones. Yet as president, he ended up governing as a relative moderate on many social and economic issues, accepting compromises or pursuing moderate lines on issues such as environmental regulation, labor protection, and entitlement programs.

Nixon's political downfall in the Watergate scandal helped clear the way for the continued strengthening of the more conservative forces in the party. Conservative activist groups, fighting the culture wars across a swath of sociocultural issues, continued to bring their energy and determination into the party. They mobilized around Ronald Reagan in 1976 when he challenged the more moderate Gerald Ford for the party nomination. Ford managed to hold on against Reagan, but his defeat by Georgia governor Jimmy Carter in the 1976 election paved the path for more conservative forces within the party. During their years in opposition, they worked to institute internal changes to party structures and rules to strengthen their role. Reforms centralized power within the party, creating new policy "issue councils" that set forth party positions on hot-button conservative issues like fighting progressive family law policies, advocating tax cuts for the wealthy, and resisting the growing environmental movement. Growing centralized control over candidate recruitment and fundraising further enabled the Republican National Committee to coordinate party support for conservative policies.[4] By 1980, more conservative forces, including conservative social activists and public figures, as well as wealthy party donors, had become strong, even dominant voices and actors within the party, contributing significantly to Ronald Reagan's successful bid for the Republican nomination and then to his successful presidential campaign.

THE DEMOCRATIC PARTY   The Democratic Party went through a similar process of ideological self-definition and centralization at the national level. During the mid-1960s, President Lyndon Johnson sought to maintain a "big tent" approach in his efforts to lead sweeping domestic reforms, known as the Great Society, addressing poverty and racial injustice. Many national Democratic Party elites felt that some ideological flexibility and compromise was a strategic necessity for the party as a whole, because the Democrats' status as the majority party would be threatened if the more conservative Southern Democrats were to leave the fold. But progressive forces gaining strength in different parts of U.S. society began pushing for the party to more clearly represent their views and to reject significant compromises with conservative Democrats. Since the late 1930s, African American activists and labor union leaders had worked to incorporate support for civil rights into the positions of party organizations throughout the northern states. This pressure from below from within the Democratic Party pushed President Johnson and other national party leaders to embrace more racially liberal policies, as exemplified by the passage of the Civil Rights Act of 1964.[5]

From the late 1960s on, harsh divergences over the party's positions on the civil rights movement prompted Southern Democrats to leave the party in growing numbers. This conservative flight tilted the balance within the party toward greater influence for the progressive forces and reduced ideological heterogeneity within the party. As on the Republican side, the intensifying culture wars in the broader society led to the emergence of sociocultural actors on the progressive side, such as women's rights groups, environmental groups, and minority rights groups, and these groups began looking for stronger representation and influence within the Democratic Party itself.

When President Johnson, embittered by domestic opposition to the Vietnam War, declined to seek reelection on the Democratic ticket in 1968, tensions over the direction of the party came to a head in the contest between Vice President Hubert Humphrey, a moderate, and Minnesota senator Eugene McCarthy, a progressive, for the presidential nomination. McCarthy's supporters lost that fight, but after the Democrats lost control of the White House in 1968, the progressives successfully pushed through a series of changes to party rules that increased their influence. These changes included opening up the process of selecting delegates to presidential nominating conventions and strengthening the role of the national party organization, which reduced the influence of the relatively conservative local- and state-level party groups throughout the South. Much as the hardline conservatives would do in the wake of Gerald Ford's defeat nearly a decade later, the progressive Democrats sought to wrest control of the party machine from those who appeared to be thwarting their agenda.

After 1968, the stance of the national party leadership swung significantly to the left. When South Dakota senator George McGovern made a successful bid for the party's presidential nomination in 1972, centered around opposition to the Vietnam War, his victory reflected the growing strength of progressive forces within the party. McGovern's triumph, however, was short-lived: he would lose to sitting President Nixon in a massive landslide, a resounding defeat that seemed to indicate the tenuous hold that progressive elements had on society more generally. Yet Nixon's political demise, coupled with the antiwar movement's success in pushing for President Ford to fully withdraw all U.S. military forces from Vietnam, strengthened the more liberal forces within the party. The ideological crystallization and narrowing of the Democratic Party was not as sharp as that of the Republican Party—the progressive forces were more an amalgam of different sociopolitical groups, while movement conservatives displayed a greater sense of commonality—but the general trend was similar.

Jimmy Carter's dark horse bid for the party nomination in 1976 and his electoral victory over Gerald Ford helped strengthen the progressive forces. They played a major role in writing the party platform that year, and although Carter was not himself a liberal in the mold of Eugene McCarthy or George McGovern, he governed in basic accordance with progressive ideals, particularly in terms of his advocacy for human rights at home and abroad. The electoral contest between him and Ronald Reagan in 1980 further heightened the sense among progressive Democrats that a clear, wide ideological gap now lay between them and the Republicans.

Political Polarization Intensifies: The 1980s to the Present

With the country's two main political parties having become more ideologically defined by the end of the 1970s, the story of the next forty years has been one of intensifying polarization, to the point of serious political dysfunction. Polarization at the political level has fed and intensified polarization within society more generally, as different political actors use polarization, effectively weaponizing it, to advance their political fortunes.

THE SLIDE INTO SEVERE POLARIZATION The ideological division between the parties widened during the presidency of Ronald Reagan. Reagan advanced several strongly conservative positions, including tax reduction, a more militant "war on drugs" that disproportionately affected minorities and the disadvantaged, and a confrontational stance toward the

Soviet Union. His tenure established greater differentiation between what Republican rule and Democratic rule meant in practice for the country, effectively raising the stakes for politicians on both sides in terms of obtaining and asserting political power. Yet even though Reagan advanced these conservative tenets, his presidency and that of George H. W. Bush still involved considerable legislative compromise and basic political civility between the two sides. More marked polarization set in during the 1990s, when the Republicans moved back into an oppositional role and movement conservatives pushed for tougher political tactics. As has been much analyzed, the rise of Newt Gingrich and the Republican takeover of the House of Representatives in 1994 brought about a scorched-earth approach to political opposition.[6] Gingrich's obstructionist tactics exploited the fact that governmental dysfunction tended to advance the Republicans' goal of smaller government by discrediting the apparent worth or possibility of more activist government.

This hard-edged Republican approach of the 1990s took place even as the Democratic Party made efforts to rein in its progressive wing. After their bruising defeat by President Reagan in the 1984 presidential election, Democratic leaders feared that the party had moved too far to the left and formed the Democratic Leadership Council to empower more moderate candidates.[7] During the 1990s, most leading Democrats, including President Bill Clinton, Vice President Al Gore, and Nevada senator Harry Reid, were relative moderates within the larger Democratic Party world. During the Clinton presidency, the Democrats also compromised on some major issues, advancing policies that promoted free trade, reformed welfare programs, and catered to more conservative "law and order" voters. But for the movement conservatives, both President Clinton and his wife Hillary Rodham Clinton were cultural and political embodiments of a liberalism they loathed. They interpreted some of the Clinton administration's goals, like health care reform, as calls for "big government." Thus, the Republicans' strategy included not just fierce opposition to the Democrats' legislative agenda but sharp, persistent attacks on the legitimacy and credibility of both Bill and Hillary Clinton. In 1998, the Monica Lewinsky scandal exemplified the rapidly polarizing environment, as congressional Republicans latched onto allegations of the president's serial sexual misconduct to initiate impeachment proceedings against him on charges of perjury and obstruction of justice. Although Clinton was acquitted by the House and served the remainder of his second term, the disputed 2000 presidential election balloting and the Supreme Court's intervention on the side of Republican presidential candidate George W. Bush underlined the trend of intensifying polarization.

Following the terrorist attacks of September 11, 2001, heightened calls for unity across the political spectrum seemed to offer the promise of a return to a more bipartisan approach to governance. But bitter partisan divisions soon emerged over the Bush administration's response to those events, its "Global War on Terror," which included the passage of controversial national security legislation like the Patriot Act of October 2001 and the invasion of Afghanistan in late 2001 and Iraq in early 2003. Throughout the Bush years, polarization tightened its grip on U.S. political life, with legislative gridlock, the weakening of norms of compromise and restraint in the Congress, and harsher criticisms and questioning of the president appearing as particular symptoms of conflict.

THE OBAMA AND TRUMP YEARS At the start of the Obama administration, Republican legislators made clear their intention to fully oppose President Barack Obama's legislative agenda and damage his presidency enough to limit it to one term. Throughout his presidency, political figures and media voices on the right questioned his legitimacy as president, focusing on personal issues such as his citizenship and religion. Senate Republicans devoted themselves to blocking as many of his judicial appointments as possible, determined to limit the appointment of judges they considered antithetical to their sociopolitical vision of the country. The emergence of the Tea Party faction within the Republican Party reflected continuing movement in the party toward the right wing.[8] When Republicans regained control of Congress in 2010 and almost completely blocked Obama's legislative agenda, the president resorted with increasing frequency to executive orders to work around their obstructionist tactics. This approach in turn provoked charges of "imperial" presidential behavior from his opponents, further inflaming partisan tensions. When the issue of police violence against African Americans erupted during Obama's second term, the extreme divisiveness of public debates and political treatment of the issue was a testament to the severity of the country's polarization, not just at the elite level but also throughout American society.

During Obama's presidency, Democrats and Republicans grew more divided along the lines of identities and attitudes tied to race, ethnicity, and religion.[9] With an African American president leading the Democrats, racial divides gained salience, and voters became more aware of which party stood for more liberal racial policies and adjusted their allegiances accordingly. Nonwhites, particularly Asians and Latinos, became increasingly aligned with the Democratic Party. At the same time, whites without a college degree moved into the Republican camp. Between 1992 and 2008, whites who had a high school degree or less were just as likely to identify with the Democrats as with the Republicans, but by 2015 they favored the Republicans by a margin of 24 percentage points. As the parties came to represent different demographics and visions of American social identity, political debate became more emotionally charged and divisive.

The election of Donald Trump to the U.S. presidency in November 2016 vividly demonstrated and increased the severity of polarization. Many voters and political elites showed that they were willing to support a candidate who had displayed a series of personal characteristics that normally would have derailed a presidential campaign—as evidenced, for example, in an audio recording in which he mentioned taking pleasure in sexually harassing women—for the sake of advancing their partisan agenda. Trump's campaign further entrenched the racial basis of polarization by appealing explicitly to white resentment toward the growing influence of ethnic minorities, particularly among white working-class voters.[10]

As president, Trump has purposefully amplified polarization. Despite having obtained a smaller share of the popular vote than his opponent, he has not tried to appeal to the center and instead has governed from the far right, using the issue of immigration, for example, to maintain and energize his political base. He has made harsh and uncivil attacks on political opponents and critics, engaged in frequent partisan attacks on nonpartisan institutions, and treated the media with a hostility and vituperation unprecedented for a modern U.S. president. His political language and style—his crudeness, bellicosity, mendacity, proclivity to attack private individuals who disagree with him, excoriation of political opponents in extreme terms, demonization of mainstream media, and much else—have been strongly polarizing. The campaign-style rallies that he has continued to hold during his presidency, at which he revels in calls to lock up his former campaign opponent and urges the crowd to jeer and boo at representatives of the press, are vivid examples of how political elites can actively fuel societal division and rancor.

CONTESTED DIMENSIONS Given the severity of U.S. polarization, debates over its causes naturally are polarized as well. Politicians and activists on opposing sides accuse one another of having violated consensual norms and moved to the extreme. Some political scientists argue that the story is one of symmetric polarization. For example, James Campbell argues in his book *Polarized* that polarization has been staggered between the left and right, with the Democrats moving further to the left in the 1970s and the Republican shift to the right coming later. He characterizes the polarization of the parties as "a two-step dance."[11] Others view polarization as primarily the fault of conservatives. For example, Thomas Mann argues in *American Gridlock* that

> the polarization is asymmetric. Republicans have become a radical insurgency: ideologically extreme, contemptuous of the inherited policy regime, scornful of compromise, unpersuaded by conventional understanding of facts, evidence, and science and dismissive of the legitimacy of [their] political opposition.[12]

In a detailed argument supporting Mann's view, Jacob Hacker and Paul Pierson note, "Elite discourse—in journalism, academia, foundations—is intensely resistant to the very strong evidence that polarization is primarily about steadily increasing GOP extremism."[13]

Scholars also debate whether the hyperpolarization of political elites reflects (and has resulted from) increasing polarization among the American public. On the one hand, Morris Fiorina points out that most Americans place themselves near the center of the ideological spectrum and that mass polarization, whether measured in terms of Americans' policy positions or ideological self-identification, has not increased over the past three decades.[14] Fiorina thus concludes that rising elite polarization does not reflect the attitudes of the American public as a whole. On the other hand, Alan Abramowitz counters that the "engaged public," composed of those Americans who turn out in primaries, work on campaigns, or call their representatives, is much more polarized than the population at large.[15] Polarization at the elite level largely reflects polarization among these politically engaged citizens, to whom candidates and elected officials are disproportionately accountable. This chapter aligns more closely with Abramowitz's view, in highlighting how activists, party reformers, and other politically engaged citizens transformed America's political parties from the bottom up.

Additional Drivers

The story set out above—in which polarization stemmed from tensions between deep forces of sociocultural change that translated into the political domain, where political parties hardwired them into political life—is a complex one. A full picture, however, must include a number of other factors, including the design of key political institutions and changes in the media landscape.

Political Institutions

Some basic institutional features of U.S. democracy have contributed to the rise of polarization. One of these is the two-party system. The use of first-past-the-post voting for virtually all legislative seats, as well as the existence of a (more or less) directly elected president and state governors, make it difficult for third parties to gain any sort of real national viability or broader political traction. This means that there is no real chance that a centrist party or other less obstructionist alternatives will be able to challenge the two main parties, regardless of their growing unpopularity. The two-party system also blocks the potential for coalition governments that might encourage members of different parties to cooperate and see one another more as partners in government than as enemies.

Competitive primary elections for legislative and executive candidates, a reform from the 1970s that was designed to open up the political arena, have also facilitated polarization. More partisan voters tend to be more motivated voters, and primary elections as a result encourage candidates to appeal to partisan bases rather than the center. Of equal importance, the reforms to the primary system in the 1970s weakened the capacity of party elites to serve as "gatekeepers" who historically had prevented extremists and demagogues from running on the party ticket.[16]

Another driver of polarization has been the growing role of money in politics and the lack of transparency surrounding its sources and uses. The campaign finance reform efforts of the 1970s, which aimed to limit the role of money in elections and in governing, failed to stop its flow. In the past ten years, political action committees have helped open up political financing to unlimited amounts of corporate and individual "dark money," providing a steady stream of partisan funding. The rapid increase in the amount of money that has gone into financing political campaigns is not a polarizing development in itself, but in the U.S. context certain aspects of it have contributed, directly or indirectly, to polarization.[17] For example, wealthy individuals who are highly motivated to fund explicitly partisan political agendas have taken advantage of the effective elimination of limits on political contributions to funnel vast sums of money into the political causes that they champion. In some cases, the most extreme causes have benefited disproportionately from this influx of funding.

Yet another telling development has been the rise of partisan gerrymandering by state governments of state and national legislative districts. By drawing legislative districts in a partisan fashion, state governments create more districts that are "safe seats" for one side or the other, which facilitates victories by candidates who hew to the edges of the political spectrum rather than the center. Attempts to reshape these gerrymandered districts along more bipartisan lines have faced severe opposition, forcing the courts to weigh in on the legality of the processes that drew these political lines. Gerrymandering thus has been both a reflection and a driver of polarization.[18]

The Media Landscape

The changed media and information landscape is another powerful factor fueling the rise of polarization. For most of the radio and television age, a small number of relatively nonpartisan national broadcasters had dominated the airwaves, but in the 1990s cable television channels multiplied, and highly partisan television and radio stations or networks emerged. These changes amplified partisan voices and reduced the common information space through which citizens obtained their news. The growth of the internet in the 2000s further fragmented the information space, reduced the role of traditional gatekeepers of news and information, and allowed individuals to create their own information spaces in which they could receive or broadcast news and opinions. The powerful surge of social media in the 2010s amplified extreme perspectives, corroded civility, and particularized information gathering to an unprecedented degree.[19] The new information landscape has also opened up opportunities for foreign powers to fan the flames of polarization by covertly inserting divisive commentary onto U.S. platforms or spreading disinformation intended to confuse and distort information about real events.

Geographic Sorting

Also significant, as both a reflection and a driver of polarization, has been the geographic sorting of citizens along partisan lines.[20] During the past twenty years, Americans have come to live around persons who share their basic political orientation and identify with the same party as they do. The number of counties where the presidential vote was decided by a single-digit margin dropped from 1,096 counties in 1992 to just 303 counties in 2016.[21] Psychological and sociological studies have shown that living among people with whom one disagrees politically tends to reduce the intensity of such disagreements.[22] Therefore, as people come to live in more politically homogenous communities, opportunities to reduce partisan divisions are lost.

Consequences

Polarization has become so pervasive in U.S. politics and the society more widely that it is difficult to fully capture all of its effects. Some of the major negative consequences have affected not only a wide range of U.S. political institutions, but also the fabric of U.S. society as a whole.

Legislature and Executive

Perhaps the most obvious negative effects of polarization appear in both houses of the U.S. Congress. Political polarization contributes to legislative gridlock—the reduced ability of Congress to pass legislation, especially on major policy issues, and to carry out other basic functions, like agreeing on a budget. The United States faces any number of serious social, economic, and political challenges, yet in the past fifteen years Congress has struggled to pass major reform bills. The few it has passed, such as Obama's health care reform and Trump's tax reform, gained little to no buy-in from the other side, weakening the legitimacy and hold of these measures. Polarization has also degraded the functioning of Congress in other basic ways, such as by weakening traditional norms of restraint and comity and by stimulating efforts to change basic rules for partisan advantage.[23]

Furthermore, polarization is undercutting the essential role Congress plays as a check on the presidency. With only rare exceptions, Republican senators and representatives have not been criticizing or trying to limit President Trump's antidemocratic impulses and actions, in part out of their belief that his value in advancing the Republican policy agenda outweighs the damage he is doing to democratic norms. In other words, the sharper polarization has become, the more willing many politicians have been to overlook violations of democratic norms and forgo traditional checks and balances for the sake of preserving and supporting their view.

Polarization is also damaging the institution of the presidency itself. Intense partisanship has led to a slew of attacks on the legitimacy of successive U.S. presidents, from political figures and many citizens more generally. The traditional idea of the U.S. president as the president of all Americans is being replaced with a partisan view that the president is the leader only of those who voted for him or her. Polarization has also rendered it much more difficult for a U.S. president to implement a legislative agenda. Presidents are more frequently failing to put into place the policies that they promised in their campaigns, which contributes to rising public disrespect for the political system and a tendency to gravitate toward outsider candidates who promise to disrupt the existing order. In some cases, presidents have to play "constitutional hardball" to force their intended policies through a blocked legislative system, which degrades democratic norms in other ways.[24]

It is worth noting that the institutional design of U.S. democracy is uniquely ill-suited to passing legislation and accomplishing other basic tasks of governance under conditions of severe partisan polarization.

Both houses of Congress can block legislation, and they are elected on different cycles. Moreover, the head of government (who can veto legislation) is elected separately by voters, rather than being chosen by the legislature as in parliamentary systems. As Juan Linz has argued, this system of separate elections for the presidency and legislature often precipitates conflict between the two branches, since both can claim to have a popular mandate even when they champion conflicting agendas.[25] Given the different electoral timelines for the presidency and both houses of Congress, it is unusual for either party to control all three for any period of time. The Senate filibuster further complicates the policymaking process, as it effectively requires a three-fifths supermajority to pass most legislation—a tall order in such a closely divided country. Gerrymandering and the geographic sorting of the electorate, which give both parties large numbers of safe seats that cannot plausibly be lost in any election, have made it even more difficult for parties to win majorities that are large enough to pass legislation without bipartisan support. For example, during Barack Obama's two-term presidency, the Democrats had a functional partisan majority (meaning control of the presidency, the House of Representatives, and a filibuster-proof Senate majority) only from July 2009 to February 2010—even though the Democratic Party had won two presidential elections, received the greater part of the popular vote for the House of Representatives in 2008 and 2012, and controlled the Senate until 2015.[26] Beyond these eight months, the Obama administration had to use special loopholes, change congressional rules, or win the support of at least some Republicans to carry out virtually all its desired congressional tasks.

Parties, Courts, and Other Institutions

Growing political acrimony has inflicted particular damage on the core actors involved in the process of polarization: the political parties. Partisan rancor has heightened the image of the parties as needlessly combative, unproductive, negative institutions that foster more problems than they solve, and has contributed to the low regard in which U.S. citizens on the whole hold their main political parties. Over the past thirty years, negative partisanship has increasingly motivated party loyalty, as large proportions of Democrats and Republicans have come to dislike the opposing party more than they like their own.[27]

Polarization is also hurting the judiciary. Because polarization in the United States is based on clashing sociocultural visions of society, and the U.S. legal system gives courts a decisive role on polarizing social issues like abortion rights and gun control, the judiciary naturally becomes a flashpoint of polarization. Over the pasty thirty years, partisan considerations in the appointment of judges have intensified, as have harsh partisan battles over the appointment of Supreme Court justices and even appeals court and district court judges. At times, this has slowed the appointments process and created persistent shortages of judges, which hurts the overall operation of the system. Even more significantly, it decreases public faith in the judicial system, as citizens come to see the judiciary not as the preserve of independent legal action, but rather as one more theater of partisan politics. Popular perceptions of the Supreme Court have become extremely partisan. From 2015 to 2018, as Trump was elected, appointed one Supreme Court justice, and prepared to choose a second, the percentage of Republicans who approved of the Supreme Court increased from 23 percent to 73 percent. Meanwhile, Democratic support for the Supreme Court dropped from 64 percent to 24 percent.[28]

Beyond the legislature, presidency, and courts, polarization has spread to other governing institutions and processes, breaking down traditional norms and practices of bipartisanship or nonpartisanship. The Federal Election Commission, for example, has been wracked by gridlock for years, undermining its work and contributing to the growing partisanship in election administration. Fights over state laws regulating voter access requirements— with Republicans favoring more restrictive access requirements and Democrats less restrictive ones—are another part of the significant intrusion of partisan politics into basic election administration. Preparations for the 2020 national census have become embroiled in disputes regarding the questions to be asked, and whether the Trump administration is modifying the census to try to reduce the counting of Americans who are more likely to vote Democratic. Some observers also felt that the recently revised income tax code's provision relating to the deductibility of state taxes, which had a greater negative effect on states that are generally Democratic, injected partisanship into the nominally nonpartisan tax system.

Society

The harmful effects of polarization on U.S. society are somewhat more diffuse than those on specific political and legal institutions. Severe societal polarization produces lower levels of social trust and cooperation and higher levels of anger and conflict. It is enough to read the online comments section of any article on U.S. politics in a major newspaper to get a vivid taste of the hyperbolic tone of discussions among many Americans over basic political issues. Partisan anger is particularly severe over divisive issues such as gun control and immigration. Efforts to measure broad patterns of affective polarization—the extent to which people on one side of the partisan divide dislike people on the other—also show significant increases in the intensity of partisan rancor. In 1960, only 5 percent of Republicans and 4 percent of Democrats reported that they would feel displeased if one of their children married someone who votes for the other party. By 2010, nearly half of Republicans and one-third of Democrats expressed unhappiness at the prospect of such a cross-party marriage.[29]

Polarization is undermining civic conversation across party lines, both among individuals and in the media. A majority of Americans now say that talking about politics with people they disagree with is stressful and frustrating. Nearly two-thirds report that when they discuss politics with those on the other side, they usually find they have less in common politically than they previously thought.[30] Polarization has decreased faith in media institutions and reduced the domain of civic discourse. Thus, at the same time that changes in the media contribute in significant ways to polarization, polarization hurts the media overall, even as it benefits specific media outlets. As polarization has spread into many elements or institutions of sociocultural life, such as universities, sports, and family life, it has caused greater conflict, anger among opposing camps, and dysfunctionality. For instance, whereas 72 percent of Democrats think that colleges have a positive effect on the country, 58 percent of Republicans feel they are a negative influence, reflecting a growing conservative view that many colleges are hostile to conservative viewpoints.[31] Democrats and Republicans have a decreasing number of cultural overlaps—more and more they eat different types of food, have different hobbies, read different books and magazines, watch different media, travel to different places, and go to different colleges and universities. With less exposure to differing viewpoints comes a greater reluctance to entertain ideas and opinions that differ from one's own.

More recently, severe polarization has contributed to a concerning increase in hate crimes and politically motivated violence.[32] Hate crime reports rose for three consecutive years between 2015 and 2017.[33] The polarizing political climate has contributed significantly to this increase, as evidenced by the fact that in November 2016, the month of Donald Trump's election as president, hate crime reports rose by almost two-thirds relative to the previous November.[34] The United States has also experienced several recent incidents of political violence, such as an attack on members of a Republican congressional baseball team in June 2017 and a wave of mail bombs sent to critics of President Trump in October 2018.

Remedial Actions

As polarization has intensified over the past twenty years, efforts to limit or reduce it have multiplied.[35] Most of these are being undertaken by civic actors, such as nongovernmental advocacy groups, community-based organizations, private philanthropists, and academic experts. This section surveys the different domains in which these initiatives are concentrated.

Civic Dialogue

Hundreds, even thousands of initiatives exist in the United States to foster civic dialogue through formal and informal conversations that bring people together across partisan lines. These exist within specific communities and operate at the state and national levels. The Bridge Alliance, composed of more than ninety organizations, seeks to create a common platform for information sharing and cooperation among such initiatives. Numerous university centers, such as the recently established Agora Institute at Johns Hopkins University, have initiated projects to address political polarization through dialogue. Although these initiatives are important, they are relatively small compared to the overall size of the country, and have made only dispersed and tentative inroads on the overall partisan divide.

Political Leadership

In recent years, political leaders from both the Democratic and Republican parties have made some efforts to transcend and heal partisan divisions. On the Democratic side, President Obama sought to set a bipartisan tone during the first few days of his administration, inviting three Republicans to join his cabinet and seeking support from across the aisle for his economic stimulus package. On the Republican side, President George W. Bush made similarly conciliatory overtures at the start of his first term, though influential officials like Vice President Dick Cheney and senior adviser Karl Rove pushed a more hardline conservative agenda. Various structural constraints, however, have rendered such efforts to cultivate bipartisanship short-lived and ineffective. For one, partisan loyalties have become so entrenched within the electorate that presidents quickly learn they have more to gain from rallying their base than appealing to the dwindling number of swing voters. The opposing party, meanwhile, has strong political incentives to use antimajoritarian tools like the Senate filibuster to deprive the president of bipartisan legislative achievements. Several recent works of popular history have underscored how the leadership of great presidents like Abraham Lincoln and Lyndon Johnson united the country in times of division, but modern presidents face daunting, ingrained challenges to such a task.[36]

Congress

Existing efforts to reduce gridlock in Congress can be divided into two general approaches. One aims to restrict opportunities for minority obstructionism in the legislative process in order to facilitate majoritarian policymaking. Along these lines, some political scientists have recommended that the Senate eliminate or at least weaken the filibuster.[37] Starting in 2013, Democratic and Republican Senate majority leaders curtailed filibuster rights on presidential nominations for executive and judicial posts, such that nominees can now be confirmed with a simple majority rather than a sixty-vote supermajority. Although the weakening of the filibuster has facilitated the appointment process, it has also rendered nominations more partisan and divisive, as the confirmation process of Supreme Court justice Brett Kavanaugh illustrated. Paradoxically, this approach to reducing gridlock has exacerbated the underlying problem of polarization even as it has attempted to ameliorate one of its symptoms.

The other, more promising strategy involves efforts to facilitate bipartisan legislative processes in Congress. Various nongovernmental groups have worked to do so by bringing together congressional representatives and their staff across partisan lines to get to know one another better and work together on common projects. Some efforts within Congress itself have sought to do the same, such as the Bipartisan Working Group and the Problem Solvers Caucus, founded in 2011 and 2017 respectively. However, many in Congress have expressed concern that the Problem Solvers Caucus in particular has done little to produce policy compromises and instead merely offers its members a useful veneer of bipartisanship.[38] Some nongovernmental organizations, such as the Bipartisan Policy Center, promote cooperation across the aisle by offering bipartisan policy research and solutions to Congress. This has become a large area of activity. In a similar vein, the recently created Bipartisan Index encourages collaboration by providing voters with information on their representatives' bipartisan activity (or lack thereof). These initiatives undoubtedly have made positive contributions to creating at least some cross-partisan linkages and activities within Congress, but the larger dynamic of intense polarization still holds sway.

Media

Journalism and social media organizations have responded to the intense polarization of many parts of the media landscape in several ways. Attempts to reduce polarization through the media include initiatives to refocus journalism on substantive reporting that engages readers, as opposed to ideological coverage that emphasizes partisan divisions. Some publications are training journalists to listen more to citizens and let their desires and preferences drive reporting. Innovative models include the Public Insight Network, which seeks to help ordinary people with useful information cooperate with journalists, and ProPublica, an independent nonprofit media group focusing on investigative reporting. Some new news apps and establishment publications like the *New York Times* are trying to engage more with stories from alternative viewpoints and encourage readers to do the same.

In response to public criticism, some social media sites have also adopted new measures to combat the pervasiveness of polarizing rhetoric on their platforms. Facebook has changed its algorithm to prioritize content shared by users' families and friends and deemphasize content shared by media companies, and has announced a plan to rank publishers by trustworthiness. Google has similarly deployed a variety of strategies to identify and combat misinformation and sensationalism. Both of these efforts have the potential to reduce the partisan bubble effect of social media.

Electoral System

Many different groups in the United States are working on electoral system reform. Some of these efforts have a particular focus on reducing polarization. Such efforts include challenging gerrymandering through legal action, running public information campaigns, and engaging in advocacy at the state level. Campaign finance reform efforts also have as part of their purpose reducing polarization, but legal constraints have prevented these efforts from making significant progress in recent years.

Another major area has been the promotion of alternative voting methods that can work to reduce polarization. In the past decade, momentum has gathered behind local and statewide campaigns for ranked-choice voting (RCV), in which voters rank the candidates rather than simply indicating their top choice. The logic is that candidates must move to the center to appeal for second- and third-choice votes, since these votes will be used to determine the winner if no candidate receives an outright majority of first-choice votes. U.S. cities such as San Francisco, Berkeley, Santa Fe, and Minneapolis have adopted RCV, and most recently, in June 2018 Maine conducted the first-ever statewide election using this system. Proponents argue that RCV discourages negative campaigning, reduces the influence of money in politics, and helps ensure that the victorious candidate is broadly acceptable to most voters.[39]

Similarly, the "top-two primary system," implemented in the state of Washington since 2008 and in California since 2012, has been championed as a means of reducing polarization. Rather than having each party nominate a (frequently extreme) candidate, this open, nonpartisan primary system allows voters from across the spectrum to select their first- and second-choice candidates, regardless of which party they represent. Although leaders such as Senator Chuck Schumer and Governor Arnold Schwarzenegger have enthusiastically endorsed the top-two primary system, research suggests that it does little, if anything, to temper polarization.[40] Severe polarization is the product of divergent sociocultural outlooks, not simply of problematic institutional arrangements and particular polarizing politicians. Nonetheless, reforms to the electoral system offer the prospect of making a large-scale impact on America's current polarization.

More generally, this review of attempted remedial actions highlights the fact that many different parts of the U.S. political community and American society as a whole are now seized by the seriousness of the problems that polarization presents and are seeking meaningful ways to address the issue. At the same time, it indicates the degree to which the tide of polarization is overwhelming the attempted solutions. Many Americans would dearly like their country to be a less polarized place, but do not yet know how it might become one.

NOTES

1. On America's culture wars, see James Davison Hunter, *Culture Wars: The Struggle to Define America* (New York: Basic Books, 1991).

2. In contrast to the emphasis here on the role of activists and party organizers in providing ideological definition for the parties, Matthew Levendusky argues that politicians holding elected office primarily sent the cues that caused voters to sort ideologically. See Matthew Levendusky, *The Partisan Sort: How Liberals Became Democrats and Conservatives Became Republicans* (Chicago: University of Chicago Press, 2009).

3. On the rise of movement conservatives in the Republican Party, see Geoffrey M. Kabaservice, *Rule and Ruin: The Downfall of Moderation and the Destruction of the Republican Party, From Eisenhower to the Tea Party* (New York: Oxford University Press, 2012).

4. For an account of the transformation of both the Republican and Democratic parties in the 1960s and 1970s, see Sam Rosenfeld, *The Polarizers: Postwar Architects of Our Partisan Era* (Chicago: University of Chicago Press, 2018), 201–8.

5. Eric Schickler, *Racial Realignment: The Transformation of American Liberalism, 1932–1965* (Princeton, NJ: Princeton University Press, 2016).

6. Steve Kornacki, *The Red and the Blue: The 1990s and the Birth of Political Tribalism* (New York: Ecco, 2018).

7. Jacob S. Hacker and Paul Pierson, "Confronting Asymmetric Polarization," in *Solutions to Political Polarization in America*, ed. Nathaniel Persily (New York: Cambridge University Press, 2015), 64–65.

8. Theda Skocpol and Vanessa Williamson, *The Tea Party and the Remaking of Republican Conservatism* (New York: Oxford University Press, 2012).

9. John Sides, Michael Tesler, and Lynn Vavreck, *Identity Crisis: The 2016 Presidential Campaign and the Battle for the Meaning of America* (Princeton, NJ: Princeton University Press, 2018).

10. Alan I. Abramowitz, and Jennifer McCoy, "United States: Racial Resentment, Negative Partisanship, and Polarization in Trump's America," *The ANNALS of the American Academy of Political and Social Science* 681, no. 1 (2019): 140–46.

11. James E. Campbell, *Polarized: Making Sense of a Divided America* (Princeton, NJ: Princeton University Press, 2016), 10.

12. Thomas E. Mann, "Foreword," in *American Gridlock: The Sources, Character, and Impact of Political Polarization*, ed. James A. Thurber and Antoine Yoshinaka (New York: Cambridge University Press, 2015), xxiv.

13. Hacker and Pierson, "Confronting Asymmetric Polarization," 61.

14. Morris P. Fiorina and Samuel J. Abrams, "Political Polarization in the American Public," *Annual Review of Political Science* 11 (2008): 563–88.

15. Alan I. Abramowitz, *The Disappearing Center: Engaged Citizens, Polarization, and American Democracy* (New Haven, CT: Yale University Press, 2010).

16. Steven Levitsky and Daniel Ziblatt, *How Democracies Die* (New York: Crown, 2018), 41–52.

17. Raymond J. La Raja and Brian F. Schaffner, *Campaign Finance and Political Polarization: When Purists Prevail* (Ann Arbor, MI: University of Michigan Press, 2015).

18. For a contrary perspective, see Nolan McCarty, Keith T. Poole, and Howard Rosenthal, "Does Gerrymandering Cause Polarization?," *American Journal of Political Science* 53, no. 3 (2009): 666–80.

19. Cass R. Sunstein, *#Republic: Divided Democracy in the Age of Social Media* (Princeton, NJ: Princeton University Press, 2017).

20. David A. Hopkins, *Red Fighting Blue: How Geography and Electoral Rules Polarize American Politics* (New York: Cambridge University Press, 2017).

21. David Wasserman, "Purple America Has All But Disappeared," *FiveThirtyEight*, March 8, 2017 (https://fivethirtyeight.com/features/purple-america-has-all-but-disappeared/).

22. Thomas F. Pettigrew, and Linda R. Tropp, "A Meta-Analytic Test of Intergroup Contact Theory," *Journal of Personality and Social Psychology* 90, no. 5 (2006): 751–83.

23. Derek Willis and Paul Kane, "How Congress Stopped Working," *Pro-*

Publica, November 5, 2018 (www.propublica.org/article/how-congress-stopped-working).

24. Mark Tushnet, "Constitutional Hardball," *The John Marshall Law Review* 37 (2004): 523–53.

25. Juan J. Linz, "The Perils of Presidentialism," *Journal of Democracy* 1, no. 1 (1990): 51–69.

26. A party also theoretically could pass legislation even if did not control the White House, if it had a two-thirds majority in both houses of Congress. In practice, this scenario is deeply implausible.

27. Abramowitz and McCoy, "United States," 146–49.

28. "Supreme Court," Gallup (https://news.gallup.com/poll/4732/supreme-court.aspx); and Ariel Edwards-Levy, "Republicans and Democrats Flip Views on the Supreme Court," *Huffington Post*, July 6, 2018 (www.huffingtonpost.com/entry/republicans-democrats-supreme-court_us_5b3bf493e4b09e4a8b285df0).

29. Shanto Iyengar, Gaurav Sood, and Yphtach Lelkes, "Affect, Not Ideology: A Social Identity Perspective on Polarization," *Public Opinion Quarterly* 76, no. 3 (2012): 405–31.

30. "More Now Say It's 'Stressful' to Discuss Politics with People They Disagree With," Pew Research Center, November 5, 2018 (www.people-press.org/2018/11/05/more-now-say-its-stressful-to-discuss-politics-with-people-they-disagree-with/).

31. Hannah Fingerhut, "Republicans Skeptical of Colleges' Impact on U.S., but Most See Benefits for Workforce Preparation," Pew Research Center, July 20, 2017 (www.pewresearch.org/fact-tank/2017/07/20/republicans-skeptical-of-colleges-impact-on-u-s-but-most-see-benefits-for-workforce-preparation/).

32. The Federal Bureau of Investigation (FBI) classifies as hate crimes "criminal offenses motivated, in whole or in part, by the offender's bias against a race, religion, disability, sexual orientation, ethnicity, gender, or gender identity." See FBI Uniform Crime Reporting Program, "Hate Crime Data Collection Guidelines and Training Manual," February 27, 2015, 4.

33. John Eligon, "Hate Crimes Increase for the Third Consecutive Year, F.B.I. Reports," *New York Times*, November 13, 2018 (www.nytimes.com/2018/11/13/us/hate-crimes-fbi-2017.html).

34. Brian Levin and John Reitzel, "Special Status Report: Hate Crime in the US – 1992 to 2016," Center for the Study of Hate & Extremism, 2018 (https://csbs.csusb.edu/sites/csusb_csbs/files/Special%20Status%20Report%20FBI%20Data%20on%20Bias%20Crime%201992%20to%202016%20Final%20Draft%2022218.pdf).

35. For a broad collection of ideas about ways to reduce polarization in the United States, see Nathaniel Persily, ed., *Solutions to Political Polarization in America* (New York: Cambridge University Press, 2015).

36. Doris Kearns Goodwin, *Leadership: In Turbulent Times* (New York: Simon

& Schuster, 2018); and Jon Meacham, *The Soul of America: The Battle for Our Better Angels* (New York: Random House, 2018).

37. See, for instance, Alan I. Abramowitz, "Beyond Confrontation and Gridlock: Making Democracy Work for the American People," in Persily, *Solutions to Political Polarization in America*, 197–207.

38. Jeff Stein, "House Problem Solvers Caucus Has Solved Few Problems, Bipartisan Critics Allege," *Washington Post*, November 5, 2018 (www.washingtonpost.com/business/2018/11/05/house-problem-solvers-caucus-has-solved-few-problems-bipartisan-critics-allege/).

39. Regarding RCV's impact on negative campaigning, see Todd Donovan, Caroline Tolbert, and Kellen Gracey, "Campaign Civility under Preferential and Plurality Voting," *Electoral Studies* 42 (2016): 157–63.

40. Eric McGhee and Boris Shor, "Has the Top Two Primary Elected More Moderates?" *Perspectives on Politics* 15, no. 4 (2017): 1053–66; and Thad Kousser, Justin Phillips, and Boris Shor, "Reform and Representation: A New Method Applied to Recent Electoral Changes," *Political Science Research and Methods* 6, no. 4 (2018): 1–19.

FOUR

Hindu Nationalism and Political Polarization in India

NIRANJAN SAHOO

Given its mind-boggling diversity in terms of religions, languages, castes, regions, and other identity markers, India has almost inevitably experienced polarization across different axes throughout its history. However, since the late nineteenth century, the primary source of political and societal polarization in the country has been a fundamental question of nationhood: should India be a secular country or a Hindu Rashtra (Hindu nation), given that more than three-quarters of the population is Hindu?[1] Although many cleavages mark Indian society, Hindu nationalism is the one dividing force that can pose an existential threat to pluralist democracy in India.

Political parties and associations have organized on opposite sides of the divide between secularism and Hindu nationalism since the early 1900s. Since the 1980s, however, the rising prominence of Hindu nationalist organizations has rapidly escalated polarization, with serious negative effects on the country's fragile ethnic and social relations. Up until the late 1970s, the political hegemony of the secular and pluralist Congress Party succeeded in tempering polarization over competing visions of Indian nationhood, even after the traumatic partition of British India on the basis of religion in 1947. The Congress' politics should not be idealized, however, and the party's failings set the stage in significant ways for the subsequent rise of Hindu nationalism. After a long period of Congress hegemony, skilled political leadership within the Hindu nationalist camp—coupled with India's economic transformation, changes related to traditional and social media, and the rise of competitive caste politics—brought this polarizing divide over Indian identity to the fore.

Particularly since the landslide victory of the Hindu nationalist Bharatiya Janata Party (BJP) in 2014, the consequences of severe polarization have grown ever more worrisome. National political dialogue has become increasingly caustic, a growing culture of intolerance has resulted in rising incidences of violence against minority communities, and the main opposition Congress Party has begun to embrace a soft version of Hindu nationalism. Severe polarization has also taken a toll on India's political institutions: the parliament has grown dysfunctional, essential questions of national security have become politicized, and institutions once respected as impartial, such as the electoral commission and the press, are increasingly distrusted. Polarization has reopened the old fault lines of the young nation, and the ruling party and main opposition now treat each other not as political competitors but as enemies. The great divide, as a noted analyst observed recently, is reflected in nearly every area of India's democracy: parliament, key decision-making bodies, the public sphere, and even private life.[2] Though efforts are being made to counter the country's majoritarian turn and to improve civic dialogue, India and its democracy remain in a situation of prolonged polarization with no clear end in sight. The divide between the two dominant parties has only deepened since the 2019 general elections, in which the Hindu nationalist BJP won a decisive victory and received a larger parliamentary majority than it had in 2014.[3] The resounding success of Hindu nationalism as an electoral strategy has led many to fear that severe polarization may remain a fixture of Indian political life for the foreseeable future.

Roots

The division between secular and Hindu nationalist visions of national identity forms the central axis of polarization in India today. This is not to ignore polarization based on differences in caste, region, language, or class. These other cleavages, however, tend to be cross-cutting, and India's myriad divisions along these lines have created a kind of equilibrium, because no one difference is able to dominate.[4] Divisions based on these characteristics thus have never posed an existential threat to India's pluralist democracy, as the issue of Hindu nationalism now does.

Contemporary polarization over national identity has its roots in the colonial period and the two clashing visions of the "idea of India" that emerged then.[5] While one strain of thinking envisioned India as a secular and pluralist nation, the other defined India as a Hindu Rashtra. During British colonial rule in the late nineteenth century, this binary choice became an increasingly prominent issue in the writings of Gopal Krishna Gokhale (1866–1915), the moderate face of the Indian National Congress (INC), and Bal Gangadhar Tilak (1856–1920), the right-wing champion of a Hindu way of life.[6] Whereas Gokhale (whom Mahatma Gandhi called his political guru) advocated for Indian nationhood based on territoriality, Tilak defined it based on the culture and religion of India's Hindu majority.[7]

The competition between these two visions intensified as Gandhi began leading the struggle for Indian independence. At a time when Gandhi was trying to transform the INC into a mass organization to resist British colonialism, Hindu nationalism began to offer a political alternative that challenged Gandhi's commitment to nonviolence and his conception of Indian nationhood. Contrary to the perspective of Gokhale and other Congress leaders, Gandhi, though a devout Hindu himself, viewed the Indian nation as a harmonious collection of religious communities that deserved to be treated as equals. He promoted a syncretic and spiritual brand of the Hindu religion.[8] Other notable Congress Party leaders also firmly opposed Hindu nationalism. In particular, Jawaharlal Nehru, who would serve as India's first prime minister (1947–64), criticized Hindu nationalism as a "communal" ideology that resembled those of Muslim and Sikh separatists.[9]

In marked opposition to Gandhi and Nehru's vision, during the 1920s Hindu nationalists argued that Hindu culture defined Indian identity and that minorities needed to assimilate by showing allegiance to the symbols of this majority culture. Many Hindu nationalists coalesced behind the

Akhil Bharatiya Hindu Mahasabha (All-India Hindu Grand Assembly), a conservative, Hindu nationalist party founded in 1915. V. D. Savarkar, a self-styled atheist and revolutionary who was leading the then Hindu Mahasabha, coined the term "Hindutva" (Hindu nationalism) to challenge Nehru's territorial and secular conception of Indian nationhood.[10] In his book *Hindutva: Who is a Hindu?* published in 1923, Savarkar argued for the idea of the Hindu Rashtra. Hindutva appears similar to many European nationalisms that are based on religious identity, and Savarkar defined the concept in terms of three essential elements: a common nation, a common race, and a common culture or civilization.[11]

In 1925, the political activist K. B. Hedgewar turned Savarkar's idea of Hindutva into a mass movement when he founded the Rashtriya Swayamsevak Sangh (RSS), a paramilitary volunteer organization dedicated to promoting Hindu nationalism. The main thrust in founding the RSS was more centralized and assertive promotion of Hindutva.[12] The RSS soon emerged as the fountainhead of the Hindu nationalist movement and the staunchest critic of Gandhi and Nehru's idea of a secular India. The RSS was able to rally diversified support behind its idea of a Hindu Rashtra from sister organizations commonly known as the Sangh Parivar, or "Family of Organizations."[13] Thus, whereas Gandhi and Nehru's idea of India was secular and plural, the Savarkarite idea of India can be characterized as ethnonationalist in the way it elevates the concept of Hinduness. Savarkar's idea of India as an ethnostate has continued to drive polarization in postcolonial India. The very essence of India as a multi-religious, multi-lingual, and multi-cultural nation is under serious threat today.

Trajectory

Political leadership has played a dominant role in shaping the trajectory of polarization in postcolonial India. The hegemony of the Congress Party until the late 1970s allowed premiers such as Jawaharlal Nehru to temper polarization even after a traumatizing partition based on religious lines. The failings of the Congress, however, eroded the space for secular politics and contributed to the rise of Hindu nationalism. At times, the Congress practiced a form of pseudosecularism, manipulating religion when it benefited the party, and used religious minorities as a vote bank rather than treating them as genuine constituencies. Starting in the 1980s, Hindu nationalist leadership brought debates over the "idea of India" to the fore, and in recent years the polarizing leadership of Narendra Modi has fanned the flames of debates over India's identity. Along with political leadership, India's economic modernization, rapid changes in traditional and social media, and the rise of caste-based politics have all fueled the rise of polarization since the 1980s.

Congress Party Hegemony Tempers Polarization, 1947 to 1980

Although the bloody partition of India and Pakistan in 1947 escalated sectarian tensions, until the late 1970s the hegemony of the Congress Party kept Hindu nationalism from occupying center stage in national politics. The deft political leadership of Jawaharlal Nehru, who served as India's first prime minister between 1947 and 1964, further tempered polarization.

Polarization between the two conflicting visions of India increased dramatically when the partition created Pakistan as a Muslim state. Tensions only rose further when a former *pracharak* (propagandist) of the RSS assassinated Gandhi in 1948 over the issue of the latter's alleged "sympathy" for the Muslim-majority Pakistan.[14] The interim government under Jawaharlal Nehru immediately banned the RSS and its affiliated organizations and took stringent measures to check their activities. The ban was lifted shortly afterward in 1949, after the RSS agreed to respect the constitution, reject violence, and assume a nonpolitical, cultural role.[15] Moreover, nation-building and other compulsions pushed the new government to be more open to the ideas of the RSS and other Hindu nationalist organizations.[16]

In the subsequent years, the Hindu right movement moderated its extremist methods and took conscious steps to pursue its agenda culturally and politically as well. In 1951, its key leader, S. P. Mukherjee, left his post as president of the Hindu Mahasabha and formed a new political party, the Bharatiya Jana Sangh (BJS), to compete in India's first general elections, slated for 1952. The BJS and RSS accused the Nehru government of favoring religious minorities and strongly objected to the government's proposed Hindu code bills, which sought to codify Hindu personal laws (relating to issues such as marriage and inheritance) and bring them under the purview of judiciary while exempting Muslims from similar reforms.[17] The BJS and

RSS were also at the forefront of agitation against codes that allowed Muslims to have separate personal laws and to slaughter cows, a practice firmly opposed by a majority of Hindus and many others in India.[18] In 1966–67, the RSS and its sister organizations gained attention for their protests nationwide against the slaughter of cows and forced the central government to enact legislation in this regard.[19]

After years of rule by the Congress, however, the authoritarian and polarizing maneuvers of Prime Minister Indira Gandhi (1966–77, 1980–84) provided the BJS and other opposition parties with a crucial opening. Indira Gandhi, the daughter of Jawaharlal Nehru, was an extremely divisive figure, and her tenure was marked by extreme centralization of power, intolerance of the opposition and the press, and finally the imposition of a state of emergency between 1975 and 1977.[20] The state of emergency— which led to the arrests of hundreds of opposition leaders and included various other draconian measures—galvanized the entire political opposition, including the Hindu nationalist BJS, to unite and form the Janata coalition, which defeated Indira Gandhi in the 1977 general elections. Although the Janata coalition was short-lived, collapsing in 1979 under the weight of internal contradictions and the political ambitions of competing leaders, it hugely benefited the BJS and brought many of its leaders to national prominence. Yet given the secular and socialist composition of the Janata coalition government, which contained many former members of the Congress Party, the Hindu right failed to advance its ideological project during this period. Further, the Congress Party under Indira Gandhi recovered in the 1980 general elections and won a legislative majority, thereby pushing the Hindu right back into opposition.

Rising Polarization and a Rising BJP: 1980 to 2004

Between 1980 and 2004, divisions over Indian national identity became increasingly prominent with the formation of the Bharatiya Janata Party, a right-wing, Hindu nationalist political party, and the success of the RSS in mobilizing Hindu nationalist sentiment. In this period, both the political failings of the Congress and skilled political leadership within the BJP allowed Hindu nationalism to enter the political mainstream.

After repeated failures to dislodge the dominant Congress Party,

Hindu nationalists from the BJS and the Janata coalition (with which it had merged in 1977) decided to chart an independent course. They did so by establishing the BJP in 1980 under the leadership of Atal Bihari Vajpayee and Lal Krishna Advani. The Vajpayee-Advani duo brought new life to the Hindu right in India in the mid-1980s. While Advani pandered to Hindu sentiments and sought to mobilize the majority community on the basis of religious identity in the Hindi heartlands, Vajpayee employed a moderate approach to expand the new party's footprint beyond the so-called Hindi Belt, a linguistic region in north-central India where the Hindi language is widely spoken. Unsurprisingly, the RSS and its sister organizations strongly opposed Vajpayee's more moderate line.

Meanwhile, in the mid-1980s, the RSS and Sangh Parivar inflamed communal tensions by launching the Ram Janmabhoomi movement, which aimed to build a temple to the Hindu deity Rama on the site of the controversial Babri Masjid, a mosque in the city of Ayodhya. Through this movement, the RSS entered into a tacit understanding with its sister organization, the Vishwa Hindu Parishad (VHP), to relaunch an ethnoreligious project that would revive the idea of a Hindu Rashtra. The two organizations started the Ram Janmabhoomi movement to reclaim for Hindus the land upon which the Babri Masjid was built, which some Hindus believe to be the birthplace of Lord Rama. In the sixteenth century, the Mughal emperor who conquered a large part of northern India, including the city of Ayodhya, had demolished a Hindu temple there and built the Babri Masjid. Given its incendiary history, this religious site had remained a major point of conflict between Hindus and Muslims and been the focus of numerous riots.[21] With the tacit support of the BJP, the RSS and VHP launched a massive national campaign demanding the restoration of the original Hindu temple in 1989. This mobilization greatly contributed to the BJP's success in the 1989 general elections, in which the "saffron party" (so-called because the color saffron is closely associated with the Hindu religion) won a remarkable eighty-five seats and helped deprive the Congress of a legislative majority.

The Congress Party's opportunistic "soft Hindutva" turn in the late 1980s also contributed significantly to the success of the Hindu right and its polarizing tactics. As prime minister, Indira Gandhi openly stoked the anxieties of India's Hindu majority in election campaigns in the 1980s, and her son, Prime Minister Rajiv Gandhi (1984–89), also wooed the Hindu community.[22] In 1985, the Congress Party faced a backlash over its reaction to the Indian Supreme Court's decision in the *Shah Bano* case, as its critics claimed that the party was allowing Muslims to live under a very different civil code.[23] In response, Rajiv Gandhi sought to win over Hindu hardliners (who were angry with his government) by opening the gate of a Hindu temple in Ayodhya in 1988. Rajiv Gandhi's actions, which appeared to pander to the Hindu right and thus to show political weakness, emboldened the Sangh Parivar to further politicize mobilization against the Babri Masjid in Ayodhya.[24] L. K. Advani made the most of the political opening by launching a famous 10,000-kilometer *Rath Yatra* (chariot journey) to demand the construction of a temple for Rama on the disputed site. Tensions ultimately culminated in the destruction of the Babri Masjid by *kar sevaks* (Hindu religious activists) on December 6, 1992, leading to a series of violent communal riots (with 1,200 reported deaths) between Hindus and Muslims across the country. The incident led to a second ban on the RSS and its sister organizations, as well as dismissals of BJP governments in several northern states.[25]

The Babri episode isolated the BJP and made it a pariah party for some time. Between the late 1990s and the early 2000s, however, the BJP carefully shifted its strategy to capture political power. Realizing that it could not win power on its own and that it needed to form alliances with other regional parties, it toned down its inflammatory Hindu nationalist rhetoric.[26] The Vajpayee-Advani duo's deft strategy of moderating Hindutva and mixing it with promises of economic development allowed the party to gain support from fifteen coalition partners in 1998 and run the first successful non-Congress coalition to complete a full five-year term between 1999 and 2004.[27] The BJP's dependence on its coalition partners meant that the party was forced to set aside contentious proposals such as building a Hindu temple at Ayodhya, adopting a Uniform Civil Code (which would end the practice of having different civil codes for different religious communities), and repealing Article 370 of the Indian Constitution (which guarantees special status to the state of Jammu and Kashmir, the only Muslim-majority Indian state).[28]

The Rise of Narendra Modi and the Revival
of Hindutva, 2004 to the Present

The symptoms of polarization temporarily abated with a Congress-led government in power between 2004 and 2014. Since 2014, however, the polarizing leadership of Prime Minister Narendra Modi and the BJP's stunning electoral success under his watch have escalated tensions dramatically.

The BJP and its Hindutva agenda suffered a huge jolt when the party lost the 2004 general elections to the Congress. The Congress-led coalition, which held power for two consecutive terms from 2004 until 2014 under Prime Minister Manmohan Singh, made some significant programmatic interventions to temper India's growing polarization, particularly through its outreach to Muslims. To address the growing marginalization of Muslims in education and government employment, the coalition established the controversial Sachar Committee in 2006 to recommend measures to redress discrimination against Muslims.[29] This effort was well meaning, but the opposition BJP and Hindu right organizations criticized the Congress for furthering minority interests at the expense of the majority community and for driving out Hindu nationalists from positions of power (popularly characterized as a "detoxification" campaign).[30] The Congress won the next general elections in 2009 based on its record of propelling robust economic growth and providing inclusive development. Yet subsequent economic problems, a series of corruption scandals, and most importantly the party's cynical use of identity politics against the purported threat of right-wing terror created critical openings for the Hindu right in the decisive 2014 elections.[31]

The BJP's astonishing electoral comeback in 2014, in which the party secured a majority of seats in the lower house on its own, suddenly brought polarization over old ideological divides to unprecedented levels. Between 1998 and 2004, the BJP had toned down its Hindu nationalist rhetoric to ensure the survival of its coalition government, and Prime Minister Vajpayee had made relatively subtle moves to advance the BJP and Sangh Parivar's ideological agenda. Since the 2014 elections, a politically stronger party under Narendra Modi has emerged as an unapologetic advocate of Hindutva and the majority community's primacy in social, political, and economic life. While in power, the BJP has sought to rewrite Indian history to emphasize the country's Hindu heritage and its glorious past, promoted Sanskrit in education policy, and stocked important historical and cultural institutions with party ideologues or sympathizers.

The real game changer was the meteoric rise of Narendra Modi, who skillfully combined promises of economic development with Hindu nationalist appeals. A three-time chief minister in the state of Gujarat, Modi was known as an able administrator, strong leader, and progrowth politician who singlehandedly turned Gujarat into one of India's top investment destinations. Modi's prodevelopment record gave the BJP formidable electoral appeal, and the rising "aspirations of the new Indian masses" contributed significantly to the party's landslide victory in 2014.[32] Yet the single biggest factor explaining the BJP's phenomenal performance was sharp polarization in the Hindi heartland states.[33] Modi was a deeply polarizing figure due to his strong stance on Hindutva and his alleged role in the 2002 Gujarat riots.[34] Crucial to the BJP's success was Modi's image as an unapologetic Hindu nationalist, whose his followers fondly address him as *Hindu Hriday Samrat*, or "ruler of Hindu hearts." Thus, not only has Modi reversed the gradual slide of the Hindu right after its lackluster electoral performances in 2004 and 2009, but also under his leadership the BJP has witnessed a phenomenal surge across all regions of the country, except the south. Together with its allies, in 2017 the BJP was in power in twenty-one out of twenty-nine states, a feat that once seemed impossible for the Hindu right.[35]

After the BJP's landslide victory in 2014, ethnonationalism gained greater traction as a core component of the party's electoral strategy. Top leaders of the Sangh Parivar and even senior leaders of the BJP have openly called to amend the constitution to make India a Hindu nation.[36] Important functionaries of the party and its affiliates regularly make controversial remarks regarding this ideological project. The government is openly and aggressively pursuing its cultural and political agenda by stocking key cultural and educational institutions with its own ideologues and sympathizers, taking a leaf from the Congress Party's book in this regard.[37] The BJP's open advocacy of Hindu nationalism has greatly alarmed India's minorities and caused considerable anxiety among opposition parties, many of which decided to form a Mahagathbandhan (Grand Alliance) to defeat the right-wing party and check its majoritarian style of governance.[38]

In the run-up to the 2019 general elections, in which the BJP won a historic victory, the country witnessed an unprecedented level of polarization between the leading political parties. The ruling BJP and affiliated Hindu nationalist organizations announced their intention to build a Hindu temple on the disputed site where the Babri Masjid once stood in Ayodhya.[39] The Congress Party under the new leadership of Rahul Gandhi not only brought its opposition to the temple's construction to the Supreme Court, but also tried to match the BJP's toxicity with toxicity.[40] Importantly, Prime Minister Modi ran a "presidential-style campaign" that sought to turn the election into a referendum on his leadership, and he employed various tactics to polarize the electorate for political gain.[41] A particularly striking example of the ruling party's polarizing tactics was the nomination of Pragya Singh Thakur as a candidate for parliament, even as she was awaiting trial for her alleged role in a 2008 terrorist attack perpetrated by alleged Hindu extremists.[42] To fan the flames of polarization further, the BJP specifically chose to have Thakur run against the Congress parliamentarian who had coined the term "Hindu terror" after the same 2008 attack.[43] Numerous top leaders of the saffron party, including the BJP's president Amit Shah, campaigned for Thakur, who won a landslide victory in the prestigious Bhopal constituency. In short, the 2019 general elections saw extreme levels of polarization and a surge in majoritarian discourse based on Hindu nationalism, both of which heavily benefited the right-wing BJP.

Key Drivers of Polarization

Three crucial drivers of increasing polarization have been India's ongoing economic transformation, changes in traditional and social media, and the rise of competitive caste politics. Hindu nationalist organizations have been able to harness the power of each of these drivers in ways that their social and political rivals find difficult to match.

ECONOMIC TRANSFORMATION   Among the key drivers of polarization in India, the least debated one is the country's economic transformation over the last three decades. The economic liberalization pursued by the Congress-led coalition government in the early 1990s transformed India's economy, moving it away from central planning and toward a more mixed and liberalized system. However, the economic reforms, which accelerated urbanization and created a sizeable middle class in the late 1990s, proved to be a huge boon for the identity politics of the BJP and its affiliates.[44] Urban voters tended to be inclined to support the BJP's cultural narratives based on Hindu nationalism.[45] According to Jaffrelot, "Urbanization has transformed Hinduism more than any other development. In the village you live together. You can't miss the muezzin or the bells of the temple and you have syncretic (mixed) cults. For example, Hindus will go to Sufi places for healing. . . . When you go to the city that's over."[46] The BJP's disproportionate support base in urban areas demonstrates that urbanization has fueled support for Hindu nationalism. With the exception of the 2009 general elections, in which the Congress cut into the saffron party's share of the urban vote, since 1996 the BJP has received a high share of its support from urban voters. In the 2014 general elections, the BJP under Modi's leadership swept most of the urban constituencies that it contested.[47]

Further, the key indirect contributing factors that led middle- and upper-caste Hindus, as well as the urban population, to support the BJP were the demolition of the Babri Masjid and the implementation of the Mandal Commission Report in the early 1990s, which raised politically charged questions about the status of socially and educationally backward classes.[48] These two critical political developments led the political scientist Yogendra Yadav to coin the expression "the three Ms of Indian politics": Mandal, Mandir (meaning "temple"), and Market.[49]

TRADITIONAL AND SOCIAL MEDIA   Changes to both traditional and social media have also fanned the flames of polarization, particularly in the past decade. Today, the most significant driver of polarization in India is biased and partisan media, whose impact has grown exponentially in the bourgeoning social media ecosystem.

In the realm of traditional media, impartial and objective reporting has become increasingly rare.[50] India's media outlets used to take pride in their objective reporting, but today they generally are split by political affiliation. In this changing media ecosystem, profit-driven partisan outlets openly support the ideological affiliation of mainstream parties and selectively circulate news. The political battles fought in 9 p.m. debates on television largely resemble those on American channels such as Fox News and MSNBC in how they sensationalize smaller issues to create false binary choices or divisions. Changes in media ownership likely play a role in this transformation, as more and more business houses now own Indian media outlets.[51]

Compounding these effects, social media has recently emerged as a major driver of polarization. Although India still has a low level of Internet penetration compared to many other large countries, the exponentially increasing use of smartphones with Internet connectivity has transformed the social media landscape, as India now has more than 450 million Internet users. Social media outlets, particularly Facebook and WhatsApp, have accelerated the pace at which distorted, unreliable, and false information spreads. While Facebook and Twitter remain key platforms for the spread of fake news among the urban and mostly English-speaking population, WhatsApp has emerged as the favorite tool for disseminating misinformation to create communal animosity. Social media thus contributes to a toxic environment of intolerance, mistrust, and hate.

Furthermore, political parties routinely employ troll armies and bots to target rival groups and spread propaganda, often with dangerous consequences.[52] Fake news and hate speech are routinely disseminated through social media platforms to foment intercommunal discord for parties' electoral advantage. Experts argue that social media is playing a crucial role in sharpening the division between the idea of secular democracy and Hindutva.[53] On this front, the BJP has acted most quickly and skillfully to exploit the potential of social media, which it did to great effect in the 2014 general elections, in its landslide victory in the state of Uttar Pradesh in 2017, and in the 2019 general elections.[54] Compared to the Congress and other parties, the BJP has been particularly effective at spreading its message via social media, and Prime Minister Modi has largely bypassed traditional media by using Facebook, Twitter, and other means of digital communication. The ruling party outspent the opposition Congress on social media advertising by more than a factor of fifteen in the recent 2019 elections.[55]

CASTE POLITICS Because caste and other primordial identities often play a decisive role in a voter's choice of candidates, political parties dole out patronage to woo caste groups to win elections.[56] Major parties in India often have been identified with the caste group they represent—a phenomenon that is especially palpable in regional politics, where caste-based parties have long flourished. In the first two decades after India's independence, caste divisions were not particularly salient in national politics, because the Congress acted as a big tent or catch-all party and drew support from across caste lines. Over time, however, tensions between the interests of the different castes represented by the Congress grew more apparent. Starting in the late 1960s, these tensions and the decline of the once-dominant Congress led to a dramatic expansion in regional and caste-based parties. In response, the Congress sought to win back its stature by appealing to Dalits and other oppressed communities.

With the upsurge of intermediary peasant castes or Other Backward Classes (OBCs) in the early 1980s, the game changed for both the major parties, as competition intensified for support from different castes and caste parties. With new OBC parties cutting into the vote base of both national parties, the BJP felt a desperate need to reinvent itself to undo the damage done by the Mandal Commission report.[57] In fact, the report was the key event that led the BJP and Sangh Parivar to decide to double down on religious polarization by stoking tensions over the Babri Masjid. Fearing that the rise of these caste-based parties would divide Hindus, the BJP sought to play into the anxieties of upper-caste Hindu voters and mobilize this constituency through the Ram Janmabhoomi movement. The BJP thus used religion to temper caste divisions.[58]

Given the handsome electoral returns that the BJP received in the intervening years, there was no turning back on this strategy. In the 2014 elections, the BJP deftly used the issue of Hindu nationalism to win over voters who otherwise might have cast their ballots along caste lines, and it benefited tremendously in the populous northern states.[59] Poll data suggest that many Dalits and OBCs abandoned their caste leaders for the BJP.[60] Notably, the BJP's polarizing rhetoric has helped it overcome caste and other primordial divisions to win elections in Uttar Pradesh and other Hindi heartland states. Data from the 2019 general elections suggest that the party's deft use of Hindu nationalism played a key role in blunting caste divisions and securing a landslide victory for the BJP.[61] The surest proof is the failure of a supposedly formidable coalition of caste-based parties to stop the BJP from winning more than two-thirds of the parliamentary seats in India's largest state, Uttar Pradesh, in 2019.[62] The success of this strategy is producing a counter-response among opposition parties, including the Congress and regional parties, which have increasingly abandoned minorities (or at least avoided taking up their cause) and embraced soft Hindutva.[63]

Consequences

Rising polarization has sharply affected Indian society and political life. Along with the rise of divisive and dismissive rhetoric, India has experienced increasing intolerance toward and violence against minority groups. Consequences in the political realm have been no less severe and include the marginalization of minority communities; bitter political contestation over historical memory, national security issues, and legislation; and attacks on independent institutions.

Sharp Change in National Conversation

The most visible impact of severe political polarization is the decreasing civility of national political discourse. Political debate has often been reduced to name-calling, uncivil exchanges, and ad hominem attacks. Liberal and secular ideologues often disparage pro-Hindutva figures as *bhakts* and *Sanghis* (both terms for "blind followers"); the latter reply by referring to the former with highly derogatory terms such as *libtards*, *sickular*, and *presstitutes* (a derogatory term for journalists). In addition, the national conversation increasingly presupposes a binary opposition between nationalists and antinationalists. Moderate political debate over ideas or even policies has little place in this atmosphere of growing hate and incivility.

Growing Culture of Intolerance

Severe polarization is damaging social relations among communities through stigmatization, abuses, and demonization, often followed by violence and intimidation. Majoritarian violence orchestrated by vigilante groups with impunity is unleashing deep anxieties and insecurities among minorities and groups that are antithetical to the Hindu right's ideology.

A significant casualty of deep polarization affecting people-to-people and intercommunity relations is declining social capital, which is vital to maintaining a cohesive social fabric in an extremely diverse and large country.

In recent years, India has seen a rising tide of violence perpetrated by vigilante groups acting as thought police or moral police.[64] As these attacks demonstrate, democracy can be put in danger not only by the state, but also by vigilante groups that are allowed to determine what people should think, write, eat, drink, and wear. Writers, scientists, and intellectuals are being attacked and routinely derided with abusive language for expressing even the slightest differences in perspective on political or cultural matters. That said, the ruling BJP and its affiliates are not exclusively to blame for such abuses, as the Congress and many regional parties are responsible for their share of hate stories.

The scale and intensity of the intolerance seen in India today are extremely high in historical perspective. Majoritarian mobs have attacked minorities, human rights advocates, and activists with impunity. For instance, according to *IndiaSpend*, 97 percent of cow-related hate crimes reported between 2010 and 2017 occurred after the BJP government assumed power in May 2014. In 2017 alone, as many as eleven Muslims were killed in incidents of cow vigilantism across the country, the highest toll on record in recent years.[65] Similarly, hateful references to minorities (with taunts such as "Muslims, go to Pakistan") have become commonplace. Even Dalits, who have special constitutional and legal protections based on their outcast status in the Hindu religion, are not spared. In recent years, there have been several cases of lynching and murderous attacks against Dalits in the states of Gujarat and Maharashtra.

In short, with political leaders and social media contributing to a spiral of increasing polarization, intolerance and hatred have become the new normal in today's India.[66] The role of political elites is best illustrated by the example of a prominent minister in Modi's cabinet giving garlands to vigilantes accused of murdering a cattle trader.[67] Intolerance and hate crimes are not restricted to divisions over the status of cows. Even personal life is not spared, as seen by the invention of scaremongering terms such as "love jihad," used to disparage interfaith relationships and marriages by claiming that Muslim men are deliberately wooing Hindu women in order to force them to convert to Islam upon marriage. In response to rising intolerance,

in October 2015, twelve filmmakers returned their national awards to protest "growing intolerance in the country."[68]

Political Marginalization of Minorities

Yet another consequence of rising polarization is the dramatic shrinking of
minority political representation. Since the 2014 general elections, Muslim
representation in the Lok Sabha (lower house) of India's parliament and
several state assemblies has fallen drastically.[69] As an illustration, even
though Muslims represent 14 percent of India's population according to
the latest census, as of 2018 they held only 4 percent of the seats in the
Lok Sabha, the lowest share since 1957.[70] In the 2019 general elections, the
number of Muslim MPs increased only marginally, from twenty-three to
twenty-seven out of 543 members.[71]

Muslims also have minimal representation in the ruling BJP: in January 2018, of the party's 1,418 assembly members, only four were Muslim.[72]
Even more troubling is that during the 2017 elections in Uttar Pradesh, a
state where Muslims constitute as much as 20 percent of the population,
the BJP chose not to field a single Muslim candidate. As a consequence,
the largest minority community's representation fell from 17.1 percent
to 5.9 percent in the state assembly. There is only one Muslim minister
in the entire Uttar Pradesh cabinet—which is headed by a Hindu monk-
cum-politician, Yogi Adityanath of the BJP.[73] And in the wake of the 2019
general elections, none of the BJP's 303 members of the Lok Sabha are
Muslim.[74]

Increasing Prominence of Identity Politics

The success of the BJP's identity politics under Modi's leadership has not
only created fissures within the opposition, but also decisively moved the
goal posts on identity questions in a negative direction. The opposition
tried to maintain its silence over a recent barbaric hate killing of a migrant
Muslim by a bigoted Hindu in Rajasthan, and major political parties have
become wary of defending and protecting religious minorities, particularly
Muslims.[75] A noteworthy development is that the BJP's overt Hindu nationalism has pushed the Congress Party to embrace a form of soft Hin-

dutva. To counter the BJP's allegations that the Congress was always a pro-Muslim party, Rahul Gandhi, the new party president of the Congress, has made frequent visits to major Hindu temples, including an arduous pilgrimage in 2018 to Kailash Mansarovar in the Himalayas, to refurbish his party's Hindu credentials.[76] In another example of this turn toward soft Hindutva, the chief minister of a recently elected Congress government in Madhya Pradesh invoked India's National Security Act to justify draconian measures against individuals accused of cow slaughter. In short, a race to the bottom on identity politics is under way.[77] After the BJP's landslide victory in the 2019 elections, fueled in significant part by the party's appeal to Hindu nationalism, competitive appeals to identity politics may remain an enduring feature of campaigns in India's democracy.

Toward a Legacy War

For decades, leaders of the Hindu right have been nurturing deep grievances against the Congress and other secular affiliates for denying them what they view as their rightful place and recognition. Jawaharlal Nehru, Indira Gandhi, and other Congress leaders blocked the Sangh Parivar's Hindutva project, and the Congress filled key cultural and educational institutions with people sympathetic to its secular ideology. Given that the party has ruled for most of India's post-independence history, it naturally monopolized the country's historical narrative and privileged Gandhi and Nehru's legacies.

Since coming to power, Modi and affiliated Sangh Parivar leaders have derided what they call the "Congress culture of appropriating everything to the Gandhi-Nehru family" and denying recognition to leaders outside the Gandhi-Nehru clan, such as Sardar Patel, one of India's founding fathers. Furthermore, the government has moved aggressively to give recognition to its icons, such as the RSS and BJS figures Deendayal Upadhyay and Syama Prasad Mukherjee, and to fill institutions with people who support and advance its ideology. One example of this legacy war is the raging controversy over the status of the Nehru Memorial Library and Museum.[78] While the BJP has announced its plan to expand the contents and reach of the library by including other former prime ministers, the Congress has criticized this proposal as a deliberate and partisan effort to erase Nehru's legacy. The ongoing legacy war is not restricted to the appropriation of institutions of national importance; it also encompasses cultural bodies, heritage sites, and national icons—of whom Sardar Patel and B. R. Ambedkar, the architect of the Constitution of India, are the BJP's favorites.

Parliamentary Dysfunction

Severe political polarization, coupled with widening mistrust between government and opposition parties, is having serious effects on the functioning of parliament and particularly the transaction of legislative business. According to the influential parliamentary watchdog PRS Legislative, there has been a secular decline in the productivity of parliamentary business for a long time, but the last few years of the BJP government have witnessed frequent standoffs between the ruling party and opposition, often leading to the washout of entire parliamentary sessions.[79] For instance, during the 2018 budget session, a united opposition motioned without requisite numbers for a no-confidence motion against the ruling party, which then used all possible means to delay the motion, including the selective invocation of parliamentary procedures. The end result was a complete washout of legislative business, and an important finance bill was passed without discussion.[80] In a growing number of instances, the government has been turning normal bills into money bills in order to work around its lack of a majority in the Rajya Sabha (upper house). The passage in 2016 of the controversial Aadhaar bill (involving biometric identity and privacy issues) as a money bill is a case in point.[81] Although previous governments have used such tactics and parliamentary business has suffered on a number of occasions, the situation was not as dire as it is today. The debates have become shriller, and the government and opposition frequently treat each other as enemies and existential threats.

Politicization of National Security

India's polarized politics do not spare matters related to national security. The recent controversies surrounding the purchase of French-made Rafale fighter jets have seen the ruling party and opposition discussing sensitive national security issues in public with little regard for the detrimental effects such discussions might have on the country's security.[82] The same is true for a much discussed surgical strike launched against Pakistan-based terror camps in September 2016.[83] The 2019 Pulwama terror attack in Jammu and Kashmir, which killed forty Indian police force personnel and precipitated a tense standoff between India and Pakistan, resulted in an even more pernicious politicization of national security issues by the ruling BJP and the opposition in the recent general elections.[84] Matters related to terrorism and internal insurgencies are routinely polarized, as the major parties do not trust each other and are intent on scoring political points and painting the other as the villain. National security matters are discussed in hypernationalistic rhetorical terms. An example is that the BJP and the Congress wield the terms "Jihadi terror" and "Hindu terror," respectively, to try to cast one another in the worst light possible. Also worrisome is the brazen misuse of vital security and strategic institutions such as the Central Bureau of Investigation and National Investigating Agency for partisan political purposes.[85]

Attacks on Independent Institutions

In this polarized political slugfest, India's independent institutions have suffered dearly. From the Supreme Court to the Reserve Bank of India to the Election Commission, most elite institutions have come under heavy partisan attack from either the government or the opposition.[86] The most telling examples of such an onslaught are the unprecedented press conference held by the four most senior judges of the highest court to highlight growing attacks on judicial freedom, a politically motivated impeachment motion against the chief justice of India by the main opposition, and the BJP-led coalition's attempt to pack the higher judiciary.[87] More recently, in December 2018 the governor of India's central reserve bank stunned the nation by resigning from the coveted office, largely over the issue of attacks on its autonomy by the central government.[88]

However, the most undesirable and unexpected fallout of growing distrust among government and opposition parties has been the shrill, baseless misinformation campaigns carried out against the electoral commission. Even though the institution is known for its exemplary and credible record of conducting elections in a country as large and diverse as India across multiple decades, in recent years political actors, especially on the BJP side, have raised doubts about the integrity of these elections. Politicians who fail to win (or are turned out of) office increasingly suggest that the possible malfunctioning or hacking of electronic voting machines may have played a role in their defeat.[89] In the latest controversy, nearly all opposition parties, including the Congress, have demanded that the country switch to paper ballots, even though the commission has already introduced a voter-verified paper audit trail to ensure the accuracy of the voting system.

Remedial Actions

Polarization has built-in dynamics that can make it self-propagating and can lead it to spiral out of control.[90] By all estimates, political polarization in India has become severe, and if not addressed it will become even more difficult to reverse. Given that the structural and institutional foundations of this polarization are widespread and entrenched, it will not be easy to find workable solutions. Mitigating polarization will require a response at multiple levels—institutional, societal, and individual. Fortunately, both the larger society and some political institutions have begun responding in multiple ways to address the causes of polarization. Current efforts to reduce polarization can be roughly divided into two categories: those that seek to reform political institutions, and those that seek to improve civic dialogue.

Political and Institutional Responses

Even though political parties and government institutions have helped contribute to India's polarization, they also form part of the bulwark against it. Opposition coalition-building and judicial activism have been the primary strategies through which political actors have sought to address rising polarization.

OPPOSITION ALLIANCES India's sharp political polarization has created space for political counter-mobilization. The powerful threat to the viability of the current opposition posed by the Hindu right has alarmed not only the main political opposition, but also many regional parties, leading them to form alliances and electoral partnerships to contain the BJP. In their first opportunity to unseat the BJP, the united opposition put up joint candidates in by-elections in Uttar Pradesh, who went on to decisively defeat BJP candidates.[91] The 2019 general elections witnessed the joining together of several prominent leaders of regional parties to form a Mahagathbandhan (Grand Alliance) in the populous state of Uttar Pradesh to challenge the dominant BJP. Similarly, Chandrababu Naidu, the chief minister in the state of Andhra Pradesh, ended a bitter thirty-five-year rivalry with the Congress Party and forged an alliance to fight the saffron party in the 2019 elections.[92] These efforts at both the state and national levels failed to stop the BJP from winning a parliamentary majority in back-to-back elections for the first time since 1984, but the country's political process is alive nonetheless in creating counter-measures to stop the pro-Hindutva majoritarian turn.[93] Opposition coalition-building remains a work in progress, but paradoxically the BJP's electoral success may facilitate this process by pushing more opposition parties into united coalitions, as occurred in the 1970s when the Congress under Indira Gandhi completely dominated Indian politics.

JUDICIAL ACTIVISM   In various institutions, there are signs of resistance to majoritarianism and the politics of polarization. In a rare show of defiance, the four most senior judges of the Supreme Court held a press conference in 2018 to critique many of the government's policies.[94] On issues such as maintaining the rule of law and ensuring that the state and its agencies deliver justice, the Supreme Court has created a special bench to monitor hate crimes, especially incidents of mob lynching.[95] Recently, the bench asked the parliament to enact legislation on the issue of hate crimes and issued notices to several state governments to submit status reports. On numerous occasions, the court has called upon the ruling party and government departments to desist from majoritarianism and hate mongering. Similarly, the Supreme Court resisted political pressure and delivered several landmark judgments, including decisions in 2018 to overturn a colonial law known as Section 377, which criminalized consensual gay sex, and to prevent the Sabarimala Hindu temple from barring women of menstruating age (contrary to what the Hindu right government had desired).[96] Thus, an independent judiciary remains the most critical institutional check against majoritarianism and the potential erosion of democratic principles, including the rights of minorities.

Improving Civic Dialogue

Various political and nonpolitical actors in India, from journalists to technology companies, have sought to counter the divisiveness of political discourse through public protest, the regulation of social media, and interfaith dialogue.

RAISING CONSCIOUSNESS   While the rise of the Hindu right under Narendra Modi has sharply divided India's civil society into "left-liberal" and "right-wing," social conservative camps, the spreading culture of intolerance and majoritarianism has greatly alarmed a sizeable portion of public intellectuals, writers, artists, journalists, academics, and activists. Since 2014, writers have called for surrendering their awards and medals (*award wapasi*) on numerous occasions, while press associations have held vigils and candlelight protests against hate crimes and violations of press freedom.[97]

REGULATING SOCIAL MEDIA   It is not an easy or straightforward task to address the dangerous role of social media in inciting violence and hatred as well as spreading fake news and misinformation. However, after constant prodding from the highest court and civil society, the government has come out with a guideline recently to counter fake news and spurious WhatsApp messages that foster social and communal discord.[98] Social media companies such as Facebook and WhatsApp have also responded by regulating and monitoring content on their platforms, particularly by disabling "bulk messaging" and "organized spamming" to prevent the distribution of fake or incendiary messages.[99]

PROMOTING INTERFAITH DIALOGUE   In a deeply divided country with animosities rooted in a complex history, regular interfaith dialogue can have far-reaching positive effects in preventing the emergence of hatred and violence. In recent years, interfaith dialogue has proven useful in checking communal riots in several Indian cities, such as Hyderabad and

Mumbai.[100] Activists and civil society actors have drawn upon the much-discussed metaphor of *Ganga-Jamuni Tehzeeb* (Ganges-Yamuna culture), which invokes the image of two rivers flowing together to suggest the possibility of harmony between Hindus and Muslims, to maintain communal harmony in Varanasi and other diverse cities.[101] In short, the syncretic Hindu religion can work as a limiting force against polarization.

The politics of polarization are keeping India in a permanent state of tension and conflict. India's civic sphere resembles a war zone in which rival parties and groups are constantly waging harsh battles. Given the coarseness of the exchanges, this divide is beginning to take a heavy toll on the fragile social relations in the country, which has weathered riots, ethnic skirmishes, and interreligious conflicts in previous decades.[102] Even at the height of the polarization resulting from the Ram Janmabhoomi movement, which caused many deaths and rioting, the divide was never as toxic and deep as it is now. Not only is there a complete breakdown of communication between the ruling party and the main opposition Congress, but also an "us-versus-them" mentality has come to define entire political and social spaces. The severity of contemporary polarization has serious implications for public policy, institutions, and the overall stability of Indian democracy. With the exception of the National Emergency in 1975–77, there has been no instance in which India's democracy has seemed so fragile. And in the 2019 general elections, polarization took a still uglier turn: key figures from the major parties repeatedly violated norms of decorum and civility, to the extent that observers characterized the election as "one of the most vitriolic campaigns ever in India."[103] The main hope for positive change comes from India's independent institutions and a resilient society, which have rejected threats to democracy in the past. In addition, a deeply hierarchical and segregated Hindu religion and its innate ethos of tolerance may act as a check against majoritarianism. At the same time, India's strong culture of interfaith dialogue can help heal the growing hatred and animosity in society. Yet time may be running out for India and its democracy, and the results of the 2019 polls offer a dire warning. With polarization now reaching alarming heights, Indian democracy may have entered into uncharted territory.

NOTES

1. Census 2011, "Religion Census 2011" (www.census2011.co.in/religion.php).

2. Ashutosh Varshney, "Narendra Modi's Illiberal Drift Threatens Indian Democracy," *Financial Times*, August 17, 2017 (www.ft.com/content/0015a59e-80e2 -11e7-94e2-c5b903247afd).

3. As per the declared results, the BJP on its own won 303 seats out of 543, securing an even larger parliamentary majority than it had in the 2014 elections. Meanwhile, the BJP-led National Democratic Alliance clinched 352 seats. The BJP also significantly improved its vote share from 31 percent in 2014 to 37.4 percent in 2019, and it surprised many observers by winning seats in eastern and southern states outside of its usual political turf. See Gilles Verniers, "Verdict 2019 in Charts and Maps: BJP Started Poorly, Congress Nearly Drew a Blank from Phases 4 to 6," *Scroll*, May 29, 2019 (https://scroll.in/article/925074/verdict-2019-in-charts-and -maps-bjp-started-poorly-congress-nearly-drew-a-blank-from-phases-4-to-6).

4. Sunil Khilnani, *The Idea of India* (New York: Farrar, Straus, and Giroux, 1998).

5. Christophe Jaffrelot, *The Hindu Nationalist Movement and Indian Politics: 1925 to the 1990s* (London: C. Hurst & Co., 1996).

6. B. D. Graham, "The Congress and Hindu Nationalism," in *The Indian National Congress: Centenary Hindsights*, ed. D. A. Low (Delhi: Oxford University Press, 1988), 170–87; and Gyanendra Pandey, *The Construction of Communalism in Colonial North India* (Delhi: Oxford University Press, 1990).

7. The ideological roots of Hindu nationalism can be found in religious revivalist and reform movements that emerged among educated Hindus in the nineteenth century. Two prominent figures behind these movements were Ram Mohan Roy and Dayananda Saraswati. While the former was keen to reform an ossified, caste-ridden Hindu religion, the latter focused on reviving religious dimensions of the Vedic Golden Age and promoting Sanskrit as the fount of Indo-European languages. These reformers sought to purify Hinduism, make it look more civilized in Western eyes, and revive its lost glories. This movement later gained further fillip from nationalists such as Tilak and Lajpat Rai, who began promoting the idea of a Hindu Rashtra. See Arun R. Swamy, "Ideology, Organization and Electoral Strategy of Hindu Nationalism: What's Religion Got to Do with It?" in *Religious Radicalism and Security in South Asia*, eds. Satu P. Limaye, Mohan Malik, and Robert G. Wirsing (Honolulu: Asia-Pacific Center for Security Studies, 2004), 73–100; Christophe Jaffrelot, "Hindu Nationalism: Strategic Syncretism in Ideology Building," *Economic & Political Weekly* 28, no. 12–13 (1993): 517–24; and Ramchandra Guha, *Gandhi: The Years That Changed the World, 1914–1948* (Delhi: Penguin Random House, 2018).

8. Christophe Jaffrelot, ed., *Hindu Nationalism: A Reader* (Princeton, NJ: Princeton University Press, 2007).

9. Christophe Jaffrelot, *The Hindu Nationalist Movement and Indian Politics*

(New Delhi: Penguin Books, 1999); and Swamy, "Ideology, Organization and Electoral Strategy."

10. Savarkar's writings on Hindutva were in large part a reaction to the pan-Islamic mobilization of the Khilafat Movement (1919–24). Most of his thoughts derived from his deep distrust of Islam and its followers. For him, Muslims, who constituted one-fifth of the population, were loyal to Mecca and Istanbul rather than India. Through Hindutva, he strove to unify Hindus, who historically had been subject first to Muslim and then to British rulers. See Richard Gordon, "The Hindu Mahasabha and the Indian National Congress, 1915 to 1926," *Modern Asian Studies* 9, no. 2 (1975): 145–203; and Ashutosh Varshney, "Contested Meanings: India's National Identity, Hindu Nationalism, and the Politics of Anxiety," *Daedalus* 122, no. 3 (1993): 227–61.

11. Pandey, *The Construction of Communalism*; and "Contested Meaning."

12. Walter K. Anderson and Shridhar D. Damle, *The Brotherhood in Saffron: The Rashtriya Swayamsevak Sangh and Hindu Revivalism* (New Delhi: Vistaar Publications, 1987).

13. For an excellent discussion of Sangh Parivar, see Gautam Mehta, "Changing Character of the Sangh Parivar," *The Hindu Businessline*, December 5, 2017 (www.thehindubusinessline.com/opinion/columns/changing-character-of-sangh-parivar/article9983293.ece).

14. The Hindu right suspected that Gandhi was inclined to favor Muslim Pakistan. See Guha, *Gandhi*.

15. Vidya Subrahmaniam, "Written Constitution Was Indeed a Pre-Condition," *The Hindu*, October 16, 2013 (www.thehindu.com/opinion/op-ed/written-constitution-was-indeed-a-precondition/article5237953.ece).

16. Thomas Blom Hansen, *The Saffron Wave: Democracy and Hindu Nationalism in Modern India* (Princeton, NJ: Princeton University Press, 1999); and Walter K. Anderson and Shridhar D. Damle, *The RSS: A View to the Inside* (Delhi: Penguin, 2018).

17. For a detailed discussion of Hindu personal laws, see Partha S. Ghosh, "Politics of Personal Law in India: The Hindu–Muslim Dichotomy," *South Asia Research* 29, no. 1 (2009): 1–17.

18. However, many lower-caste Hindus or Dalits do not support the ban on cow slaughter, as many of them derive their livelihood from cow slaughter. On this subject, see Jawhar Sircar, "Contending with Contentious Cows," The Hindu Centre for Politics and Public Policy, February 9, 2019 (www.thehinducentre.com/the-arena/current-issues/article26203100.ece).

19. For an illustration of the incident, see Shoaib Daniyal, "Looking Back: The First Parliament Attack Took Place in 1966—And Was Carried Out by Gau Rakshaks," *Scroll*, August 28, 2016 (https://scroll.in/article/814368/did-you-know-the-first-parliament-attack-took-place-in-1966-and-was-carried-out-by-gau-rakshaks).

20. Kuldip Nayar, *The Judgement: Inside Story of the Emergency in India* (Delhi: Vikas Publishing House, 1977).

21. Pandey, *The Construction of Communalism.*

22. Kanchan Chandra, "The Triumph of Hindu Majoritarianism: A Requiem for an Old Idea of India," *Foreign Affairs*, November 23, 2018 (www.foreignaffairs .com/articles/india/2018-11-23/triumph-hindu-majoritarianism).

23. In dealing with Muslim personal law in the 1985 *Shah Bano* case, the Indian Supreme Court upheld the lower court's ruling directing Shah Bano's husband to pay alimony under a provision of Indian law applicable to all communities. This pathbreaking ruling created a huge uproar within the Muslim community, especially among Muslim males, which prompted the Rajiv Gandhi government to quickly enact the Muslim Women (Protection of Rights on Divorce) Act in 1986 to roll back the progressive judgment and appease members of the minority community. See "What Is *Shah Bano* Case," *The Indian Express*, August 23, 2017 (https:// indianexpress.com/article/what-is/what-is-shah-bano-case-4809632/).

24. Hansen, *The Saffron Wave.*

25. Ibid.

26. Anderson and Damle, *The RSS.*

27. Together with more than a dozen regional parties, the BJP formed a coalition called the National Democratic Alliance to form governments in 1998 and 1999.

28. Anderson and Damle, *The RSS.*

29. For a comprehensive review of the Sachar Committee's report, see Rakesh Basant, "Social, Economic and Educational Conditions of Indian Muslims," *Economic & Political Weekly* 42, no. 10 (2007): 828–32.

30. For a discussion of Modi's rise in this period, see Atul Singh and Manu Sharma, "Atal Bihari Vajpayee Paved the Way for Narendra Modi," *Fair Observer*, August 20, 2018 (www.fairobserver.com/region/central_south_asia/atal-bihari -vajpayee-death-bjp-narendra-modi-indian-politics-news-today-23491/).

31. Among other things, Congress politicians invented terms such as "Hindu terror" and "saffron terror" to stir up fears about the BJP. See "How 'Saffron Terror' Was Coined: A Rundown of 2008 Malegaon Blasts," June 5, 2018, *The Quint* (www. thequint.com/videos/news-videos/how-saffron-terror-was-coined-a-rundown-of -2008-malegaon-blasts).

32. Ashutosh Varshney, "2014, like 1952," *The Indian Express*, May 19, 2014 (https://indianexpress.com/article/opinion/columns/2014-like-1952/).

33. For instance, in the Hindi-speaking states such as Uttar Pradesh (UP), Bihar, Rajasthan, Madhya Pradesh, Chhattisgarh, Haryana, Delhi, Jharkhand, Himachal Pradesh, and Uttarakhand, the BJP won 190 out of 225 seats. In UP, the BJP broke all past records by capturing seventy-three out of eighty seats.

34. The Gujarat riots happened in 2002 when Modi was the chief minister of the state. The statewide communal riots led to more than a thousand deaths, mostly within the Muslim community. Although the Supreme Court appointed a special investigation team that exonerated Modi in 2012, many accuse him of not taking sufficient action to quell violence against Muslims. For an update, see Manas Das-

gupta, "SIT Finds No Proof against Modi, Says Court," *The Hindu*, April 10, 2010 (www.thehindu.com/news/national/sit-finds-no-proof-against-modi-says-court/article3300175.ece).

35. However, the saffron party received a major jolt in 2018 when it lost three key Hindi heartland states to the Congress. As of December 2018, the BJP's tally was down to sixteen states. See also Suhas Palshikar, "Towards Hegemony: BJP beyond Electoral Dominance," *Economic & Political Weekly* 53, no. 33 (2018): 36–42.

36. See Varshney, "Narendra Modi's Illiberal Drift;" and Zoya Hasan, "Politics without Minorities," *The Hindu*, September 5, 2014 (www.thehindu.com/opinion/lead/politics-without-the-minorities/article6380445.ece).

37. The Congress has a long record of filling important institutions with cadres supportive of its ideology and close to the Nehru-Gandhi family. This has been a major complaint of Sangh Parivar ideologues, who seek to "detoxify" institutions by filling them with people of their own liking.

38. Abhiram Ghadyalpatil, "Regional Parties Set the Anti-Modi Narrative with Aggressive Posturing," *LiveMint*, February 14, 2019 (www.livemint.com/politics/news/regional-parties-set-the-anti-modi-narrative-with-aggressive-posturing-1550081046875.html).

39. The BJP has also openly challenged the judges of India's Supreme Court on this issue. See "Ayodhya: Indresh of RSS Slams CJI-Bench, Claims Govt Is Ready with a Law," *The Indian Express*, November 28, 2018 (https://indianexpress.com/article/india/ayodhya-ram-temple-rss-supreme-court-indresh-vhp-5468030/).

40. Aria Thaker, "The Toxic Politics inside the Congress Party's Social Media Team," *Scroll*, October 25, 2018 (https://qz.com/india/1436914/the-chaos-inside-divya-spandanas-congress-social-media-team/).

41. Iain Marlow, "Modi Has Turned India's Elections into a U.S.-Style Presidential Race," *Bloomberg*, March 25, 2019 (www.bloomberg.com/news/articles/2019-03-25/modi-vs-who-india-s-ruling-party-pushes-presidential-election).

42. Sagarika Ghose, "With Pragya Thakur in the Fray, Hindutva No Longer Needs to Wear a Mask," *Times of India*, April 28, 2019 (https://timesofindia.indiatimes.com/blogs/bloody-mary/with-pragya-thakur-in-the-fray-hindutva-no-longer-needs-to-wear-a-mask/).

43. The BJP and its allies have accused the Congress of falsely framing Thakur, as well as the monk Swami Aseemanand, in terror cases and inventing the term "Hindu terror" to defame the majority community. Although India's top investigative agencies and higher judiciary handled these terror cases, the BJP maintains that the Congress politicized them to maintain its secular and pro-minority image for electoral gain. For a review of the controversy, see Abhiram Ghadyalpatil, "Battle for Bhopal and Its Message to India," *LiveMint*, June 2, 2019 (www.livemint.com/news/india/battle-for-bhopal-and-its-message-to-india-1559477427779.html).

44. Kalpesh Damor and Vinay Umarji, "New Middle Class Supports the BJP More Than Cong: Christophe Jaffrelot," *Business Standard*, April 20, 2014 (www

.business-standard.com/article/opinion/new-middle-class-supports-the-bjp-more-than-cong-christophe-jaffrelot-114041900883_1.html).

45. On the intersection of economic policy and identity politics, see Priya Chacko, "Marketizing Hindutva: The State, Society, and Markets in Hindu Nationalism," *Modern Asian Studies* 53, no. 2 (2019): 377–410.

46. Michael Goldfarb, "Why India's Leading Political Party Believes Hinduism 'Must Prevail,'" *PRI*, February 12, 2014 (www.pri.org/stories/2014-02-12/why-indias-leading-political-party-believes-hinduism-must-prevail).

47. Christophe Jaffrelot and Sanjay Kumar, "The Impact of Urbanization on the Electoral Results of the 2014 Indian Elections: With Special Reference to the BJP Vote," *Studies in Indian Politics* 3, no. 1 (2015): 39–49.

48. The Janata government established the Mandal Commission in 1979 to study and recommend measures to address the situation of educationally and economically disadvantaged castes (referred to as "other backward classes," or OBCs). The commission recommended that 27 percent of government jobs and positions in public universities should be reserved for the OBCs. This policy led to violent riots by the upper castes across India in the 1990s. See the National Commission for Backward Classes, "Report of the Backward Classes Commission," 1980 (www.ncbc.nic.in/User_Panel/UserView.aspx?TypeID=1161).

49. Yogendra Yadav, "Electoral Politics in the Time of Change: India's Third Electoral System, 1989–99," *Economic & Political Weekly* 34, no. 34/35 (1999): 2393–99.

50. The rising instances of paid news in recent years have contributed to traditional media's loss of credibility. See the Press Council of India, "'Paid News:' How Corruption in the Indian Media Undermines Democracy," April 1, 2010 (http://presscouncil.nic.in/OldWebsite/Sub-CommitteeReport.pdf).

51. See Murali Krishnan, "Indian Media Facing a Crisis of Credibility," *DW*, June 5, 2017 (www.dw.com/en/indian-media-facing-a-crisis-of-credibility/a-39120228).

52. Taberez A. Neyazi, "Social Media and Political Polarisation in India," *Seminar*, no. 699 (2017): 31–35.

53. Maya Mirchandani, "Digital Hatred, Real Violence: Majoritarian Radicalisation and Social Media in India," *ORF Occasional Paper*, August 2018 (www.orfonline.org/research/43665-digital-hatred-real-violence-majoritarian-radicalisation-and-social-media-in-india/).

54. Prashant Jha, *How the BJP Wins: Inside India's Greatest Election Machine* (Delhi: Juggernaut, 2017).

55. Vidhi Choudhary, "BJP Outspends Congress, Others in Social Media Advertising," *Hindustan Times*, May 3, 2019 (www.hindustantimes.com/lok-sabha-elections/bjp-outspends-congress-others-in-social-media-advertising/story-FHByCC5vUfs7xCvD9kDY5L.html).

56. Rajni Kothari, ed., *Caste in Indian Politics* (New Delhi: Orient Longman, 1970).

57. For an informative review of the controversial Mandal Commission report

that recommended affirmative action for middle castes, leading to caste riots in 1990, see Pankaj Pachauri, "India Today Presents Varied Opinions on Mandal Commission Implementation," *India Today*, September 30, 1990 (www.indiatoday.in/magazine/special-report/story/19900930-india-today-presents-varied-opinions-on-mandal-commission-implementation-813086-1990-09-30).

58. Jaffrelot, *The Hindu Nationalist Movement*; and Hansen, *The Saffron Wave*.

59. For instance, the two large states of Bihar and UP together send 120 members to parliament. Out of these 120 seats, the BJP won 105 in the 2014 elections.

60. See Center for the Study of Developing Societies, *India National Election Study 2014* (New Delhi: CSDS, 2014).

61. Shreyas Sardesai and Vibha Attri, "Post-Poll Survey: The 2019 Verdict Is a Manifestation of the Deepening Religious Divide in India," *The Hindu*, May 30, 2019 (www.thehindu.com/elections/lok-sabha-2019/the-verdict-is-a-manifestation-of-the-deepening-religious-divide-in-india/article27297239.ece).

62. Preetha Nair, "In Caste-Strong Uttar Pradesh, Why SP-BSP-RLD Alliance Suffered a Jumbo Setback vs BJP & Co.," *Outlook*, May 24, 2019 (www.outlookindia.com/magazine/story/india-news-in-caste-strong-uttar-pradesh-why-sp-bsp-rld-alliance-suffered-a-jumbo-setback-vs-bjp-co/301667).

63. Ahead of the 2018 elections in Gujarat and Karnataka, Congress president Rahul Gandhi made several visits to Hindu temples in these states and avoided association with minority groups.

64. L. K. Sharma, "A Vote against Religious Hate," *Open Democracy*, November 9, 2015 (www.opendemocracy.net/openindia/l-k-sharma/vote-against-religious-hate).

65. Data have been collected since 2010. See Alison Saldanha, "2017 Deadliest Year for Cow-Related Hate Crime Since 2010, 86% of Those Killed Muslim," *IndiaSpend*, December 8, 2017 (www.indiaspend.com/2017-deadliest-year-for-cow-related-hate-crime-since-2010-86-of-those-killed-muslim-12662/).

66. Khushboo Upreti, "Has India Forgotten about the Art of Democratic Debate?" *Qrius*, July 25, 2018 (https://qrius.com/has-india-forgotten-about-the-art-of-democratic-debate/).

67. "Minister in Modi's Cabinet Garlands Cow Vigilantes Convicted for Lynching a Muslim Trader in Jharkhand," *Huffington Post*, July 7, 2018 (www.huffingtonpost.in/2018/07/06/union-minister-jayant-singh-garlands-cow-vigilantes-convicted-for-lynching-a-muslim-trader-in-jharkhand_a_23476652/).

68. Humaira Ansari, "12 Filmmakers Return National Awards, Protest 'Growing Intolerance,'" *Hindustan Times*, October 29, 2015 (www.hindustantimes.com/india/10-filmmakers-return-national-awards-over-growing-intolerance-ftii-row/story-9N1XOrEe1NAIDcZ4dLlNLP.html).

69. Christophe Jaffrelot and Gilles Verniers, "The Dwindling Minority," *The Indian Express*, July 30, 2018 (https://indianexpress.com/article/opinion/columns/muslims-politicians-in-india-bjp-narendra-modi-government-5282128/).

70. Rasheed Kidwai, "Need for Major CVE Program to Engage with Muslim

Community," ORF Analysis, June 20, 2018 (www.orfonline.org/expert-speak/need-for-major-cve-programme-to-engage-with-muslim-community/).

71. "2019 Lok Sabha Election Results: Only 27 Muslim MPs Elected to Parliament, None from the BJP," *Scroll*, May 24, 2019 (https://scroll.in/latest/924627/2019-lok-sabha-election-results-only-24-muslim-mps-elected-to-parliament-none-from-the-bjp).

72. Jaffrelot and Verniers, "The Dwindling Minority."

73. Nissim Mannathukkaren, "The Fast Disappearing Muslim in the Indian Republic," *The Indian Express*, January 22, 2018 (https://indianexpress.com/article/opinion/the-fast-disappearing-muslim-in-the-indian-republic-bjp-mla-hindu-saffron-religion-5034205/).

74. "2019 Lok Sabha Election Results: Only 27 Muslim MPs Elected to Parliament, None from the BJP," *Scroll*, May 24, 2019 (https://scroll.in/latest/924627/2019-lok-sabha-election-results-only-24-muslim-mps-elected-to-parliament-none-from-the-bjp).

75. Shoaib Daniyal, "Opposition's Silence on Rajasthan Hate Murder Is a Troubling Sign for India," *Scroll*, December 20, 2017 (https://scroll.in/article/862076/the-daily-fix-oppositions-silence-on-rajasthan-hate-murder-is-a-troubling-sign-for-india); and Hasan, "Politics without Minorities."

76. See "From Flag Is My Religion to Shiv Bhakt," *Dailyhunt*, September 20, 2018 (https://m.dailyhunt.in/news/india/english/india+press+agency-epaper-indpres/from+flag+is+my+religion+to+shiv+bhakt+how+rahul+gandhi+is+using+hindutva+lite+to+make+a+comeback-newsid-97368100).

77. "The Return of Identity Politics and Its Hefty Cost," *LiveMint*, April 10, 2018 (www.livemint.com/Opinion/x42E8WuLHwYaGk1N1DoiiN/The-return-of-identity-politics-and-its-hefty-cost.html).

78. The Nehru Library was once the first prime minister's residence. After Nehru's death, to preserve his memory, his residence was declared a museum and library, which has come to house archives and Nehru's own writings.

79. According to a study conducted by PRS Legislative, the Lok Sabha (lower house) spent just 1 percent of its allotted time on legislative business, while the Rajya Sabha (upper house) spent 6 percent of its time on legislative business in the recently concluded budget session in April 2018, making it the least productive budget session since 2000. See Upreti, "Has India Forgotten?"

80. "Broken Houses: On the State of Parliament," *The Hindu*, April 9, 2018 (www.thehindu.com/opinion/editorial/state-of-parliament-broken-houses/article23475032.ece).

81. Alok Prasanna Kumar, "Why the Centre's Dubious Use of Money Bills Must Not Go Unchallenged," *Scroll*, May 11, 2016 (https://scroll.in/article/807861/why-the-centres-dubious-use-of-money-bills-must-not-go-unchallenged).

82. For details on the Rafale deal controversy, see "What Is Rafale Deal Controversy? All You Need to Know," *NDTV*, February 9, 2018 (www.ndtv.com/india-news/what-is-rafale-deal-controversy-all-you-need-to-know-1810706).

83. Pravin Sawhney, "Politicising Surgical Strikes Erodes the Army's Potency and Deterrent Value," *The Wire*, October 1, 2018 (https://thewire.in/security/politicising-surgical-strikes-erodes-the-armys-potency-and-deterrent-value).

84. Shraddha Chowdhury, "Balakot Air Strikes Shouldn't Be Politicised amid India-Pakistan Hostilities; National Interest Needs Precedence," *Firstpost*, March 4, 2019 (www.firstpost.com/india/balakot-air-strikes-shouldnt-be-politicised-amid-india-pakistan-hostilities-national-interest-needs-to-take-precedence-6189631.html).

85. On the "Hindu terror" controversy, see "Congress Does Balancing Act on 'Saffron' Terror," *India Today*, August 27, 2010 (www.indiatoday.in/india/story/congress-does-balancing-act-on-saffron-terror-81049-2010-08-27).

86. Milan Vaishnav, "India's Elite Institutions Are Facing a Credibility Crisis," *LiveMint*, February 20, 2018 (www.livemint.com/Opinion/vvPejHxB52AVzqQBRLoIWL/Indias-elite-institutions-are-facing-a-credibility-crisis.html).

87. Michael Safi, "India's Top Judges Issue Unprecedented Warning over Integrity of Supreme Court," *The Guardian*, January 12, 2018 (www.theguardian.com/world/2018/jan/12/india-supreme-court-judges-integrity-dipak-misra); and Amy Kazmin, "India's Opposition Moves to Impeach Supreme Court Chief Justice," *Financial Times*, April 20, 2018 (www.ft.com/content/90ca99ba-4486-11e8-803a-295c97e6fd0b).

88. Gopika Gopakumar, Shayan Ghosh, and Asit Ranjan Mishra, "RBI Governor Urjit Patel Resigns amid Messy Face-Off with Govt," *LiveMint*, December 11, 2018 (www.livemint.com/Politics/6KnAp2KO0asOVOvnemGjGP/Urjit-Patel-resigns-as-RBI-governor.html).

89. Saubhadra Chatterji and Smriti Kak Ramachandran, "17 Opposition Parties to Ask Poll Panel to Use Ballot Papers for 2019 Elections," *Hindustan Times*, August 3, 2018 (www.hindustantimes.com/india-news/17-opposition-parties-to-ask-poll-panel-to-use-ballot-papers-for-2019-elections/story-Wp98rSBO0eRPkgqnFoBoKK.html).

90. Murat Somer, "Cascades of Ethnic Polarization: Lessons from Yugoslavia," *The ANNALS of the American Academy of Political and Social Science* 573, no. 1 (2001): 127–51.

91. Rakesh Mohan Chaturvedi, "In Face of United Opposition, BJP Needs Out-of-Box Idea to Win 2019 Polls," *Economic Times*, June 1, 2018 (https://economictimes.indiatimes.com/news/politics-and-nation/in-face-of-united-opposition-bjp-needs-out-of-box-idea-to-win-2019-polls/articleshow/64408763.cms).

92. Yunus Y. Lasania, "Rahul, Chandrababu Naidu to Jointly Address Meetings in Telangana," *LiveMint*, November 27, 2018 (www.livemint.com/Politics/1AyezTgv9FaO8i9MCCUIcP/Rahul-Chandrababu-Naidu-to-jointly-address-meetings-in-Tela.html).

93. Pretika Khanna and Gyan Varma, "Mayawati Dumps Congress, Puts Mahagathbandhan on Notice," *LiveMint*, October 3, 2018 (www.livemint.

com/Politics/IDGiYk1UF3N67y7nvKBjpK/Mayawati-dumps-Congress-puts-mahagathbandhan-on-notice.html).

94. "SC Judges Press Conference: Legal Fraternity Says It's Unprecedented, Shocking," *The Hindu*, January 12, 2018 (www.thehindu.com/news/national/sc-judges-press-conference-legal-fraternity-says-its-unprecedented-shocking/article 22429811.ece).

95. Ananthakrishnan G, "Mobocracy Can't Be the New Normal, Get a Law to Punish Lynching: SC to Govt," *Indian Express*, July 18, 2018 (https://indianex-press.com/article/india/cji-condemns-lynchings-across-country-asks-parliament-to-make-new-law/).

96. Shashank Bengali, "With a String of Historic Judgments, India's Top Court Nudges the Country Forward—Sort of," *Los Angeles Times*, October 2, 2018 (www.latimes.com/world/asia/la-fg-india-supreme-court-explainer-20181002-story.html).

97. "'Award Wapasi' Campaign a Success: Nayantara Sahgal," *Indian Express*, January 24, 2016 (https://indianexpress.com/article/india/india-news-india/award-wapasi-campaign-a-success-nayantara-sahgal/).

98. For the government's guideline on social media, see Department of Electronics and Information Technology, "Framework & Guidelines for Use of Social Media for Government Organisations," n.d. (https://archive.india.gov.in/allimp frms/alldocs/16484.pdf).

99. On measures taken by WhatsApp in India, see Venkat Ananth, "#Election2019: How WhatsApp and Political Parties Are Playing Cat and Mouse over Spamming," *ET Prime*, November 28, 2018 (https://prime.economictimes.in-diatimes.com/news/66837159/technology-startups/election2019-how-whatsapp-and-political-parties-are-playing-cat-and-mouse-over-spamming).

100. For a recent report by a Hyderabad-based volunteer organization promoting interfaith dialogue, see M. A. Moid et al., "Summary Report: A Study of Communal Conflict and Peace Initiatives in Hyderabad: Past and Present," COVA, 2018 (http://amanpanchayat.org/wp-content/uploads/2018/01/Communal-con-flict_Hyderabad.pdf).

101. Priyankar Upadhyaya, "Communal Peace in India: Lessons from Multicultural Banaras," in *Religion and Security in South and Central Asia*, ed. K. Warikoo (New York: Routledge, 2011), 83–95.

102. Murali Krishnan, "India's Intolerance Is Hurting the Country," *The Interpreter*, February 2, 2018 (www.lowyinstitute.org/the-interpreter/indias-intoler-ance-hurting-country).

103. Jeffrey Gettleman and others, "Under Modi, a Hindu Nationalist Surge Has Further Divided India," *New York Times*, April 11, 2019 (www.nytimes.com/2019/04/11/world/asia/modi-india-elections.html); and "Can Indian Politics Recover from the Toxicity of the 2019 Lok Sabha Election Campaign?" *The Print*, May 17, 2019 (https://theprint.in/talk-point/can-indian-politics-recover-from-the-toxicity-of-the-2019-lok-sabha-election-campaign/236713/).

FIVE

Of "Patriots" and Citizens: Asymmetric Populist Polarization in Poland

JOANNA FOMINA

In 2017, the late Professor Karol Modzelewski, an academic and a prominent figure of Poland's Solidarity movement, observed: "There are now two Polands. We don't get the same news. We don't read events in the same way. Nor do we have the same values. It's as if we are losing our common language. We no longer listen to one another, and we no longer talk to each other. Worse, we don't even want to talk to each other."[1] Indeed, while social and political differences are present in any democratic society, Poland's governing party, Law and Justice (Prawo i Sprawiedliwość; PiS), has managed to reformulate the main dividing line of political life and turn its followers and critics into two unyielding hostile camps. These factions disagree not only about an increasing number of social, economic, and cultural issues, but also about their basic diagnosis of contemporary Polish realities—which makes it increasingly impossible to establish a political consensus.

The political polarization in Poland is asymmetric and populist. There is a visible asymmetry between the two rival camps: whereas the PiS camp is ideologically cohesive, tightly knit, and politically mobilized, the opposition is fragmented and mobilizes primarily in reaction to the government's policies and rhetoric.[2] Further, PiS's populist tactics have given political contestation in Poland a "Machiavellian" character by raising highly contentious issues such as identity and belonging and advancing the narrative that one group of Poles has been marginalized in the democratic transformation of Poland that began in 1989.[3]

The government camp has been reinvigorating old divisive narratives and opening up new battlefields to keep its electoral base mobilized, ensure its continuing grip on power, and remake the Polish state in a majoritarian and illiberal fashion. As a result, affective polarization—the degree to which people on one side of the partisan divide dislike those on the other— has reached an unprecedented level in Polish society at large. In addition to fueling societal anger, severe polarization has undermined trust in public institutions, damaged the quality of policy processes, and facilitated the government's efforts to erode checks and balances. Societal and political divisions benefit the ruling party, which holds almost all the instruments necessary to remain in power. Hence, it is unlikely that any initiatives aimed at bridging the gap between the two camps can effectively reduce polarization. In terms of remedial actions, it is most important to make sure that the public has access to fact-based and unbiased sources of information. While the opposition needs to address the asymmetric character of the polarization by uniting around a set of democratic values threatened by the populism of the ruling party, new political initiatives are needed to reach out to the people who are alienated by both sides of the present conflict.

Roots

Currently, about one-third of Poles identify as supporters of the PiS-led government, another third identify as opponents, and the rest state that they do not support either side.[4] Analysts and sociologists have often described the PiS and anti-PiS camps using traditional socioeconomic categories such as wealth, education, and residence (urban versus rural). But these distinctions seem to be secondary to the political and ideological orientations of the inhabitants of the "two Polands," which in this chapter will be identified as, respectively, "patriots" and "citizens." The former tend to be collectivistic and to have a predominantly ethnic and religious (exclusivist) view of Poland's national identity, as well as a strong attachment to their political representatives—that is, PiS. On the other side, the "citizens" tend to be both individualistic and pluralistic, with divergent political and ideological loyalties, and to adhere to a nonexclusivist definition of identity, such as being both Polish and European. What defines the "citizens" as a group is predominantly political, namely, their strong rejection of the PiS government, its ideology, and its illiberal politics.

At the heart of this conflict lies a disagreement about the assessment of Poland's democratic transition as well as the current and future character of the shared political community. PiS has mobilized its supporters around the claim that former communist and liberal elites conspired to deny particular groups (true Poles, or simply, "the people") the benefits of Poland's postcommunist transformation. PiS employs this narrative to exploit and reinforce existing resentments, prejudices, fears, and frustrations shared by some groups (whether justifiably or not), while providing them with a shared identity.[5] The party has all the main features of populism, defined as "a general protest against the checks and balances introduced to prevent 'the people's' direct rule."[6] It contrasts the presumably morally superior "people" with corrupt elites (and their supporters) and challenges liberal democracy and its respect for minority rights, while seeking to abolish or control its watchdog institutions. The party's definition of "the people" is highly exclusionary: the populist elites get to decide who is a "true Pole" and who is "of the worse sort."[7] The PiS camp is much more ideologically cohesive and less likely to question the decisions of its party leaders.

By contrast, a rejection of PiS and its populism, nationalism, and authoritarianism unites the anti-PiS camp. Although this camp is mostly associated with liberal and center-left-oriented elites who are politically sympathetic to Civic Platform (PO) and the recently formed *Nowoczesna* (Modern) party,[8] it comprises people and organizations across the ideological spectrum, including some groups formed with the particular aim of stopping the "PiS assault against democracy."[9] The opposition camp's actions are predominately reactive to various political discourses and policies of the PiS government, as is most vividly illustrated by a series of mass rallies in response to the government's concrete policy steps. This camp is much more fragmented, and not all issues are equally salient for the various groups within it. The two camps are thus asymmetric in terms of their level of mobilization, their internal cohesion, and the extent to which they are proactive or reactive.

These camps are strongly divided in terms of their perceptions of the current political reality. For example, whereas 80 percent of the opposition camp is convinced that the government aims to curtail the rights and freedoms of people whose political views differ from those of the ruling coalition, 78 percent of PiS supporters are convinced to the contrary. Those in the middle ground are divided on this point.[10]

The political differences between the two camps overlap with sociodemographic differences. Government supporters are less educated, older, less affluent, much more religious, and more frequently from rural areas.[11] Interestingly, research conducted before the 2015 elections also demonstrated important differences in terms of psychological characteristics between the PiS and PO electorates, which largely correspond to the two camps. The PiS electorate appears to be much more prone to authoritarianism (as demonstrated by characteristics such as a conviction about the hierarchical organization of human relations, faith in the effectiveness of solutions based on force, and respect for authority) and political paranoia (understood as receptiveness toward conspiracy theories and belief in the existence of hidden forces that rule the world). What is more, anomia and political alienation are also more prevalent within the PiS electorate. PiS voters more often feel that they are lost in the social world and are uncertain of the values and rules governing it; they also tend to feel that they lack influence in this sphere and are distrustful of its mechanisms and political elites.[12]

Certain ideological and sociodemographic differences between the electorates of PiS and PO were visible already in 2005, but at that time both electorates shared a right-wing orientation and relatively high level of religiosity, with 51 percent of PO voters regularly participating in religious practices. This has changed, as today self-identified right-wingers overwhelmingly support PiS (69 percent), while 58 percent of supporters of the left and 40 percent of supporters of the political center identify with the opposition camp. What is more, in 2005 about half of PO voters mentioned PiS as their second-choice vote, and vice versa.[13] A decade later, these two camps have become sharply divided, and anger has become an immanent feature of Poland's political life. PiS engenders negative and hostile emotions among 32 percent of the population, most often among the PO electorate (76 percent) and the left-of-center electorate (63 percent). Civic Platform evokes a negative reaction from 22 percent of the electorate, especially among PiS voters (56 percent), deeply religious people who participate in religious practices several times a week (46 percent), and right-wing voters (45 percent).[14] A tendency exists among a large section of the society toward political Manicheism. For example, according to a 2018 study, a plurality of Poles agree that "politics is ultimately a struggle between good and evil."[15]

The "leftist" and "rightist" labels have become both derogatory terms used to refer to opponents and terms of self-identification reclaimed by both camps. Yet these terms may be misleading. In Poland, as in some other younger democracies, a right-wing orientation on sociocultural issues often correlates with a left-wing economic orientation, and vice versa. Other labels for the two conflicting camps used in public debates are "Poland of social solidarity" vs. "liberal Poland," "populists" vs. "democrats," "true Poles" vs. "Poles of the worse sort," or "Poland B" (the Eastern part) vs. "Poland A" (the Western part).

Trajectory

Political polarization has arguably been characteristic of Poland's entire post-1989 history. Nevertheless, the nature and types of political cleavages have evolved considerably over the past thirty years. Initially, the main dividing line was between political camps originating from either the former communist party or the democratic opposition to the communist system in the 1980s. These two camps, often labeled as postcommunist and post-Solidarity, respectively, alternated in power throughout the 1990s. The end of this political bipolarity came about in the mid-2000s, with the near-demise of the postcommunist left, and resulted in a split within the post-Solidarity camp. Political entrepreneurs such as Jarosław Kaczyński skillfully exploited conflicting ideas about how to deal with Poland's communist past, and this issue became a major dividing line within the elite and the society. For some, joining the European Union (EU) in 2004 marked the end of Poland's postcommunist transformation, whereas for others the end of the postcommunist period required a purge of the people, institutions, and ideas that they saw as responsible for Poland's postcommunist malaise. After 2010, a new set of discourses centered on support for or opposition to nativist populism subsumed the earlier partisan divides and narratives, and since 2015, PiS control of the presidency and parliament has brought polarization to unprecedented heights.

The Democratic Transition and Its Discontents, 1989 to 2005

The path to Poland's democratic transition was paved by the so-called Round Table negotiations, when in order to mitigate serious social unrest, the communist government agreed in 1989 to discussions with the opposition, including the banned Solidarity trade union. The resulting Round Table Agreement made possible partially free legislative elections (to 35 percent of the seats in the lower chamber of Parliament and all the seats in the newly established Senate). After the Solidarity camp's landslide victory marking the fall of communism in Poland in 1989 and the subsequent transition to liberal democracy, the Polish political scene was dominated by the rivalry between two camps: postcommunist and post-Solidarity. The first camp organized politically into a center-left coalition, known as the Democratic Left Alliance (Sojusz Lewicy Demokratyczne; SLD), whereas the post-Solidarity camp comprised a plethora of political parties defining themselves as right-of-center to varying degrees. For the next sixteen years, both camps alternated in power. Two political groupings partly escaped this clear division: the agrarian Polish People's Party (Polskie Stronnictwo Ludowe; PSL) and the Freedom Union (Unia Wolności), the party of the post-Solidarity intelligentsia.

The first post-1989 Polish prime minister, Tadeusz Mazowiecki of the Freedom Union, spoke of the need to establish "a thick line" between Poland's communist past and democratic present.[16] Already in the early 1990s, the right wing of the post-Solidarity camp started to intentionally misinterpret this idea as a blanket overlooking of communist-era wrongs—symbolized by the negotiated transition to democracy through the Round Table Agreement. Though praised in Poland and abroad as a way of avoiding bloodshed and building a new democratic and inclusive society, the Round Table Agreement evoked deep resentment among parts of the society, which political entrepreneurs carefully fueled. Lustration—

the purging of former communist officials from state institutions—and de-communization were major topics of Polish political debates in the 1990s.

"Shock therapy," a set of radical free market reforms adopted in the early 1990s, contributed vitally to Poland's economic recovery, but its benefits came with high social costs, at least initially. More than a million people, for example, lost their jobs at inefficient state-owned firms that were privatized.[17] The reforms hit rural areas especially hard, while they brought considerable opportunities for young urbanites with entrepreneurial skills and knowledge of foreign languages. Moreover, the process of privatizing state-owned giants was not always fully transparent, which gave rise to suspicions of corruption and further contributed to the discourse of the "winners and losers" of the transition.

After this initial period of sharp-edged economic reform, which divided the main political camps, the postcommunist and post-Solidarity parties evolved to embrace rather moderate and largely consensual positions on economic issues, including tax policy, unemployment, and privatization. Crucially, economic growth had picked up by 1992, reducing political tensions over economic policy. As a result, the cultural axis became the dominant dividing line and primary determinant of voters' behavior. The two camps increasingly clashed over sociocultural issues such as the relations between church and state, minority and women's rights, and earlier points of contention regarding decommunization, lustration, and transitional justice in general.

"The End of Post-Communism in Poland,"[18] 2005 to 2010

By 2005, the postcommunist SLD had nearly collapsed, destroyed by a string of corruption scandals, and the division between the post-Solidarity and postcommunist camps became obsolete. A powerful new political division emerged *within* the post-Solidarity camp, catalyzed by internal personal conflicts between two relatively new parties, Law and Justice and Civic Platform. Initially perceived by many of their supporters as programmatically rather similar, they grew apart with the realization that they needed to run against each other.

The 2005 elections took place in the crucial context of Poland's accession to the EU, which had been preceded by the 2003 EU membership referendum. EU accession unleashed fears related to modernization and globalization and strengthened the voices of the transition's discontents. The populist discourse that dominates politics today emerged in these years. Its main proponent and beneficiary was PiS, which was founded in the early 2000s by two twin brothers, Lech and Jarosław Kaczyński. Though their political lineage was in the post-Solidarity camp, the two had built their post-1989 political careers questioning the tenets of the democratic transition.

Three main strands of thought defined the PiS-led coalition government of 2005–07: economic populism, radical anticommunism, and nationalistic "identity" populism.[19] Whereas other political actors such as the populist Self-Defense party mainly focused on purely antielitist and antiestablishment rhetoric, PiS underscored the need to do away with the *układ* ("arrangement"), a purported conspiracy between the ex-communist elites, businesses, the media, and even some representatives of the post-Solidarity movement.[20] PiS thus combined anticommunist and anticorruption rhetoric and purported to explain the bitter conflict within the post-Solidarity camp. The party's public relations specialists labeled the new axis of political competition a clash between the "Poland of social solidarity" and "liberal Poland," attacking PO for its alleged disregard for the more economically vulnerable and promising to take care of the "victims of the transition." On the cultural axis, PiS mostly avoided making openly antisemitic or xenophobic remarks, but it framed the LGBT (lesbian, gay, bisexual, and transgender) community as an enemy within. The party's nationalist discourse depended strongly on its virulent homophobic rhetoric, underpinned by the Euroskeptic stance that all such "aberrations" came from a "godless, morally corrupt" Europe.

The early elections called in the autumn of 2007 following the collapse of the PiS-led coalition government brought victory to the PO. The key to the latter's success was using political polarization to its advantage with a clear narrative of "taking back the country" from the personally unpopular Kaczyński twins. The personal charisma of the opposition leader, Donald Tusk, and his strongly pro-European rhetoric appealed in particular to young voters, who appreciated the freedoms brought by EU membership as well as the booming postaccession economy.

Numerous conflicts marked the three years of cohabitation of the PO government (in coalition with the agrarian and Christian democratic PSL) with PiS president Lech Kaczyński. The president used his veto power extensively against government legislation and faced considerable criticism and ridicule for his perceived ineptitude and confrontational political style. He was widely expected to lose the 2010 presidential election.

The Aftermath of Smoleńsk: The Rise of "True Patriots," 2010 to 2015

Though the popularity of PiS was clearly waning by early 2010, a combination of sheer contingency, voters' fatigue with the incumbents, divisions within PO, the weakness of the left, and PiS's economic and nativist populism dramatically strengthened PiS and propelled Poland down a path of increasingly severe polarization.[21] One of the most potent factors was a contingency: in April 2010, the presidential airplane crashed in an attempted landing near Smoleńsk, Russia, resulting in the deaths of the presidential couple as well as almost a hundred Polish officials and members of the crew. The massive outpouring of grief from the society, amplified by the media, relaunched the waning political career of the deceased president's brother, Jarosław Kaczyński. It allowed PiS to create a highly emotional narrative built around the tragic event, which presented the late Lech Kaczyński as a fallen national hero.

Although the tragic event proved to have been an accident resulting from bad weather conditions and negligence of basic security rules and regulations, PiS leaders presented it as a conspiracy plotted by government elites, the "postcommunist secret services," and Russia.[22] This narrative fit perfectly into Poland's messianic tradition and culture of martyrdom, according to which Poland's independence requires victims, which is deeply rooted in the collective consciousness. It was also consistent with the earlier PiS narrative about deeply corrupted, treacherous Polish elites colluding with foreign powers, and it tapped into a wellspring of anti-Russian sentiment. The accusatory and resentful way in which PiS exploited the event gave rise to the derogatory term the "Smoleńsk religion," referring to the supposed cult surrounding the plane crash victims. PiS's framing of the event has served as an effective means of mobilizing and consolidating the right-wing populist electorate, helping to secure Kaczyński's leadership on the right wing of the political spectrum. Although Jarosław Kaczyński ultimately lost the 2010 presidential election by six percentage points, the Smoleńsk tragedy reinvigorated PiS.

The Smoleńsk plane crash conspiracy theory was not the only "post-truth" narrative that PiS political elites pushed in order to secure power. Despite Poland's ten years of uninterrupted economic growth in the 2000s, with the lowest unemployment rate on record since 1989 and a doubling of the minimum wage during PO's time in government, PiS's dominant narrative referred to "Poland in ruin" and claimed that only new, uncorrupted political elites (namely, PiS) could repair the country. PiS's "fact-resistant" campaign relied on presenting the entire period after the 1989 transition and in particular the last eight years of PO government in the bleakest possible terms: as a period when a small elite enriched itself and did little for the great majority of the society. As Hubert Tworzecki has recently argued, PiS's harsh criticism of the status quo had particular resonance given that a significant majority of Poles (among both PiS and PO voters) did not regard the political system as legitimate or fair and wanted systemic change.[23] At the same time, PiS skillfully stoked Poles' fears related to the refugee crisis as well as fears of social change among conservative voters, with the aid of the Catholic Church.

Other factors that contributed to PiS's success in the 2015 presidential and parliamentary elections included PO's often indolent maneuvering between the right and left wings, the "lost" center-left votes cast for the left-wing coalition that failed to pass the 8 percent threshold for entry into parliament, and the move by young voters to antiestablishment parties.

Escalating Polarization under PiS Rule, 2015 to the Present

With PiS in control of the presidency and parliament since 2015, Poland has entered an even more severe phase of polarization, as PiS has used its control over the legislative process to push through deeply controversial legislation. In particular, PiS has attacked the independent institutions that constitute the last meaningful check on its power and pushed through sweeping reforms in areas from education to social welfare. These reforms often have been hastily and poorly prepared and passed along party lines without robust public debate. And PiS policy has inflamed sociocultural divisions through a focus on certain divisive social issues, such as women's rights, Polish historical memory, and the refugee crisis. The opposition, meanwhile, has had recourse only to the courts and to the streets.

The primary political divide in Poland is no longer about who has reaped the benefits of Poland's transformation or about dealing with Poland's communist past, although it inherits many traits from these older political conflicts. It is a struggle to define Poland's future: while "patriots" claim to defend traditional national and religious values, defined in relation to Poland's history as a "Christian civilization," "citizens" want to see Poland in the family of democratic and pluralistic Western societies. Thus far, "patriots" seem to have the upper hand, but the strength and resilience of "citizens" should not be underestimated. Poland's political polarization is not likely to subside any time soon, and in recent years, the PiS government has intensified conflict on numerous fronts, the most important of which include the following.

THE ASSAULT ON CONSTITUTIONAL CHECKS AND BALANCES   A series of reforms that effectively aim to limit the checks and balances system and introduce full partisan political control over public institutions has increased polarization among political elites and in the society and provoked mass protests in a number of Polish cities. The two camps follow two different logics: PiS supporters interpret democracy as majoritarian rule, whereby the parliamentary majority has the right to implement any changes it deems necessary "for the good of the people," whereas the opposition sees democracy as a system of checks and balances limiting the power of elected authorities, as enshrined in the country's constitution.

The PiS government has attempted to bring the judiciary, "the bastion of everything in Poland that is bad,"[24] in Jarosław Kaczyński's words, under explicit political control. In recent years, the party has passed a series of so-called reforms to the Constitutional Tribunal, the National Council of the Judiciary, and the Supreme Court, as well as legislation putting courts of general jurisdiction under the strict control of the government-appointed minister of justice (who is at the same time supposed to serve an impartial function as public prosecutor general). The opposition and a plethora of Polish and international civic organizations and expert bodies, including the Venice Commission of the Council of Europe, the European Commission (EC), and the U.S. Department of State, have criticized these efforts.

SOCIAL CONSERVATISM AND THE TOTAL ABORTION BAN PiS has found itself under pressure from the Catholic Church and illiberal civil society groups (e.g., the Ordo Iuris Foundation) to tighten Poland's abortion law, which is already one of the most restrictive in Europe. The Church supported PiS during the last electoral campaign, and pro-church groups twice collected hundreds of thousands of signatures petitioning the parliament to introduce a total ban on abortion. PiS's "anti-gender crusade,"[25] as its opponents call it, has included repeated attempts to introduce such legislation in 2016 and again in 2018. These efforts were met with huge "black marches" across the whole country and gave birth to several new grassroots initiatives, including the group Women's Strike. The protests have succeeded in putting the legislative process on hold. Instead, the government and the parliamentary majority have introduced other elements of their "traditional values" agenda. For example, the health ministry took steps to restrict access to contraception pills and endorsed a "conscience clause" (such that doctors may refuse to perform an abortion on the grounds of their religious convictions) that made it practically impossible to have an abortion in the public health care system.[26] These restrictions have effectively amounted to the government's desired total ban.

THE POLITICS OF HISTORICAL MEMORY PiS has fueled polarizing cultural debates by promulgating a narrative of Polish history that absolves the nation of responsibility for past atrocities and casts it as a victim that has been denied justice. Although historically PiS and President Lech Kaczyński were part of the political consensus around the policy of reconciliation with Poland's neighbors, after the Smoleńsk crash, Jarosław Kaczyński adopted an alternative narrative on historical memory—the politics of "standing up from our knees." This one-sided nationalist narrative maintains that Poland has always been a nation of hero-martyrs, unfailingly noble to all its neighbors and generous to its ethnic and national minorities, yet frequently betrayed by those who benefited from Polish largesse. Such appeals to Polish national pride have helped to mobilize PiS's nationalistically-minded electorate while further antagonizing the opposition camp. Kaczyński famously called apologizing for the 1941 Jedwabne pogrom, in which more than 300 Polish Jews were murdered by their Polish neighbors during the Nazi occupation, an example of the "pedagogy of shame" and appealed to the Polish people not to apologize for their history. Kaczyński has also inflamed grievances related to the country's occupation during World War II. He has demanded that Germany, for instance, pay up to $850 billion in "long-overdue" war reparations. He has stated that Ukraine, in turn, needs to apologize for the wartime "Volhynia genocide," in which Ukrainian nationalists carried out ethnic cleansing in southeastern Poland, and to stop treating the fighters of the underground Ukrainian Insurgent Army responsible for this violence as national heroes. The new 2018 antidefamation law made "the defamation of the Polish nation" a criminal offense and allowed for the prosecution of people who "against the facts" ascribe "responsibility and co-responsibility" for the Holocaust to the Polish nation or the state, dividing the public along familiar lines.[27]

EDUCATION REFORM   PiS has exploited its control over the presidency and parliament to enact a sweeping overhaul of Poland's education system. These reforms have been deeply polarizing, as PiS—a party that received less than 40 percent of the vote in the 2015 parliamentary elections—has acted as though it had a mandate for radical change. Among other elements, the PiS reform brought back some communist-era institutional elements; made significant changes to the core curriculum, such as including a strong focus on nationalism and conservative values; and merged some schools while closing others, which meant that some school staff and in particular school headmasters lost their jobs. The Teachers' Trade Union and many parents' committees staunchly opposed the reform. Opponents of the reform argued that it was unnecessary, costly, highly ideological, and badly prepared. Protesters gathered over 100,000 signatures for a petition that called for a referendum on the reform, but the PiS-controlled parliament flatly rejected this idea. Public opinion regarding the reform also reflected the country's political divisions. Whereas 82 percent of PiS voters and 63 percent of voters for the antiestablishment, right-wing Kukiz'15 movement supported it, the majority of PO and Nowoczesna voters rejected it (76 percent and 81 percent, respectively).[28]

BACKLASH AGAINST ENVIRONMENTAL PROTECTION   PiS has also deliberately antagonized environmentalist groups, which it has sought to characterize as a threat to traditional values and national security. The government sparked public protests in 2017 when it authorized the intensive logging of the Białowieża Forest. Although the environment minister justified the logging by citing the presence of woodworm, environmental activists argued that the policy was commercially motivated. A group of ecologists and their supporters started a peaceful civil disobedience protest, blocking the heavy machinery used for the logging. Criticized by the UNESCO World Heritage Committee and the EC, it was stopped only after a contrary ruling by the European Court of Justice. The destruction of the Białowieza Forest was symbolic of PiS attitudes toward environmental protection. In the ruling party ideology, environmentalists, like feminists or proponents of LGBT rights, are part of the process of destruction of Europe's "traditional Christian values." Coal-based energy production is presented as essential to national security, and any policies aimed at reducing climate change are cast as part of a vast left-wing conspiracy that threatens the well-being and safety of ordinary Poles.

THE REFUGEE CRISIS PiS has rallied its base by stoking fears about an influx of refugees and has rapidly changed public attitudes toward migration in the process. In September 2015, Polish society was almost equally divided over whether Poland should support the EU deal on the handling of the refugee crisis and accept some of the refugees. By June 2017, not even two years later, less than one-fifth of the society still supported receiving refugees.[29] Driving this change in public opinion was the vitriolic campaign against refugees that PiS and Kukiz'15 members mounted ahead of the parliamentary elections in October 2015 and continued after the elections, now with great help from the public media. This campaign has resulted in a deep politicization not only of the response to the European refugee crisis of 2015, but also of migration policy in general—previously a largely apolitical issue. Anti-refugee, racist, and xenophobic slogans have become part of Poland's annual independence marches. A number of prodemocratic and antiracism grassroots organizations have been organizing pro-refugee rallies and demonstrations, but the ruling party and right-wing media have widely promoted the narrative that refugees are a threat to both national security and cultural identity.

POLAND AND EUROPE   PiS has further polarized Polish society by attacking the EU as a threat to Poland's national sovereignty and traditional values. After the Polish government ignored several EC warnings regarding its so-called judicial reform, in December 2017 the EC triggered Article 7 of the Treaty of the European Union against Poland, a measure that may result in sanctions and the suspension of Poland's voting rights. In a separate development, the Commission launched "infringement proceedings," whereby in September 2018 it sued Poland in the European Court of Justice on the grounds that the new Polish Law on the Supreme Court undermined judicial independence. In October 2018, the court ordered Poland to suspend the changes to its judicial system.

Polish society is divided over whether the country should deepen EU integration, but not over whether it should remain an EU member. The vast majority of Poles, irrespective of their political affiliation, support Poland's EU membership. However, this support is often pragmatically motivated and shallow. Whereas 66 percent of PO voters support deeper EU integration, only 27 percent of PiS supporters are in favor, with half of this group set against it.[30] A considerable part of Polish society opposes deeper integration with the EU out of fear of losing national sovereignty, rejects the introduction of the euro, and sees Europe as the source of unwelcome social changes that contravene traditional Catholic values. The refugee crisis has also armed Euroskeptics with another argument for maintaining cautious relations with Europe. Predictably, Polish society is also divided along party lines about the EU's use of Article 7 and its criticism of the PiS government for undermining the rule of law.

Consequences

The deepening of political and societal divisions benefits PiS, helping it to keep its electorate mobilized as well as to avoid accountability by using the excuse that all criticisms are "the unjustified attacks of the biased and hostile opposition."[31] Polarization has also taken a toll on the democratic process by diminishing governmental accountability, destroying checks and balances, crippling public debate, and by extension creating more opportunities for political corruption. The growth of what is known in Poland as a "tribe mentality,"[32] coupled with the political withdrawal of a considerable section of the society, has been unprecedented. Anger and xenophobia have been on the rise, and trust in public institutions has become dependent on political preferences.

A Spiraling "Tribe Mentality" and Political Withdrawal

Poles increasingly live in bubbles where the media they read and the people they discuss politics with align closely with their political views. As a result, public opinion has splintered, and individuals have become locked in a "tribe mentality"; more and more they cannot find common ground with the opposing side and do not make an effort to seek it.

Polish media are strongly polarized not only with respect to their content, but also with respect to their audiences, who increasingly distrust the opposing side's sources of information. In addition, public television is firmly under the government's control and extremely partial in its reporting, to the point of verging on disinformation. While PiS government supporters mainly watch government-controlled public television (67 percent), the opposition relies on the news from the private TVN and TVN24 channels (64 percent).[33] The same is true about printed media. Media consumed by the pro-PiS camp are never critical of the ruling party and never fail to demonize the opposition (usually described as "total opposition"), but the anti-PiS media are critical not only of the government, but also of the opposition parties, whom they regularly deride for failing to stand up to PiS. Even though the "patriots" and "citizens" inhabit two different media bubbles, the opposition's bubble is more heterogeneous.

Beyond polarization in the news media, the PiS and anti-PiS camps each have their own theaters, cabarets, museums, and even books and films. Writers, singers, and actors are expected to take a stand in the current conflict or are sometimes dragged into it, most often through right-wing harassment on social media. Thus, the Oscar-winning 2013 film *Ida*, directed by Paweł Pawlikowski, was accused by right-wing media (and the PiS culture minister) of promoting "anti-Polish" stereotypes, whereas *Volhynia*, a 2016 movie by an equally accomplished director, Wojciech Smarzowski, was praised for embracing right-wing narratives of Ukrainian cruelty and Polish nobleness surrounding the previously mentioned controversy of the wartime killings in Volhynia.

Given the divided media and cultural environment, Poles increasingly differ not only in their political views, but also in their understandings of the country's social and political realities. Whereas PiS supporters are convinced that the government fully upholds democratic standards and respects the rights and freedoms of all, the opposition camp believes exactly the opposite. When the political realities are interpreted in completely conflicting terms, with no agreement on facts, it is very difficult to identify a basis for compromise or rapprochement.

A related consequence is the avoidance of direct confrontation between representatives of the two camps in everyday life as well as the tendency to surround oneself with people who share similar political views. Seventy-six percent of people who believe that the society is divided prefer to avoid political discussions.[34] A majority of Poles say they do not have people whose views they cannot tolerate among their family, friends, and acquaintances, while 64 percent report that they are afraid to talk about politics with people whose political views they do not know.[35] At the same time, the atmosphere of heated conflict and the "false equivalence" discourse (mistakenly attributing equal responsibility for the ongoing conflict to both camps) have left many people with deep disdain for all politics and politicians. They either withdraw from political life altogether or fall into the arms of populists and demagogues who campaign as outsiders and rail against the corruption of the political class.

An Explosion of Hatred and Xenophobia

The Polish governing elites' acceptance of radical nationalism; praise for far-right marches as expressions of patriotism; vitriolic anti-migrant discourse; and public expressions of xenophobia, Islamophobia, and antisemitism have reset the parameters of acceptable discourse and unleashed an "unprecedented wave of hatred."[36] Public opinion research demonstrates an increase in negative attitudes not only toward migrants and refugees, but also toward Jews, Ukrainians, Germans, and individuals of other nationalities.[37] In 2016, a Prosecutor's Office report demonstrated an increase in the number of hate crimes in the past several years, although the government ignored this finding.[38] While prejudice may be excellent fuel for the political mobilization of selected groups of voters, it is much easier to activate than to placate, and hateful rhetoric is thus an extremely dangerous tool in the long term, potentially poisoning public life for decades to come.

Damaged Policy Processes

Polarization has dramatically reduced governmental accountability, as the government does not feel the need to justify its actions to an "alien camp" and perceives and presents any criticism as a blanket, undeserved attack. The parallel realities promoted by a divided media effectively shelter the government from hearing the opposing side's criticisms, while severe polarization allows trusted charismatic leaders to claim that they "know best what is good for [the] nation,"[39] despite the opposition's resistance. The Polish case also demonstrates that political polarization may prevent elections from serving as a check on authoritarian tendencies, as incumbents can move to abolish checks and balances without losing support from their unflinchingly loyal base. As a result, a country may still hold nominally democratic elections, accompanied by the violation of basic principles of the rule of law.[40]

Furthermore, severe polarization makes it difficult to adopt profound reforms that require wide social acceptance. In highly polarized contexts, governments may either avoid such reforms and focus instead on a populist policy agenda or ram through sweeping reforms without the required political and public debate. In the latter case, when the political tide turns, the next government often will not support and will seek to change the policies adopted by its predecessor. The educational reform in Poland is a case in point.

Political Corruption and Cronyism

Severe polarization is fostering or facilitating political corruption, cronyism, and patronage. Political loyalty has become the dominant criterion for selecting people to fill government jobs, often in the face of a limited supply of adequately qualified people. At the same time, officials' nominations and decisions have become immune to public oversight: the critical voices of the opposition are dismissed as biased, while supporters avoid criticizing their own party due to the supposed "state of war." The years of

PiS government since 2015 have been marked by illicit transfers of public money as a payoff for political support.[41] A recent example was the case of the chairperson of the Polish Financial Oversight Commission demanding a bribe of 40 million zloty (approximately US$10.5 million) from a banker. Another is the funding of the Lux Veritatis Foundation, which received 80 million zloty (roughly US$22 million) from the state budget between the time PiS formed the government in autumn 2015 and May 2018.[42] Yet another example is the checkered political and business career of Bartłomiej Misiewicz, who became a member of the board of trustees of two large state-owned companies, despite lacking adequate qualifications.[43] Yet such scandals have had a limited impact on the overall support for PiS and its government. Polarization is one explanation for this phenomenon, which some commentators call the "Teflon-like" quality of PiS.[44]

Declining Public Faith in Institutions

Severe and in Poland's case asymmetric polarization degrades public faith in key institutions. Trust in the judiciary and in particular in the Constitutional Tribunal has fallen precipitously over the past two years, as the PiS media have sought to convince the public that the courts are corrupt and that judges are merely partisan actors. Research shows that trust in the courts and in public institutions is strongly partisan.[45] PiS voters tend to trust their government and the PiS-controlled parliament (74 percent), while supporters of the opposition tend to positively rate the institutions that PiS attacks, including not just the courts but also the Human Rights Commissioner, the EC, and the European Parliament. Meanwhile, 84 percent and 85 percent of voters for Nowoczesna and PO, respectively, express distrust toward the Polish Parliament.

The Decline of Foreign Policy Consensus

A still further negative consequence of Poland's severe polarization is the gradual breaking-up of the traditionally broad elite and societal consensus on foreign policy. Poland's democratic transition, with all its successes, failures, and discontents, has been kept afloat by support from diverse parties for membership in key Western institutions, including NATO and the

EU. Even though public support for membership in these institutions is at a record high, the diplomatic skirmishes with Poland's key international partners, including Germany, France, Ukraine, Israel, the United States, and the EU, and the combative rhetoric of PiS politicians and media are bound to have polarizing effects on public opinion. One result of these developments is the increased susceptibility among part of the public and the political class to the influence of Russia's proauthoritarian, anti-Western propaganda.[46]

Remedial Actions

Poland's severe and asymmetric polarization illustrates the difficulties inherent in initiatives aimed at bridging the political gap between two warring camps and restoring democratic pluralism. The key problem is that polarization is highly beneficial to the ruling PiS (or at least is perceived as such). The party is thus unlikely to abandon its polarizing policies and rhetoric. As long as PiS remains in power and maintains its advantageous position with regard to its opponents, the situation is unlikely to change.

Most discussions about healing the political divide in Poland culminate in a call to bring the two camps to the table and allow them to find common ground in at least some areas of disagreement. Civil society groups, think tanks, and media organizations have launched a number of initiatives of this kind, but so far it is difficult to see any visible success from them. Most PiS politicians and ideologues refuse to participate in events that are not organized by "their" think tanks and nongovernmental organizations or use the opportunity to repeat their narratives rather than engage in meaningful conversation. Such initiatives also come under fire from representatives of the opposition, who complain (with some justification) that these dialogues merely provide the perpetrators of the current democratic backsliding with another platform to justify their action to new audiences.

Another group of initiatives seeks the mediation of the officials of the Catholic Church, especially the less conservative parts of the clergy. However, there is currently little evidence that the Church is willing to abandon its unwavering support for the current government and to become, like in the pre-1989 period, a mediator between the government and the opposition.

A number of left-of-center political groupings have also attempted to establish a viable alternative to the two dominant political camps. These initiatives have recently been focused on a charismatic former mayor of Słupsk, Robert Biedroń, who has launched a new center-left political party Wiosna (Spring) aimed at reaching out to those who have lost trust in the current political players. The next parliamentary elections are scheduled for no later than November 2019. If successful, Biedroń could fundamentally challenge the current divisions and become a game changer. However, his tendency to attack both sides of the polarized political spectrum has alienated many potential sympathizers; it may turn out that instead of healing Polish politics, Biedroń will only contribute to the current fragmentation of the anti-PiS opposition.

If such initiatives are to succeed, they need to address the society at large, local communities, and various social groups, rather than the key representatives of both PiS and its opponents. Even though many Poles prefer to rely on partisan media sources and distrust other outlets, some promising recent efforts have sought to make unbiased information and analysis available to all interested groups and individuals. One such relatively recent initiative is Oko.press, a web-based portal that provides reactions and objective analysis in real time and free of charge to tens of thousands of readers. Although Oko.press is strongly associated with the opposition camp, it keeps politicians at arm's length. It has adopted as a motto the words of the late Polish war hero and social activist Władysław Bartoszewski: "The truth does not lie in the middle; it lies where it lies."

NOTES

1. Laure Mandeville, "Dark and Dynamic: A Tale of Two Polands," *World-Crunch*, October 23, 2017 (www.worldcrunch.com/world-affairs/dark-and-dynamic-a-tale-of-two-polands).

2. For a comparative perspective on why anti-populist forces frequently struggle to form a cohesive political front, see Brandon Van Dyck, "Why Not Anti-Populist Parties? Theory with Evidence from the Andes and Thailand," *Comparative Politics* 51, no. 3 (2019): 361–88.

3. Dan Slater and Aries A. Arugay, "Polarizing Figures: Executive Power and Institutional Conflict in Asian Democracies," *American Behavioral Scientist* 62, no. 1 (2018): 92–106.

4. This group of "observers" comprises undecided voters and those who do not take part in elections, partly voters of the antiestablishment Kukiz'15 Party, who are more often supportive of the ruling party, and the agrarian Polish Peo-

ple's Party, whose electorate is generally somewhat more inclined toward the opposition. There are no left-wing parties currently in the parliament, and the left is very fragmented. See Centre for Public Opinion Research, "Suweren podzielony—sympatycy rządzących versus sympatycy opozycji oraz publiczność" [Divided sovereign—Supporters of the government versus supporters of the opposition and their audience], May 2017 (www.cbos.pl/SPISKOM.POL/2017/K_061_17.PDF).

5. Relative material deprivation has been shown to be one of the PiS supporters' shared characteristics. See Maciej Gdula, *Dobra zmiana w miastku: Neoautorytaryzm w Polskiej polityce z perspektywy małego miasta* [The good change in town: Neoauthoritarianism in Polish politics from a small town's perspective] (Warsaw: Krytyka Polityczna, 2018). However, relative group deprivation is understood much more broadly than in just a material sense. A judgment that people like oneself as a group have less resources or influence, lower status, and the like, even if one personally does not experience deprivation, appears to have considerable explanatory potential and is worth exploring further.

6. Anton Pelinka, "Right-Wing Populism: Concept and Typology," in *Right-Wing Populism in Europe: Politics and Discourse*, ed. Ruth Wodak, Majid Khosravinik, and Brigitte Mral (London: Bloomsbury, 2013), 3–22.

7. Jarosław Kaczyński infamously used the term "Poles of the worse sort" in reference to participants at anti-PiS public rallies.

8. Centre for Public Opinion Research, "O polityce, która nie buduje wspólnoty" [On politics that do not build a community], November 2017 (www.cbos.pl /SPISKOM.POL/2017/K_160_17.PDF).

9. Jan Tomasz Gross, "Gross: Kaczyński jest psujem" [Gross: Kaczyński is a breaker], *Krytyka Polityczna*, January 18, 2016 (https://krytykapolityczna.pl/kraj/ gross-kaczynski-jest-psujem/).

10. Centre for Public Opinion Research, "Suweren Podzielony."

11. Ibid. For example, the government camp enjoys support among 49 percent of those aged 65 and older, while the opposition enjoys support only among 29 percent. Voters under 45 years of age often side with the opposition. Notably, the majority of the youngest generation of voters (18 to 24 years of age) do not identify themselves either with the government or with the opposition. Sixty-three percent of people who participate in church services several times a week and 64 percent of those who identify as deeply religious support the government, while only 9 percent and 12 percent of these groups respectively support the opposition. At the same time, almost half of those who do not participate in church services at all support the opposition. Low-income individuals (who earn less than 1399 zloty, or around US$370, per person in a household on a monthly basis) are also more likely to support the government—around 40 percent of this group. They also are more likely to not support either the government or the opposition. Meanwhile, 45 percent of those who earn at least 2000 zloty or about US$536 per person in a household on a monthly basis support the opposition camp. More than 40 percent of people with only primary or vocational education support the government, with only 17 percent

supporting the opposition, while 46 percent of people with higher education support the opposition and only 22 percent support the government.

12. Centre for Public Opinion Research, "Psychologiczne charakterystyki elektoratów partyjnych" [Psychological characteristics of party electorates], October 2015 (www.cbos.pl/SPISKOM.POL/2015/K_138_15.PDF).

13. Centre for Public Opinion Research, "Układ poparcia dla partii politycznych przed wyborami do parlamentu" [Support for political parties before parliamentary elections], June 2005 (www.cbos.pl/SPISKOM.POL/2005/K_100_05.PDF).

14. Centre for Public Opinion Research, "Antypatie partyjne" [Partisan animosities], June 2017 (www.cbos.pl/SPISKOM.POL/2017/K_081_17.PDF).

15. Peter Kreko and others, "Beyond Populism: Tribalism in Poland and Hungary" (Budapest: Political Capital Institute, 2018), 36.

16. He said: "We split away the history of our recent past with *a thick line*. We will be responsible only for what we have done to help extract Poland from her current predicament, from now on." See Dominika Blachnicka-Ciacek, "Reading Mazowiecki's Expose Twenty Years Later," *Liberté!*, May 2, 2012 (http://liberte world.com/2012/05/02/reading-mazowieckis-expose-twenty-years-later/).

17. Leszek Balcerowicz, who implemented these reforms, served as finance minister in two center-right governments and later served as the president of the National Bank of Poland.

18. The quoted text here was the title of Jarosław Kaczyński's lecture at the Heritage Foundation in 2016.

19. For a more detailed analysis of the first PiS government's populism, see Joanna Fomina and Jacek Kucharczyk, "Poland after 2005 Elections: Domestic Discontent or EU Backlash?" in *Democracy and Populism in Central Europe: The Visegrad Elections and Their Aftermath*, ed. Martin Butora and others (Bratislava: IVO, 2007), 81–98.

20. For more on the negative consequences of PiS's "system-delegitimizing rhetoric," see Hubert Tworzecki, "Poland: A Case of Top-Down Polarization," *The ANNALS of the American Academy of Political and Social Science* 681, no. 1 (2019): 97–119.

21. Joanna Fomina and Jacek Kucharczyk, "The Specter Haunting Europe: Populism and Protest in Poland," *Journal of Democracy* 27, no. 1 (2016): 58.

22. Władysław Trzaska—Korowajczyk, "Smoleńsk 10 kwietnia 2010 Po dwóch latach" [Smoleńsk on April 10, 2010 after two years], *Katolickie Stowarzyszenie Dziennikarzy*, April 11, 2012 (www.katolickie.media.pl/index.php/publikacje /publikacje-czlonkow-ol-ksd/3302-wadysaw-trzaska-korowajczyk-smolesk-10 -kwietnia-2010-po-dwoch-latach).

23. Tworzecki, "Poland," 112–14.

24. Jan Cieński, "Poland's Constitutional Crisis Goes International," *Politico*, December 24, 2015 (www.politico.eu/article/poland-constitution-crisis-kaczyn ski-duda/).

25. Paweł Wiktor Ryś, "Antygenderowy katechizm" [Anti-gender catechism]

Krytyka Polityczna, February 6, 2014 (https://krytykapolityczna.pl/kraj/antygen-derowy-katechizm/).

26. See Jacek Kucharczyk and others, "Poland—When Fear Wins: Causes and Consequences of Poland's Populist Turn," in *Nothing to Fear but Fear Itself?* (London: Demos, 2017), 305–74 (www.demos.co.uk/wp-content/uploads/2017/02/Nothing-to-Fear-but-Fear-Itelf-final.pdf).

27. Adam Michnik, "Absurd goni absurd" [One absurdity after another], *Gazeta Wyborcza*, January 29, 2018 (http://wyborcza.pl/7,75968,22958506,adam-michnik-o-nowelizacji-ustawy-o-ipn-absurd-goni-absurd.html).

28. Centre for Public Opinion Research, "Czy reforma edukacji powinna zostać poddana pod głosowanie w referendum?" [Should there be a referendum on the education reform?], May 2017 (www.cbos.pl/SPISKOM.POL/2017/K_057_17.PDF).

29. Centre for Public Opinion Research, "Stosunek do przyjmowania uchodźców" [Attitudes toward receiving refugees], April 2017 (www.cbos.pl/SPIS KOM.POL/2017/K_044_17.PDF).

30. Centre for Public Opinion Research, "Reakcje na uruchomienie wobec Polski Art. 7 traktatu o Unii Europejskiej" [Reactions to the EU's triggering of Article 7 against Poland], January 2018 (www.cbos.pl/SPISKOM.POL/2018/K_014_18 .PDF).

31. "Prezes PiS: Opozycja totalna żyje w wymyślonym świecie. 'Propaganda skierowana przeciwko nam przechodzi w szaleństwo'" [PiS president: The total opposition lives in a made-up world. 'The propaganda directed against us verges on madness'"], *W Polityce*, March 31, 2017 (https://wpolityce.pl/polityka/333850 -prezes-pis-opozycja-totalna-zyje-w-wymyslonym-swiecie-propaganda-skiero wana-przeciwko-nam-przechodzi-w-szalenstwo?strona=2).

32. Magdalena Środa, "Naszyzm" [Ours-ism], *Gazeta Wyborczka*, September 7, 2016 (http://wyborcza.pl/1,75968,20653732,naszyzm.html).

33. Centre for Public Opinion Research, "Suweren podzielony."

34. Ibid.

35. Centre for Public Opinion Research, "Monolog, dialog czy kłótnia—Polaków rozmowy o polityce" [Monologue, dialogue, or squabble—Poles' discussion on politics], November 2017 (www.cbos.pl/SPISKOM.POL/2017/K_153_17.PDF).

36. Małgorzata Święchowicz, "Badacz rasizmu: Mamy falę nienawiści bez precedensu w najnowszej historii Polski" [Racism scholar: We are facing a wave of hatred unprecedented in the history of modern Poland], *Newsweek*, September 30, 2016 (www.newsweek.pl/polska/rasizm-mamy-fale-nienawisci-bez-precedensu-w-polsce/4m9te6q).

37. Centre for Public Opinion Research, "Stosunek do innych narodów" [Attitudes toward other nations], March 2018 (www.cbos.pl/SPISKOM.POL/2018 /K_037_18.PDF).

38. Grzegorz Furgo and Marta Golbik, "Interpelacja nr 2905" [Interpellation No. 2905], April 28, 2016 (www.sejm.gov.pl/sejm8.nsf/InterpelacjaTresc .xsp?key=31190AC6).

39. Rafał Białkowski, "J. Kaczyński: my w Polsce wiemy najlepiej, co jest dobre dla naszego narodu" [J. Kaczyński: We in Poland know best what is good for our people], *Polska Agencja Prasowa*, May 4, 2019 (www.pap.pl/aktualnosci/news%2C446489%2Cj-kaczynski-my-w-polsce-najlepiej-wiemy-co-dobrze-sluzy-naszemu-narodowi).

40. As Michael Meyer-Resende aptly observed, democracy without checks and balances provided by an independent judiciary is not even "illiberal democracy" but not democracy at all, as an independent judiciary is the only way to ensure free and fair elections. See Michael Meyer-Resende, "Is Europe's Problem Illiberal Majoritarianism or Creeping Authoritarianism?" *Carnegie Europe*, June 13, 2018 (https://carnegieeurope.eu/2018/06/13/is-europe-s-problem-illiberal-majoritarianism-or-creeping-authoritarianism-pub-76587).

41. Wojciech Cieśla, "Sami swoi, czyli jak żywi się rząd i jego poplecznicy," [Only ourselves, or how the government and its followers are fed], *Newsweek*, February 25, 2018 (www.newsweek.pl/biznes/gospodarka/nagrody-dla-politykow-pis-nagrody-dla-ministrow-w-rzadzie-pis/yx03ezm).

42. The Lux Veritatis Foundation was established by Tadeusz Rydzyk, a Catholic priest who built a right-wing media empire, which includes Radio Maria and TV Trwam, as well as a media academy. Highly popular with older, devout voters, Rydzyk's media outlets remain a formidable political force able to make or break the fortunes of right-wing politicians.

43. Bartłomiej Misiewicz served briefly as a Ministry of Defense spokesman and is a close associate of Antoni Macierewicz, the PiS defense minister between November 2015 and January 2018. After considerable media criticism, a government commission was formed to investigate how Misiewicz had become a career member of the board of directors of a state-owned arms manufacturer and concluded that he did not have the required qualifications.

44. Cezary Michalski, "Siła teflonu. Dlaczego PiS niemal wszystko uchodzi bezkarnie?" [The strength of Teflon. Why can PiS get away with almost anything?], *Newsweek*, May 17, 2018 (www.newsweek.pl/polska/polityka/bezkarnosc-pis-jak-pis-izoluje-kazda-grupe-spoleczna/p6q0cv9).

45. Centre for Public Opinion Research, "O nieufności i zaufaniu" [On distrust and trust], March 2018 (www.cbos.pl/SPISKOM.POL/2018/K_035_18.PDF).

46. Jacek Kucharczyk, "Exploiting Political Polarization in Poland," in *Sharp Power: Rising Authoritarian Influence*, National Endowment for Democracy, December 2017 (www.ned.org/wp-content/uploads/2017/12/Sharp-Power-Rising-Authoritarian-Influence-Full-Report.pdf), 94–123.

Part III

ELITE POLARIZATION IN RELATIVELY HOMOGENOUS SOCIETIES

SIX

Colombia's Polarizing Peace Efforts

ANDREAS E. FELDMANN

Colombia has long suffered intense periods of political and social polarization rooted in core issues of socioeconomic exclusion and the distribution of power. In the past ten years, polarization has once again flared up, fueled by conflicting views on how to end the long and bloody internal armed conflict that has consumed the country since 1964. The 2016 Peace Accord between the administration of President Juan Manuel Santos and the Revolutionary Armed Forces of Colombia (Fuerzas Armadas Revolucionarias de Colombia; FARC), the country's most emblematic and strongest guerrilla group, is the focal point of this new phase of polarization. In the 2018 presidential election, sharp disagreement over the future of the peace accord and its purported impact on the country produced the most polarized election in the country in recent decades. The winner of the election, Iván Duque of the right-wing Centro Democrático, openly criticized the accord and suggested that he might substantially amend it, while his second-round opponent, Gustavo Petro of the leftist Progressive Movement party, strongly supported it.

Colombia represents yet another instance of a growing global phenomenon in which polarization transforms social and political relations into "two unyielding hostile factions."[1] In its concentration around the issue of peace, however, Colombia's polarization differs within Latin America from the pattern of polarizing populism that arose in the 2000s, which was marked by the emergence of radical leftist reformers who gained power and challenged fundamental elements of the political system, as seen in Bolivia, Ecuador, Honduras, Nicaragua, and Venezuela.[2] Colombia also differs from the recent Brazilian experience characterized by the emergence of right-wing populism (see chapter 9 in this volume).

This chapter examines this new phase of polarization in Colombia, arguing that even though it is an elite-driven phenomenon, it has been spreading into the wider society through loyalty ties to uncompromising political factions. The roots of Colombia's contemporary polarization lie in a lengthy history of political violence, first between competing political camps and then between armed guerrilla groups and the Colombian state and paramilitary groups supporting its counterinsurgency efforts. Political polarization over peace negotiations, however, has intensified in the past two decades and is largely the result of elite-level divisions. In particular, three aspects of the 2016 Peace Accord—justice for past crimes, political participation for former guerrilla leaders, and land reform—have been intensely polarizing. As for the main consequences of polarization, Colombia has managed to avert political gridlock, but growing discord has imperiled the prospects for a lasting peace, contributed to an increase in already high levels of violence and social turmoil, and undermined trust in the judiciary as an independent institution. Although the Santos administration, the Catholic Church, and civil society groups have launched initiatives aimed at fostering dialogue and countering polarization, these have proven inadequate thus far to address the underlying causes and sheer scale of the problem.

Roots

Polarization has been a powerful and tragic feature of Colombia's political life since independence in 1810. For most of the nineteenth century and throughout the twentieth century, two parties—Liberal and Conservative—dominated Colombian politics. They emerged as a reaction to divisions between centralists allied with Simón Bolívar and federalists siding with his rival Francisco de Paula Santander during the early years of the new republic. As far as their origin and social membership, the two parties displayed only subtle differences: both represented landowners, merchants, and a rising professional middle class.[3] According to Frank Safford, the Conservative Party was slightly more aristocratic and powerful and represented the elite of the main cities, including Bogotá, Cartagena, and Popayán, while Liberals were strongest in more peripheral zones, in particular the east of the country.[4] As for their politics, both were elitist parties that differed most conspicuously on the role of the church in politics, with Liberals more inclined to support the separation of church and state. As for their economic views, Liberals were more open to integrating Colombia's economy into world markets.[5] Despite their similar origin, their bitter rivalry fueled high levels of social and political exclusion, which together with rising economic inequality triggered acute and repeated waves of violence between the opposing camps.[6] The inability to resolve socioeconomic and political grievances became a major stumbling block in the process of state formation.[7]

Although violence between conservatives and liberals was a common occurrence during the early stages of independence in many Latin American countries, in Colombia it took a particularly virulent form and lasted much longer. In the modern era, political tensions erupted into a horrifying period of civil war between 1948 and 1963 known as La Violencia, which resulted in the deaths of more than 300,000 Colombians and the displacement of numerous communities.[8] Liberal and Conservative elites eventually were able to put an end to La Violencia through a consociational formula known as the National Front (Frente Nacional), in which they agreed to share political power.[9]

Though the National Front was critical in mending relations between Liberals and Conservatives, its exclusionary nature, particularly its failure to incorporate popular sectors (including the peasantry and fast-growing urban middle and working classes), created another axis of polarization in Colombia's already fractured society. In 1964, in response to this exclusion, peasant self-defense forces in central Colombia created the FARC, while urban sectors, with Cuban support, formed the National Liberation Army (Ejército de Liberación Nacional; ELN). These groups rebelled against the central state, which they accused of disregarding their demands for social justice and in particular for land redistribution. These leftist insurgencies elicited a strong reaction from the central state and later paramilitary groups that emerged to buttress the state's counterinsurgency efforts.[10] The existence of a robust drug industry in the country, which guerrillas and paramilitary groups utilized to finance their military activities, exacerbated and prolonged the conflict.[11]

The sociopolitical and economic consequences of this phase of violence have been devastating for Colombia. According to a recent study, 262,000 people have lost their lives, and as many as seven million have been forcibly displaced from their communities.[12] The economic impact of the war has also been enormous. Indepaz, a Colombian think tank, calculates that during the 1964-2016 period, the cost of the conflict reached between $139 billion and $179 billion.[13] The conflict, moreover, has had pernicious effects on the country's social fabric, sowing the seeds of distrust in communities afflicted by violence and profound cynicism throughout the society. Colombia is thus a telling example of a country in which polarization and violence are intertwined and reinforce each other.[14] It was out of this long-running, devastating conflict that the current phase of polarization was born.

Trajectory

The contemporary phase of polarization in Colombia can be traced to the administration of President Andrés Pastrana (1998-2002). As the Colombian government began moving in the late 1990s to try to make peace with the FARC and other insurgent groups, a profound divide opened up in the country over whether and how to pursue peace. This divide intensified as the most recent peace process with the FARC advanced and came to a head in 2016 with the holding of a public referendum on the peace accord.[15] Despite the praise the accord has received abroad for its innovation, constructive spirit, and evenhandedness, Colombians bitterly argue over its content and merits.[16] Although ideological and identity-based divisions have contributed to the strength of public discord, elite rivalries have been the primary driver of polarization.

The San Vicente del Caguán Negotiations

Under President Pastrana, failed negotiations (1999-2002) with the FARC turned the peace process into a polarizing and emotionally charged issue for the Colombian public. The problem was related to the design of the talks. As a goodwill gesture to the FARC, Pastrana granted the group a demilitarized zone of 42,000 square kilometers (km²)—an area the size of Switzerland—in the southern department of Caquetá. The state and the FARC, however, were not able to agree on the terms of a cease-fire, and thus they continued military operations while the talks were being held. During the three years of negotiations, the FARC took advantage of this sanctuary to recruit and train new operatives, develop military expertise, and stage attacks, including acts of terrorism like kidnappings and bombings.[17] The FARC was also able to establish a presence in major metropolitan areas, where it committed highly visible attacks, particularly kidnappings. As security conditions worsened, public opinion turned against peace negotiations.

The Uribe Effect

The tenure of President Álvaro Uribe (2002–10), whose election in 2002 was directly linked to the failure of the abovementioned process, became another defining period for Colombia. His persona and policies contributed hugely to the deepening of political polarization in the country. A cunning politician, Uribe identified the electorate's frustration with the peace process and craving for security and campaigned on the promise to fight the FARC head on to restore security and the rule of law. Though he had long been a member of the Liberal Party, Uribe ran in 2002 as an independent candidate and as an outsider who promised to defy the political establishment dominated by powerful Bogotá families that had ruled the country almost uninterruptedly since independence. He represented the interests of the powerful landed and industrial sectors of Antioquia, an important province located in the northwest of the country that historically competed with the capital. After his election, Uribe broke ranks with the Liberal Party to create his own party, the Social Party of National Unity (Partido Social de Unidad Nacional), composed of a mix of right-wing conservatives, defectors from liberalism, and a coalition of regional forces.[18]

Feeling increasingly besieged by the simultaneous onslaught of guerrillas and paramilitaries, Uribe decided to implement the so-called Democratic Security Policy (DSP).[19] The DSP sought to address the critical security situation by increasing the numbers and capacity of troops and police units and by deploying security forces more aggressively. Pressure from the security establishment, in particular the military, with its vested institutional interest in a military solution to the conflict, reinforced Uribe's dedication to the DSP.[20] At the same time, the United States underwrote a multifaceted counterinsurgency assistance initiative, known as Plan Colombia, that buttressed the DSP. Although Plan Colombia began during the Pastrana administration, the initiative got into full swing under President Uribe.[21] The administration justified the policy by claiming that militarization was the only answer to insecurity and that the military build-up was crucial not only to support the rule of law but also to promote economic and social development.

Uribe's policies achieved important results in the realm of security. The FARC suffered heavy blows at the hands of security forces, including the capture or killing of senior and mid-rank officers and the loss of strategic areas.[22] Under pressure from a sustained military offensive, the FARC's fighting force dwindled from 16,000 combatants in 2002 to approximately 7,000 to 8,000 in 2010 following military defeats and massive desertion.[23] The security outlook also improved as a result of peace negotiations with the United Self-Defense Forces of Colombia (Autodefensas Unidas de Colombia; AUC), a confederation of regionally based paramilitary groups. A large portion of AUC troops demobilized, and hundreds of mid-ranking leaders were imprisoned while fourteen top commanders were extradited to the United States after they refused to honor their commitments under the peace agreement.[24] The weakening of guerrilla and paramilitary groups helped to lower violence and reduce (temporarily) drug cultivation and production.[25] Improved security conditions and a more business-friendly environment also provided a boost to the Colombian economy by increasing investment and employment.

Notwithstanding its positive aspects, Uribe's tenure was exceedingly controversial. Drawing on his majority in Congress and legitimized by his high approval ratings, Uribe modified the constitution to allow his reelection in 2006. His administration was also tainted by a plethora of scandals, including the use of the intelligence services to spy on opposition members, links between paramilitary groups and Uribe's allies in Congress, and a substantial increase in human rights abuses perpetrated by security forces (including torture, disappearances, and extrajudicial executions). The AUC peace process also proved controversial, as some saw it as excessively lenient toward paramilitaries.[26] Uribe's abrasive leadership style and Manichean political discourse further divided the nation. In 2018, the Colombian Supreme Court placed Uribe under investigation for allegedly making false statements and tampering with witnesses.

Although Uribe certainly has been the most influential and popular politician in modern Colombia—he had a 75 percent approval rating upon leaving office—he is arguably the most divisive political figure since former President Turbay Ayala (1978–82), whose term in office was characterized by high levels of repression.[27] Uribe's wide appeal, direct style, and rapport with ordinary Colombians won him a large base of loyal, fervent supporters. Yet his ruthless political tactics created a significant number of diehard detractors. Critics highlight Uribe's authoritarian tendencies, disregard for institutional checks and balances, and damaging human rights record; they were also dismayed by his alleged ties to extralegal paramilitary groups.[28] More importantly, his uncompromising approach to resolving the country's complex problems undermined political dialogue.[29] Particularly consequential was his militaristic rhetoric, which injected into Colombian public opinion the idea that total military victory over the FARC was within reach.[30]

President Santos's U-Turn

A third critical moment in Colombia's recent polarization was President Juan Manuel Santos's (2010–18) decision to start peace negotiations with the FARC in 2012. As defense minister during Uribe's second term, he played an important role in the execution of the DSP. Santos won the presidency running as Uribe's political heir and campaigning on a platform promising the continuation of democratic security. Santos's rise to power was due in no small part to his association with Uribe. As a result, his announcement that he would initiate peace negotiations with the FARC caught everybody by surprise and fractured the center-right coalition created during the Uribe years.

Santos's reversal created a bitter divide within the Colombian elite between those loyal to Uribe and those loyal to Santos. Uribe and his followers saw Santos's decision to open negotiations with the insurgent group as a betrayal. Acrimony grew further because in his attempt to move toward the political center, Santos deliberately marginalized Uribe and his allies in the negotiations with the FARC. Reflecting the estrangement of the two figures, in 2013 Uribe formed a new party, the Centro Democrático, and became the head of the opposition. The animosity between the two camps reached a boiling point during President Santos's reelection campaign in 2014. In a charged second round, Santos faced Óscar Iván Zuluaga, a former finance minister under Uribe who represented the Centro Democrático.[31]

The referendum on the peace accord with the FARC, held in October 2016, was another milestone in Colombia's political polarization. The Santos administration decided to organize it to bestow legitimacy upon the accord. To the surprise of many, Colombians rejected the accord by half a percentage point.[32] The reasons behind this rejection are complex. Notwithstanding a clever campaign by the "No" camp (led by former President Uribe) that transformed the vote into a referendum on the Santos administration, the results showed that Colombians remained divided over the matter. Rural and poorer areas, especially communities with a high presence of FARC forces and other armed parties, voted in favor of the agreement. Urban and more economically advanced areas gave less support to the accord, particularly in central and western regions such as Antioquia.[33]

Recriminations and acrimony spread because, following its surprising electoral defeat in the referendum, the Santos administration persevered with the objective of finalizing the agreement. To that end, it gathered the main points presented by the opposition—up to 455 concrete issues—and included most of them in a new round of negotiations with the FARC. Against all odds, in a few weeks it hammered out a new accord and, relying on its majority in Congress, approved it in a special voting session despite the vociferous objections of the Centro Democrático.[34]

The opposition charged that the new accord was flawed and that the Santos administration failed to incorporate in good faith its reservations. Some sectors on the left also voiced criticism of the modified agreement, in particular the government's last-minute changes that may allow military officers accused of serious offenses to avoid prosecution. Even though it is generally agreed that the modifications introduced in the final accord improved it, opposition to the deal has continued to grow.[35] In a recent interview, Santos regretfully admitted:

> I didn't realize that post truth, that the propaganda against the (peace) process was much more powerful and much more effective than I imagined. . . . And when I realized, it was too late.[36]

The elite-driven nature of polarization in Colombia is exemplified in the fallout between political heavyweights and former allies Uribe and Santos, which has involved intrigue and drama of a truly Shakespearean nature. Colombians supporting each camp are to some extent divided by ideological and socioeconomic cleavages: more affluent conservatives, in particular regional elites, as well as popular sectors especially in rural areas, tend to support Uribe and his political legacy. Conversely, leftist sectors, both affluent and more popular, supported Santos's attempts to reach a negotiated deal with the FARC.[37] Notwithstanding these differences, the rivalry between these camps stems mostly from their unwavering loyalties to political *caudillos* (strongmen) representing the country's political and economic elite. This has been a constant in a country where notoriously personalistic tendencies have characterized politics and political leaders' personal animosities have been transferred to the population. This was clearly the case during the bleak years of La Violencia, when factions committed atrocities in the name of the liberal and conservative values espoused by their patrons.[38] This pattern, albeit in a different guise, seems to repeat itself today: the majority of Colombians desire peace and security, but they are bitterly divided in their support for different factions within the political elite advocating for different formulas to achieve fundamentally similar goals.

The 2018 National Elections

The 2018 national elections represented the latest advance of the creeping polarization process gripping the country. Disillusioned with the Santos administration in the wake of corruption scandals and subpar economic performance—prompted partly by the end of the commodity boom—and fired up by discussions concerning the peace process with the FARC, Colombians deserted centrist parties. In the first round of the presidential election, Duque and Petro, representing the extremes of the political spectrum, defeated moderate rivals including Sergio Fajardo, a former mayor of Medellín, and Humberto de la Calle, the former chief negotiator of the 2016 Peace Accord.[39] In voting for Duque and Petro, Colombians endorsed markedly opposing worldviews.

A former leftist guerrilla commander who later became mayor of Bogotá and a senator, Petro represented a modern, urban, progressive left, advocating for structural societal changes and viewing the state as the main vehicle for bringing about this transformation. Petro was a staunch supporter of the peace accord, even though he was critical of the centrist administration of President Santos. Young, urban generations yearning for change and supportive of efforts to reach a negotiated solution to the internal armed conflict supported Petro's campaign. Rural communities, especially on the Pacific coast, in the Amazon region, and on parts of the Atlantic coast, also supported his candidacy. Petro supporters for the most part regarded the peace accord as a critical juncture, a re-foundational moment for the country. Leftist parties, the green party, and members of the centrist coalition who voted for Fajardo in the first round supported Petro.

Iván Duque, conversely, represented a broad coalition of probusiness conservatives close to former President Álvaro Uribe. The candidate of the Centro Democrático, Duque was supported by the conservative and most of the liberal parties, as well as by Cambio Radical, a small party led by conservative dissident Germán Vargas Lleras. Duque had widespread appeal among upper- and middle-class voters as well as among more conservative popular sectors such as evangelicals. He won twenty-four of Colombia's thirty-two departments, receiving especially strong support in the so-called Coffee Axis (Eje Cafetero), the eastern plains, and central Colombian departments including Antioquia.[40] His camp regarded the peace accord with the FARC as a dangerous step that undermined Colombia's existing socioeconomic and political order. Duque and his allies rejected what they regarded as the "liberal values" behind the peace accord. Duque's camp was also worried about Cuban and especially Venezuelan influence in the negotiations and, more consequentially, about the Maduro regime's ties with insurgent groups, a charge adamantly denied by Caracas.[41] Duque often attacked Petro as a "pawn" of the Venezuelan regime, prompting Petro to accuse Duque of using dirty, deceitful tactics.[42]

Discord over the Accord

Why has the 2016 Peace Accord been so divisive among Colombians? Three main issues divide the public: postconflict justice, political participation for former guerrilla leaders, and land reform in rural areas. These issues are emotionally charged for many Colombians and, particularly in the case of land reform, bring out significant ideological differences between the opposing camps. Yet as the previous section has shown, elite rivalries have played a crucial role in amplifying these divisions.

Postconflict Justice

Disagreement on how to deal with the thorny issue of postconflict justice has caused critical friction in Colombian society. Based on a transitional justice model, the accord seeks to strike a balance between peace and justice that pursues the latter to the greatest possible extent. The accord established a transitional justice mechanism known as the Special Jurisdiction for Peace (Jurisdicción Especial para la Paz; JEP). José Miguel Vivanco, the Human Rights Watch director for the Americas, describes the JEP as a "system of lenient 'transitional justice' rules."[43] As part of the accord, the FARC's rank-and-file members will be pardoned, while the group's leaders will have to appear before a tribunal and confess their alleged crimes in exchange for leniency.[44] State officials including governors, mayors, and members of Congress as well as civilians may also be asked to testify before the JEP.

As is often the case in postconflict settings, violence has hardened the views of Colombians and of victims and their relatives in particular. Throughout the conflict, all actors involved (guerrillas, paramilitary groups, and the state) committed systematic and widespread human rights abuses, including massacres, abductions, disappearances, executions, bombings, forced recruitment of minors, and population displacement.[45] The parties' furtive attempts to hide their abuses and their reluctance to show remorse for their deeds have sown a deep sense of mistrust in the population.[46] This context has provided fertile ground for increasing polarization.

The perceived leniency of the peace process toward FARC leaders has triggered a major pushback. Most Colombians deeply resent the group. In a recent poll, 58 percent of Colombians thought that the FARC was primarily responsible for violence in the country (32 percent ascribed responsibility to paramilitaries and 7 percent to the state). A paltry 6.2 percent indicated that they trusted the FARC. Interestingly, even though 67 percent of Colombians favored a negotiated solution to the conflict, only 41 percent were in favor of negotiating with the FARC.[47] It is not surprising, then, that the special treatment offered to the group's leaders upsets many Colombians.

In the opinion of the accord's detractors, the terms for administering justice to FARC members create a dangerous precedent that permits impunity for the most serious crimes. The JEP has had a slow, troubled implementation period due to its very nature as a complex parallel mechanism to administer justice, which requires the selection and training of special personnel, including judges, lawyers, and public administrators. This slowness has furthered the perception that there is no political will to deliver justice and that the government is intentionally delaying the process because it is reluctant to investigate (let alone prosecute) alleged perpetrators. Those in favor of the accord, conversely, respond that the JEP needs time to work and that some degree of leniency is a small price to pay if the end goal is the FARC's demobilization.[48]

Although the issue of justice has been divisive in past peace negotiations, Colombians' positions on any particular accord tend to reflect their loyalty to particular leaders. The 2005 demobilization of the AUC during the Uribe administration prompted similarly passionate disagreements. However, the right-wing Uribe supporters who are now crying foul over the terms of the current FARC agreement advocated for comparable mechanisms during the AUC demobilization. In a similar display of inconsistency, leftist sectors now in favor of leniency toward FARC members were extremely critical of the terms of the peace accord with the AUC. Victims' associations and a few human rights organizations have voiced their criticism of such double standards.[49]

Political Participation

A second polarizing aspect of the accord involves the political participation of the FARC in Colombia's democracy. Recognizing that a democratic deficit and lack of avenues for political participation lay at the root of the conflict, the accord devoted an entire section to political participation and democratic reform. It explicitly states that strengthening Colombian democracy is fundamental to achieving long-lasting peace. A pivotal element is the promise to promote the participation of previously marginalized social organizations to build a more representative system. In accordance with this spirit, the FARC agreed to demobilize and transition into a political party—to that end, in 2017 the group changed its name to the People's Alternative Revolutionary Force. The state, for its part, guaranteed the FARC special representation for a transitional period by allocating it five of the 172 seats in the lower house of Congress and five of the 108 seats in the Senate.[50]

Detractors contend that a group that espoused violence and attacked democratic institutions should not be allowed to participate in the system. Many people, even those who in principle favor the group's participation in politics, seem incensed about allowing the group to participate in politics before the JEP hearings begin. They claim, reasonably, that this poses the risk that people who have committed serious crimes could become elected officials. Reflecting the unpopularity of the group, the results of the congressional elections of March 2018 were dismal for the FARC: it won just 53,000 votes in the Senate election, 0.34 percent of the total. The group's presidential candidate, Rodrigo Londoño, was not faring much better in opinion polls when he dropped out of the first round of the presidential election for health reasons.[51]

Land Reform

Lastly, the peace accord's plan to address unequal land distribution and foster rural development has been controversial.[52] A significant part of the vociferous opposition to the accord comes from powerful provincial elites represented by the Centro Democrático and other rightist parties who have much to lose from the accord's proposed reforms. This group is alarmed at the prospect of being forced to yield portions of their property as part of land redistribution schemes. They also worry about higher taxation and more generally oppose efforts to enhance the presence of the state in rural areas, as this may encroach on the power they wield in some remote municipalities. Divisions on this point reflect more profound disagreements over the most desirable economic model for the country and, concomitantly, the role the state should play in the country's future development.

Colombians are divided between those who staunchly defend property rights and those who, while favoring private property, believe that these rights should fulfill a social function. Colombia's influential and powerful economic elite favors the socioeconomic status quo, predicated on a free market economy. Members of the traditional elite associated with the service and manufacturing industries, as well as middle-class professionals, comprise this group. Powerful, provincial elites with links to land and the agricultural sector—many of whom prospered despite a general context of armed conflict—also favor keeping things the same.[53] The opposing camp advocates for structural change to address socioeconomic inequality and lack of inclusion, which in its view are the main causes of violence in the country. This camp includes quite distinct groups ranging from moderate, pro-free market elites, academics, and intellectuals and sectors of the middle class to leftist parties, labor unionists, environmentalists, peasants, the working class, and civil society activists who are more critical of free markets.

The Santos administration attempted to strike a balance between these opposing positions by advocating for structural reforms to land tenure while guaranteeing a favorable environment for the country's influential agroindustrial sector. In a puzzling move, however, the Santos government passed an agrarian law that contains several contentious elements that, according to critics, go against the spirit of the accord and will make it impossible to introduce reforms. Against the backdrop of claims by thousands of dispossessed peasants, the government decided to allow agroindustrial corporations access to empty plots of state-owned land intended for redistribution. This move reinforced the perception among some progressive sectors that the government compromised with the powerful groups opposing the accord in order to block major land reform.[54]

Consequences

The current phase of polarization is having a major impact on Colombian politics and society. Contrary to what might be expected, particularly in a presidential system like Colombia's, polarization thus far has not had a crippling effect on the functioning of the Colombian government. Despite the harsh rhetoric and constant clashes between different political camps, presidents have found ways to get legislation passed. During the Santos administration, for example, collaboration on several bills emerged on strictly pragmatic terms.[55] Drawing on substantial executive powers and the capacity to disburse resources, the Colombian president has important tools to secure legislative majorities.[56] Colombia's political factions also found common ground against the backdrop of accusations that some of their leaders had received kickbacks from the Brazilian construction giant Odebrecht. These charges increased the pressure on the parties to agree to pass anticorruption legislation as a way to restore public faith in the government.

Polarization is, however, having four powerful, pernicious effects on Colombia's political institutions and society. First and most consequentially, it is ruining the prospects of a lasting peace in the country. As previously explained, objections to a settlement with the FARC have fueled polarization. To a significant degree, this rejection is informed by a narrative that the FARC could have been defeated militarily and that therefore the accord not only unfairly rewards the group but also was unnecessary. Regardless of the merits of such a view, which arguably are weakly supported, the accord nevertheless has been signed and the FARC demobilized. Yet as the opposing parties bicker over the merits and implementation of the accord, blaming each other for its problems, the accord weakens and loses public credibility, imperiling its future. In other words, the peace process has reached a point of no return—the only possible alternative is a complete collapse of the accord, which would pave the way for the FARC's return to arms. This outcome would be disastrous for the country, in which (notwithstanding improvements) security conditions remain problematic. Furthermore, several paramilitary groups and the ELN, with which the government is currently negotiating a peace agreement in Ecuador, remain armed. The ELN remains a potent force: in January 2019, the group claimed responsibility for a car bombing attack against the police academy in Bogotá, which killed twenty people.[57] Against this backdrop, reneging on the accord would render any potential future negotiated solution exceedingly unlikely, whether with the FARC or with other armed groups.

Second, attacks against human rights defenders and community organizers have significantly increased. The Office of the United Nations High

Commissioner for Human Rights reports that there were 441 attacks, 121 of them deadly, against human rights defenders and community leaders in Colombia in 2017.[58] The year before, a similar number of activists were killed. Journalists also have been routinely attacked and threatened.[59] A polarized context characterized by unsubstantiated accusations undoubtedly helps create conditions that increase the risk of attacks on such groups. Frivolous charges of complicity with the guerrillas seem particularly reckless given the existence of dangerous, right-wing extremists in the country ready to target rivals.[60]

Third, the polarized political environment has contributed to rising social tensions across the country. The Ombudsman's Office of Colombia, an agency charged with monitoring human rights, has expressed its concern over a significant increase in the level of social conflict since the signing of the peace accord in 2016. Protests, including rallies, strikes, and roadblocks, have grown in number and intensity as left-wing sectors have grown frustrated with the slow implementation of the peace accord's main points. Mobilized leftist sectors have demanded changes on issues including education, labor conditions, infrastructure, security, land, and political participation. Protests have been particularly widespread in the areas most affected by the armed conflict, such as the Atlantic and southwestern regions.[61]

Finally, as many of the case studies in this volume also highlight, political polarization has threatened the independence and credibility of the judicial system. Parties on both sides of the political spectrum have accused the judiciary of bias and favoritism due to improper influence by the executive branch. The Centro Democrático has been vocal in its criticism of the Supreme Court's investigation of former President Uribe. Leftist parties have also accused the judiciary of acting in biased ways by opening frivolous investigations.[62] Overall, observers have expressed concern about the process of nominating, selecting, and promoting judges and the behavior of the powerful Attorney General's Office (Fiscalía), which often inconsistently selects and executes investigations. The Colombian judiciary has already been losing credibility owing to serious allegations of impropriety and corruption, and now charges of politicization are further undermining the reputation of this crucial institution.[63]

Remedial Actions

Concerned about the effects that the harsh divide over the peace process is having on the country, a variety of actors, including the Santos administration; the Catholic Church; universities; and grassroots, advocacy, and human rights organizations have devised initiatives to address the problem. These efforts fall into four main categories: conflict resolution and peace mediation activities, communications campaigns to foster tolerance, gatherings and workshops to incentivize political dialogue among the opposing camps, and political leadership.

In the domain of conflict-resolution activities, the Santos administration created the National Council for Peace, Reconciliation, and Coexistence, charged with developing a national program to foster dialogue and bring about reconciliation. An important part of its mission was to share information about the peace accord and its implementation with the public. The Vatican, for its part, offered its good offices to facilitate dialogue between supporters and detractors of the peace accord in an attempt to buttress the process. In a highly symbolic move, Pope Francis traveled to Colombia on an official visit in 2017. During his time in the country, he promoted the peace accord and repeatedly urged Colombian leaders to persevere in their efforts to achieve peace despite "obstacles, differences and varying perspectives."[64]

As for communications initiatives, the Ombudsman's Office of Colombia launched a "no stigmatization" campaign to spread information about the peace process, underscoring the need to foster dialogue among the different sectors of society. The Ombudsman's Office has also conducted workshops and training sessions in rural areas, including former FARC strongholds. In the same vein, through its Episcopal Conference, the Colombian Catholic Church recently launched a nationwide Pedagogy of Peace campaign with activities in schools, community centers, and parishes to teach people the importance of dialogue and compromise. Likewise, the Colombian Agency for Reintegration has undertaken a communications campaign to disseminate information, for instance through several television ads, to promote public acceptance of combatants who are being reintegrated into Colombian society.

Regarding political dialogue, the National University of Colombia organized a successful effort in conjunction with the United Nations Development Programme to create national and regional fora to discuss postconflict scenarios in areas strongly affected by violence.[65] Topics included victims' rights, reconciliation, and illegal crop substitution schemes. Several nongovernmental organizations have promoted other initiatives to foster dialogue. Dejusticia, an influential legal watchdog based in Bogotá, launched a campaign against violence, underscoring the need to remove arms from politics. This campaign included workshops and a series of meetings between human rights and corporate lawyers.

Lastly, in contrast to the overall charged tone of the frontrunners of the 2018 presidential campaign, some presidential hopefuls deliberately strove for a centrist, conciliatory tone. Humberto de la Calle emphasized the benefits of peace and the importance of dialogue and reconciliation in his campaign. Sergio Fajardo and his running mate Claudia López made dialogue and reconciliation cornerstones of their presidential campaign, which was based on pillars including civic culture, education, security, and the fight against corruption. Fajardo's substantive proposals and constructive tone stood in contradistinction to the divisive rhetoric that characterized both the Duque and Petro presidential campaigns.

Notwithstanding the symbolic importance of these activities, initiatives to mitigate polarization have been relatively few and far between and for the most part isolated, piecemeal efforts. Predictably, their effect on diminishing polarization has been rather limited. Repairing the divisive politics engulfing Colombia will require a more concerted, multidimensional, and comprehensive strategy at the national level.

NOTES

I thank Tom Carothers and Andrew O'Donohue for their generous, substantial help in preparing this chapter. I am also grateful to Diana Guiza, Mónica Pachón, Gustavo Gallón, Román Ortiz, Felipe Botero, Carlo Nasi, Christoph Kleber, Helena Rodríguez, Nikolai Stieglitz, Matias Spektor, Richard Youngs, Maria Koomen, and the rest of the participants in the Political Polarization Workshop organized in Barcelona by Carnegie for their suggestions and comments.

1. Murat Somer and Jennifer McCoy, "Déjà Vu? Polarization and Endangered Democracies in the 21st Century," *American Behavioral Scientist* 62, no. 1 (2018): 3–15.

2. Samuel Handlin, "The Logic of Polarizing Populism: State Crises and Polarizaiton in South America," *American Behavioral Scientist* 62, no. 1 (2018): 75–91.

3. Thomas Skidmore, Peter Smith, and James Green, *Modern Latin America*, 8th ed. (Oxford: Oxford University Press, 2014), 185–87.

4. Frank Safford, "Social Aspects of Politics in Nineteenth-Century Spanish America: New Granada, 1825–1850," *Journal of Social History* 5, no. 3 (1972): 344–70.

5. David Bushnell, *The Making of Modern Colombia: A Nation in Spite of Itself* (Berkeley: University of California Press, 1993), 40.

6. David Bushnell, "Politics and Violence in 19th Century Colombia," in *Violence in Colombia: The Contemporary Crisis in Historical Perspective*, ed. Charles Bergquist, Ricardo Peñaranda, and Gonzalo Sánchez (Wilmington, DE: SR Books, 1992), 11–30.

7. Jennifer Holmes and Sheila Amin Gutiérrez de Piñeres, "Violence and the State: Lessons from Colombia," *Small Wars and Insurgencies* 25, no. 2 (2014): 372–403; Harvey Kline, *State Building and Conflict Resolution in Colombia, 1986–1999* (Tuscaloosa: University of Alabama Press, 1999); and Andreas E. Feldmann, "Measuring the Colombian 'Success' Story," *Revista de Ciencia Politica* 32, no. 3 (2012): 739–52.

8. Marco Palacio, *Entre la legitimidad y la violencia, 1875–1944* [Between legitimacy and violence, 1875–1944] (Bogotá: Norma, 1995).

9. Jonathan Hartlyn, "Colombia: The Politics of Violence and Accomodation," in *Developing Countries: Latin America*, ed. Larry Diamond, Juan J. Linz, and Seymour Martin Lipset (London: Adamantine Press, 1989), 290–334.

10. Fernando Cubides, "From Private to Public Violence: The Paramilitaries," in *Violence in Colombia: Waging War and Negotiating Peace*, ed. Charles Bergquist, Ricardo Peñaranda, and Gonzalo Sánchez (Wilmington, DE: SR Books, 2001), 127–48.

11. Daniel Pécaut, *Guerra contra la sociedad* [War against society] (Bogotá: ESPASA, 2002).

12. Centro Nacional de Memoria Histórica, "Estadísticas del conflicto armado en Colombia" [Statistics on the armed conflict in Colombia], 2017 (www.centrodememoriahistorica.gov.co/micrositios/informeGeneral/estadisticas.html).

13. Diego Otero Prada, "Gastos de guerra en Colombia" [Costs of war in Colombia], Fundación Indepaz, 2017 (www.indepaz.org.co/wp-content/uploads/2016/08/portada-los-gastos-de-la-guerra.pdf).

14. Stephen Van Evera, "Hypotheses on Nationalism and War," *International Security* 18, no. 4 (1994): 5–39.

15. Renata Segura and Delphine Mechoulan, "Made in Havana: How Colombia and the FARC Decided to End the War," International Peace Institute, Feburary 2017 (www.ipinst.org/2017/02/how-colombia-and-the-farc-ended-the-war).

16. Negotiations between the Santos administration and the FARC revolved around five major points: comprehensive agrarian reform, political participation, an end to the conflict, drug trafficking, and victims' rights.

17. Román D. Ortiz, "Insurgent Strategies in the Post-Cold War: The Case of the Revolutionary Armed Forces of Colombia," *Studies in Conflict & Terrorism* 25, no. 2 (2002): 127–43; and Andreas E. Feldmann, "Revolutionary Terror in the Colombian Civil War," *Studies in Conflict & Terrorism* 41, no. 10 (2018): 35–52.

18. Mónica Pachón, "Colombia 2008: Success, Dangers and Mistakes of the Policy of Democratic Security in the Uribe Administration," *Revista de Ciencia Política* 29, no. 2 (2010): 327–53.

19. Presidencia de la República de Colombia, *Política de defensa y seguridad democrática* [Defense and democratic security policy], Bogotá, 2003.

20. Nazih Richani, *Systems of Violence: The Political Economy of War and Peace in Colombia*, 2nd ed. (Albany: State University of New York Press, 2013).

21. Socorro Ramírez, "Colombia y sus vecinos" [Colombia and its neighbors], *Revista Nueva Sociedad* 192 (July–August 2004), 144–56; and Jonathan D. Rosen, *The Losing War: Plan Colombia and Beyond* (Albany: State University of New York Press, 2014).

22. Holmes and Piñeres, "Violence and the State."

23. María Victoria Llorente and Jeremy McDermott, "Colombia's Lessons for Mexico," in *One Goal, Two Struggles: Confronting Crime and Violence in Mexico and Colombia*, ed. Cynthia Arnson, Eric Olson, and Christine Zaino, Woodrow Wilson Center Reports on the Americas No. 32. (Washington, DC: Woodrow Wilson Center, 2014), 1–37.

24. Enzo Nussio, "Learning from Shortcomings: The Demobilisation of Paramilitaries in Colombia," *Journal of Peacebuilding & Development* 6, no. 2 (2011): 88–92.

25. The annual homicide rate dropped from 25,681 in 2002 to 17,459 in 2010. World Bank, "International Homicides" (https://data.worldbank.org/indicator/VC.IHR.PSRC.P5?locations=CO); and United Nations Office on Drugs and Crime, "Colombia Coca Cultivation Survey," 2013 (www.unodc.org/documents/crop-monitoring/Colombia/Colombia_Coca_Cultivation_Survey_2012_web .pdf).

26. Human Rights Watch, *Paramilitaries' Heirs: The New Face of Violence in Colombia* (New York: Human Rights Watch, 2010).

27. Andreas E. Feldmann and Victor Hinojosa, "Terrorism in Colombia: Logic and Sources of a Multidimensional and Ubiquitous Political Phenomenon," *Terrorism and Political Violence* 21, no. 1 (2009): 42–61.

28. Carlo Nasi and Monica Hurtado, "Las elecciones presidenciales del 2014 y las negociaciones de paz con las FARC: Cuando la estrategia de polarizar no basta para ganar" [The presidential elections of 2014 and the peace negotiations with the FARC: When the strategy of polarizing is not enough to win], in *Polarización y posconflicto: Las elecciones nacionales y locales en Colombia, 2014–2017* [Polarization and postconflict: The local and national elections in Colombia, 2014–2017], ed. Felipe Botero, Miguel García Sánchez, and Laura Wills-Otero (Bogotá: Universidad de los Andes, 2018), 229–68.

29. Plataforma Colombiana de Derechos Humanos, "El embrujo autoritario: Primer año de gobierno de Álvaro Uribe Vélez" [The authoritarian charm: The first year of the government of Álvaro Uribe Vélez], 2003 (http://pdba.georgetown .edu/Security/citizensecurity/Colombia/evaluaciones/primeranoUribe.pdf).

30. Llorente and McDermott, "Colombia's Lessons."

31. Nasi and Hurtado, "Las elecciones presidenciales."

32. The turnout in the referendum was only 37 percent, matching that of Colombian national elections in the recent past.

33. Ana Arjona, "War Dynamics and the No Vote in the Colombian Referendum," Political Violence @ a Glance, October 20, 2016 (http://political violenceataglance.org/2016/10/20/war-dynamics-and-the-no-vote-in-the-colom bian-referendum/).

34. Segura and Mechoulan, "Made in Havana."

35. Andreas E. Feldmann, "Will Colombia's Peace Accord Boost Its Democracy?," Carnegie Endowment for International Peace, Rising Democracy Network, July 13, 2017 (https://carnegieendowment.org/files/RDN_Feldman_Colum bia_07132017.pdf); and Kyle Johnson, "The Uncertainty of Peace in Colombia," International Crisis Group, February 1, 2017 (https://colombiareports.com/un certainty-peace-colombia/).

36. "Damned Is the Peacemaker," *The Economist*, July 28, 2018 (www.econo mist.com/the-americas/2018/07/28/history-will-judge-colombias-outgoing-presi dent-kindly).

37. Colombia is a relatively homogenous country. Most the population is of mestizo origin. Indigenous people represent 3.4 percent and blacks 10.3 percent of the population. The overwhelming majority of the population is Catholic. See Skidmore, Smith, and Green, *Modern Latin America*, 193.

38. Frank Safford and Marco Palacios, *Colombia: País fragmentado, sociedad dividida* [Colombia: Fragmented country, divided society] (Bogotá: Norma, 2002).

39. Duque obtained 39 percent and Petro 25 percent of the vote. Fajardo finished a close third with 23 percent and de la Calle 2 percent. Germán Vargas Lleras, seen as a staunch representative of the Conservative Party, got 7 percent. See "Así quedaron las fuerzas para la segunda vuelta presidencial" [Thus remained the forces for the presidential run-off], *El Tiempo*, June 1, 2018 (www.eltiempo.com/elec ciones-colombia-2018/presidenciales/que-partidos-apoyan-a-ivan-duque-y-gustavo -petro-en-la-segunda-vuelta-225632).

40. "El Centro Democrático ganó en 24 de los 32 departamentos y 19 capitales" [Centro Democrático won in 24 of the 32 departments and 19 capitals], *El Tiempo*, June 17, 2018 (www.eltiempo.com/elecciones-colombia-2018/presidenciales/analisis -de-la-segunda-vuelta-por-regiones-y-capitales-231930).

41. "Colombia Rejects Venezuela as Guarantor of Peace Talks with ELN Rebels," Reuters, September 27, 2018 (www.reuters.com/article/us-colombia -rebels-venezuela/colombia-rejects-venezuela-as-guarantor-of-peace-talks-with -eln-rebels-idUSKCN1M72H0).

42. Lorena Arboleda, "Mitos y realidades de Iván Duque y Gustavo Petro" [Myths and realities about Iván Duque and Gustavo Petro], *El Espectador,* June 7, 2018 (www.elespectador.com/elecciones-2018/noticias/politica/mitos-y-reali dades-de-ivan-duque-y-gustavo-petro-articulo-792936).

43. José Miguel Vivanco, "Colombia Should Think Twice Before Extraditing a Former FARC Commander," *El Tiempo,* May 7, 2018 (www.hrw.org/ news/2018/05/07/colombia-should-think-twice-extraditing-former-farc-comman der). Vivanco's portrayal of the JEP is not shared by most Colombian human rights nongovernmental organizations, who do not find it excessively forbearing.

44. The accord granted amnesty to 7,405 guerrillas, including 1,405 who were released from prison. See "Colombia Approves Amnesty Agreed in FARC Peace Deal," *BBC World,* December 28, 2016 (www.bbc.com/news/world-latin-america -38455493). Those found guilty will receive sentences ranging from two to eight years of restricted liberty but not jail time. Those who refuse to confess will not enjoy this benefit. See República de Colombia, "Acuerdo Final Para La Terminación Del Conflicto y La Construcción de una Paz Estable y Duradera" [Final accord for the termination of the conflict and construction of a stable and durable peace], point 5, 164–67 (www.altocomisionadoparalapaz.gov.co/procesos-y-conversaciones/Pa ginas/Texto-completo-del-Acuerdo-Final-para-la-Terminacion-del-conflicto.aspx).

45. Comisión Histórica del Conflicto y sus Víctimas, *Contribución al enten- dimiento del conflicto armado en Colombia* [Commission for the understanding of the armed conflict in Colombia] (Bogotá: Ediciones Desde Abajo, 2015).

46. A case in point is the famous False Positives (Falsos Positivos) scandal. During the Uribe administration, security forces executed shantytown youngsters and passed them off as guerrilla fighters to claim bounties and publicize the success of the DSP. The revelation of this scandal greatly tainted President Uribe's tenure and shattered public trust in the Colombian Armed Forces. See "Colombia: Prosecution of False Positive Cases under the Special Jurisdiction for Peace," Human Rights Watch, March 28, 2016 (www.hrw.org/news/2016/03/28/colombia-pros ecution-false-positive-cases-under-special-jurisdiction-peace#). Beyond some lukewarm apologies and promises to "never again" repeat these unlawful actions, the FARC—and other parties—have failed to sincerely acknowledge their responsibility and repent for their actions.

47. Nicolás Galvis Ramírez and others, "Barómetro de las Américas Colombia 2016: Paz, posconflicto y reconciliación" [Barometer of the Americas, Colombia 2016: Peace, post conflict, and reconciliation], Observatorio de la Democracia, 2016.

48. Johnson, "The Uncertainty of Peace in Colombia."

49. José Miguel Vivanco, the director of Human Rights Watch's Americas Division, criticized the accord and warned against the dangers of impunity in an open letter to President Santos. Vivanco was also a very vocal opponent of the previous accord with the AUC. See Human Rights Watch, "Carta al Presidente Santos sobre la Ley de Amnistía" [Letter to President Santos about the amnesty law], De-

cember 25, 2016 (www.hrw.org/es/news/2016/12/25/carta-al-presidente-santos-sobre-la-ley-de-amnistia).

50. República de Colombia, "Acuerdo Final" [Final accord], 35–45.

51. "The Contenders to Succeed Colombia's Peacemaking President," *The Economist*, March 15, 2018 (www.economist.com/the-americas/2018/03/15/the-contenders-to-succeed-colombias-peacemaking-president).

52. The rationale for land redistribution is that the armed conflict fostered systematic land grabs across rural Colombia. See Francisco Gutiérrez Sanín and Jenniffer Vargas Reina, eds., "Front Matter," in *El despojo paramilitar y su variación: ¿Quiénes, cómo, por qué?* [The paramilitary dispossession and its variation: Who, how, why?] (Bogotá: Editorial Universidad Del Rosario: 2016), i–vi. Today's provincial elites are the primary beneficiaries of these land grabs, which also generated massive population displacement in the country. See Stefanie Engel and Ana María Ibáñez, "Displacement Due to Violence in Colombia: A Household-Level Analysis," *Economic Development and Cultural Change* 55, no. 2 (2007): 335–65.

53. Some landed elites recently formed consortiums with links to shadowy armed organizations, in particularly paramilitary groups. The oil palm industry is a case in point. See Carlos Gómez, Luis Sánchez Ayala, and Gonzalo Vargas, "Armed Conflict, Land Grabs and Primitive Accumulation in Colombia: Micro Processes, Macro Trends and the Puzzles in Between," *The Journal of Peasant Studies* 42, no. 2 (2015): 255–74.

54. Feldmann, "Will Colombia's Peace Accord Boost Its Democracy?"

55. In 2016, the Colombian Congress approved 51 laws and one administrative act (a constitutional amendment), 11 of them on substantive social issues such as housing, early childhood, poverty alleviation, and labor, and four others providing the legal framework for the peace accord. These included laws for the creation of transition cantonments for demobilized FARC members, an agreement for the deployment of UN peacekeeping forces, the creation of Special Legislation for Peace, and the terms for a referendum on the final accord.

56. Felipe Botero, Gary W. Hoskin, and Mónica Pachón, "On Form and Substance: An Assessment of Electoral Democracy in Colombia," *Revista de Ciencia Política* 30, no. 1 (2010): 41–64.

57. "Bogotá Blast: Deadly Car Bomb Kills 20 in Colombian Capital," *BBC*, January 18, 2019 (www.bbc.com/news/world-latin-america-46904683).

58. United Nations High Commissioner for Human Rights, "Annual Report of the United Nations High Commissioner for Human Rights on the Situation of Human Rights in Colombia," A/HRC/37/3Add.3, March 2, 2018 (https://reliefweb.int/report/colombia/annual-report-united-nations-high-commissioner-human-rights-situation-human-rights-0).

59. In 2017, one journalist was murdered, while in 2018 two were killed. See Committee to Protect Journalists, "Journalists Killed in Colombia Since 1992" (https://cpj.org/americas/colombia/).

60. Human Rights Watch strongly criticized Senator Uribe's continued lashing

out "against journalists and other critics, accusing them, without evidence, of being complicit with guerrilla groups." See Human Rights Watch, "Colombia: Events of 2017" (www.hrw.org/world-report/2018/country-chapters/colombia).

61. Defensoría del Pueblo Colombia, "Informe del Defensor del Pueblo al Congreso" [Report of ombudsman to the Congress], 2017 (www.defensoria.gov.co/public/pdf/XXV-Informe-del-Defensor-del-Pueblo-al-Congreso.pdf).

62. "¿Está politizada la justicia en Colombia?" [Is justice politicized in Colombia?], *El País*, August 1, 2018 (www.elpais.com.co/politica/esta-politizada-la-justicia-en-colombia.html).

63. The press has unearthed that the chief prosecutor (*Fiscal General*), Néstor Humberto Martínez, may be involved in the cover-up of a major bribe scandal regarding a tender by Odebrecht. See Joshua Goodman, "New Allegations that Colombia Prosecutor Covered Up Bribes," 570 News, November 14, 2018 (www.570news.com/2018/11/14/new-allegations-that-colombia-prosecutor-covered-up-bribes/).

64. Wes Michael Tomaselli, "Pope Francis Appeals for Reconciliation in War-Scarred Colombia," *Washington Post*, September 7, 2017 (www.washingtonpost.com/world/the_americas/pope-francis-appeals-for-reconciliation-in-war-scarred-colombia/2017/09/07/a1ef2618-9327-11e7-8482-8dc9a7af29f9_story.html).

65. Helen Murphy and Luis Jaime Acosta, "Colombian Academic Seeks to Heal Divided Nation as President," Reuters, March 2, 2018 (www.reuters.com/article/us-colombia-election-fajardo/colombian-academic-seeks-to-heal-divided-nation-as-president-idUSKCN1GE2NU).

SEVEN

Winner Takes All: Elite Power Struggles and Polarization in Bangladesh

NAOMI HOSSAIN

Bangladesh has been experiencing an intensifying pattern of polarization between the two camps that have dominated the country's politics since the return to multiparty competition in 1991. The signs of this polarization include violent political competition, parliamentary and election boycotts by the opposition, and the politicization of key institutions by the ruling party. By the mid-2000s, the political divide had become so intense that the military backed a nonparty caretaker government (NPCG) in 2007–08 to halt electoral politics and attempt to restart politics on a less divisive basis.

Although the signs of Bangladesh's political divide are highly visible, its origins and nature are not immediately evident. Polarization is not new in the country's violently contentious political history, but its trajectory in recent years poses a puzzle. Why has the two-party divide led to such intense political anger and conflict? Is the divide merely an instrumental political one used by one side or the other to attract or rally voters, or is it a reflection of deeper sociopolitical divisions regarding not just party choices, but also the fundamentals of national identity?

This chapter argues that the origins of polarization in Bangladesh do not lie in any deep-rooted or identity-based difference between the opposing sides. A political history featuring two bloody partitions reduced the importance of religious, ethnic, and social differences within and between the elite and the masses in the past half-century. There are no important regional divisions in this small, relatively undifferentiated land. A robust, enduring elite consensus on economic and human development has underpinned the country's unexpected economic successes. Bangladesh presents a case where polarization—a substantial and growing distance between the main political actors and their supporters over a period of nearly thirty years—is of almost purely political origins. That is, divisions between the two main political parties have been almost entirely instrumental, having grown out of competition over who holds political power, rather than over how power is wielded or on whose behalf.

Although polarization originally emerged as the product of elite power struggles rather than important latent ideological or social differences, in the past five years, polarization has taken on a new, or rather a renewed, focus on the role of religion in public life. This issue has brought to the surface long-simmering differences with respect to the role of religion in the nation and state. The recent overdue (albeit imperfect) process of transitional justice contributed to these divisions, resulting in a toxic medley of popular movements, partisan competition, radical Islamism, and terrorist activity. The effort to contain or defuse these schisms has intensified the drive by the ruling party, the Awami League (AL), to expand its power over state institutions, politics, and civil society.

Moreover, the design and functioning of the country's political institutions have reinforced and exacerbated the process of polarization. The weakness of checks and balances in particular has dramatically raised the stakes of political competition, as electoral victors can ride roughshod over their opponents. Efforts to address this polarization or mitigate its effects, above all the military intervention of 2007–08, have arguably made it worse. Yet the end of this process of polarization may now be in sight—not because political differences have been defused or narrowed, but because in this winner-takes-all polity, a single winner has emerged in the past decade. Since coming to power in 2009, the AL, the nationalist party that led the country's struggle for independence, has consolidated its control over Bangladeshi society and state institutions.

Roots

Two catch-all parties, the AL and the Bangladesh Nationalist Party (BNP), emerged as the main players after multiparty competition was established in 1991. Since then, the two have alternated in power in a series of elections in which the incumbent never once gave up power without either an intense struggle or an intervention backed by potential force.[1] As figure 7-1 shows, the two main parties captured a growing share of the popular vote, incorporating both small and other significant parties into the alliances they dominated. The share of parliamentary seats occupied by these two parties rose from just above 50 percent in the early 1990s to almost 90 percent by 2008.[2]

This two-party system has yielded some of the benefits of what Adrienne LeBas terms "generative conflict,"[3] as the parties competed for votes on the basis of performance with respect to basic public service delivery, a matter on which a strong elite consensus developed across parties and sectors. Yet almost three decades of competitive politics have been marked by

Figure 7-1. **Vote Shares of Four Largest Parties, 1991–2008**

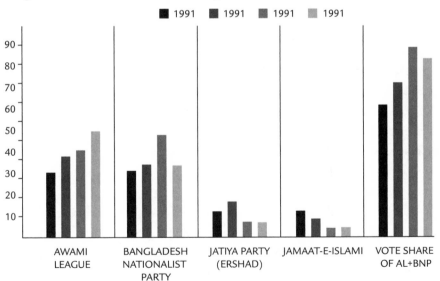

Source: Author's figure, based on reports from the Bangladesh Election Commission (www.ecs.gov.bd/category/publications). Note: This figure excludes the 2014 elections, which the BNP boycotted, as well as the 2018 elections, which were not free or fair.

a significant increase in adverse political polarization. This is apparent in high levels of political violence, including the use of mass strikes (*hartals*) as a matter of routine partisan competition, sanctioned and institutionalized in political culture by a century of anticolonial struggle and democratic movements. It further manifests itself in the inability of opposing groups to engage in key processes of governance such as legislation, maintenance of law and order, policymaking, and political transitions. Key institutions of state and society are also polarized through the "partyarchal" politicization of the bureaucracy, the media, civil society groups, trade unions, and business organizations.[4]

That the hostility between the two major parties yields unproductive responses to the many challenges facing this vast, densely packed population is an article of faith among observers of Bangladeshi politics. Calls to "rise above politics" are common, and "politicization" is widely regarded as a public bad. Both parties agree, at least in principle, that parliamentary democracy should be the basis for political governance, and yet elite competition for political power in Bangladesh has been polarized and polarizing, a high-stakes game of winner-takes-all, with the logic to win at all costs.

Until around 2013, when the struggles over the transitional justice effort by the AL government reignited historic debates over national identity, this polarization was chiefly between parties and their leaders. Voting behavior in Bangladesh suggested a large political center-ground. It is not yet clear whether political polarization will generate the kinds of ideological and social distance in the wider society seen in highly polarized polities elsewhere. In a recent article, Tahmina Rahman argues that rising polarization over competing views of national identity has in fact fueled polarization at the mass level and divided Bangladeshi society.[5] Yet as the following analysis will show, the homogeneity of the population tends to militate against such broad divisions.

Despite its high visibility, the full nature of this political polarization is uncertain. Are the two opposition camps simply political groupings with no deep differences that are locked in a fight over political power, or do they represent groupings with a deeper and genuinely irreconcilable divide? Any such division is not easily located in any profound social fissures within this comparatively homogenous society, and no political party has successfully politicized any perceived social differences based on class, region, or status.

The absence of important social differences reflects the political history of Bangladesh, the arc of which has tended toward erasing or eradicating structural social differences in an attack on the social foundations of economic and political subjugation. "Foreign" elites and their supporters were removed or neutralized in a two-stage partition, first from West Bengal and India in 1947, and then from Pakistan in 1971. Mushtaq Khan views these partitions as the outcome of conflicts over purely material matters, as the result of "elites' inability to agree about the distribution of rents."[6] But social distinctions between the elite and the masses always mattered for political mobilization and organization, with the foreignness of ruling elites framed as the reason for their inability to rule in the interests of the mainly Bengali-speaking Muslim rural masses. From the time of independence in 1971, political elites (regardless of partisan affiliation) have tended to deny the existence of primordial distinctions within society in an effort to assert their legitimacy. They have emphasized a common identity and their own affinity with the masses as the basis for national integration.[7] The national elite is itself homogenous and closely knit, interrelated through multiple bonds of kinship, marriage, and place as well as common socializing experiences of education and culture.

Conventional left-right ideological differences also fail to explain Bangladesh's political polarization. The AL and the BNP both occupy a broad centrist position in Bangladeshi political ideology. Early differences with respect to left-right orientation disappeared when the AL embraced the market in 1996, abandoning the "socialistic" principles it had adopted as a tactical response to postwar radicalism rather than out of conviction or as a result of class mobilization. Both parties have historically represented a range of staunchly middle- and upper-class interests, from the rich peasantry that founded the AL in 1949 to the industrial and state elites that founded the BNP to civilianize military rule in 1978.[8]

The most credible source of ideological difference relates to the parties' ideologies of nationhood. As M. Moniruzzaman notes, the AL and BNP have diverged with respect to whether national identity is founded on Bengali cultural identity and language, as the AL has historically framed it, or on language and territory, as the BNP argues. They also disagree over whether the state should be secular, as stipulated in the constitution established under AL rule, or whether Islam should be the religion of the state, as most other parties believe. Both parties place great weight on their own versions of nationalist ideology. Given that former AL leader and nationalist hero Sheikh Mujibur Rahman is regarded as the founding father of Bangladesh—and that the AL's current leader, Sheikh Hasina, is his daughter—the AL claims undisputed leadership of the independence struggle. The importance of this symbol of nationhood is so great, however, that the BNP has also attempted to assert its more meager claims on the part of its founder, Ziaur Rahman, a general and freedom fighter in the liberation war.

Yet even though the parties differ in their ideologies of nationhood in ways that sharply divide elites, this difference has not to date proved substantial enough to constitute the root of a genuinely identity-based pattern of polarization among the wider population. Bangladeshi scholars and politicos perceive ideological differences regarding national identity and the liberation struggle to be of great and enduring significance, but to the outsider they can appear slight. These differences sometimes have been trivialized as nothing more than personal antagonisms between two women leaders seeking vengeance for the traumas of political violence in their own lives and families.

Enduring tensions around the role of religion in Bengali Muslim identity and in public life periodically resurface to intensify partisan differences. These tensions were amplified most recently through the prosecution of Islamic party leaders starting in 2009 for crimes committed during the liberation war.[9] The trials gave rise in 2013 to the iconic Shahbag movement, which demanded capital punishment for the convicted war criminals in the name of defending secular values. This movement was met in turn by an equally disruptive counter-movement orchestrated by well-organized groups under the Hefazat Islamist platform. A series of terror attacks and the mass murder of foreigners and champions of free speech by radical Islamist groups at this time heightened tensions around the issue of secularism. The security crisis provoked by the 2016 Holey Café attack arguably created space for extralegal measures against the government's political opponents more generally.[10]

Yet differences over the issue of religion have not generated a deep and polarizing cleavage in Bangladesh. As the role of religion and associated social matters have taken a more dominant position in national politics since 2008, the AL has moved toward the center-ground with respect to the role of religion in public life. By easing its commitment to secularism, the party has aimed to incorporate a customarily more devout rural majority as well as a newly Islamicized urban middle class into its support base.[11]

In short, political polarization in Bangladesh is an almost purely political phenomenon; it reflects nothing but a struggle between competing elite groups over who gets to hold, or hold on to, political power.[12] This competition is frequently seen in personalistic terms, as "not ideological at all but personal, in the form of the enmity between the 'two begums'—party leaders Sheikh Hasina [of the AL] and Khaleda Zia [of the BNP]."[13] Differing conceptions of national identity may deepen this polarization at different moments, but elite power struggles lie at the root of political conflict.

Trajectory

Polarization of an extreme and confrontational nature is not a new feature of Bangladeshi politics. Moments of rupture and political settlement have followed periods of widening political divisions at key historical junctures. These ruptures divide Bangladeshi history into four primary periods, each with its own defining conflict. Growing political divisions culminated in the founding of independent Bangladesh in 1971. Subsequently, political instability wracked the new nation and peaked with the assassination of Sheikh Mujib and a series of military coups in 1975, followed by fifteen years of military rule. Between 1991 and 2007, the country saw fierce but balanced competition between the AL and BNP in multiparty elections. Since 2008, the AL has emerged as the dominant party, with growing power over state institutions, politics, and civil society. Likewise, the drivers of polarization have differed significantly across historical periods. Religious and ethnic divisions served as the dominant source of political conflict until 1971, while economic crisis and weak institutions fomented discord in the early years after Bengali independence. Since the return to multiparty elections in 1991, however, personalistic political competition has led polarization to reach new heights.

From East Bengal to East Pakistan

Until the achievement of Bengali independence in 1971, political conflict arose primarily between Bengali Muslims and perceived outsiders, rather than among Bengali Muslims themselves. The Muslim League, which fought for a Muslim state to be carved out of British India, was founded in Dhaka, and Bengali Muslim politicians were at the forefront of the struggles that established the state of Pakistan. In the period before the partition of India in 1947, this eastern part of the province of Bengal featured prominently in the communal divisions, including the deadly Noakhali riots of 1946, in which thousands of people were killed; the partition itself then led to the deaths of a million people and the displacement of 15 million more.[14]

After partition, the newly created dominion of Pakistan contained modern-day Bangladesh and Pakistan, yet political and economic power was disproportionately concentrated in the west. Political divisions between Bengalis in the east and the Pakistani elite in the west of the country emerged first with the Language Movement of 1954, when the military regime killed Bengali students protesting a policy to install Urdu as the national language. Bengali politicians were prominent in the democracy struggles through the 1960s and were instrumental in pushing for Pakistan's first democratic elections, held in 1970. Bengalis argued that the west dominated state and private investment and opportunities, while in the east, the agrarian economy stagnated and the local elite saw few benefits from development.

Political differences came to a head in the weeks before the 1970 general election, when one of the deadliest tropical storms in world history struck Bhola, in the Bay of Bengal, killing around 300,000 people, mostly peasants and fisherfolk. The callous and delayed response of the Pakistani officials was seen as an outrage in the east and became a central campaign issue. Sheikh Mujibur Rahman's AL overwhelmingly won the election in what one observer described as "possibly the greatest victory of any party in a free and contested election anywhere."[15] The West Pakistani elite had no intention of allowing a Bengali-majority party to rule, and the impasse ended in a declaration of Bengali independence, a military crackdown in the east, and a civil war that ended in 1971 when a vast refugee crisis triggered Indian intervention on the side of the Bengalis.

It should be noted that the international community denied Bangladesh justice for the atrocities of a war widely seen as genocidal in intent. The United States notoriously turned a blind eye to Pakistan's war crimes during the conflict, and subsequently it was disinclined to permit the poor and aid-dependent new nation to hold its ally to account, using its leverage over food and multilateral aid to make its point.[16] To a significant extent, the divisions that have emerged in the past ten years reflect the long festering of old war wounds.

Postwar Crisis and Military Rule, 1971 to 1990

Economic crisis, famine, and increasing radicalization on the left rudely curtailed a brief period of apparent unity after the achievement of nationhood in 1971. This period of polarization reflected the unresolved tensions between the bourgeois–rich peasant supporters of the AL and the radicalized left, including in the army and the student population, which the euphoria of the liberation struggle had temporarily suppressed. By 1974, the AL government, which had two years earlier been elected with a huge popular mandate, was using paramilitary forces to fight leftist guerrilla groups, placing hungry rural migrants in camps, and struggling for its political and economic survival. By 1975, the AL had ended Bangladesh's democratic experiment: the constitution had been amended to allow a single-party state, incorporating peasant and worker groups into the old AL, and to establish a presidential system.

After 1975, a series of coups and countercoups ushered in a period of military regimes presided over by generals and civilianized military regimes that lasted until 1990. In August 1975, military officers staged a coup and brutally assassinated the nationalist hero Sheikh Mujibur Rahman, now known as Bangabandhu (or "Friend of the Bengalis"), along with all of the members of his family present at the time.[17] In the fifteen years that followed, the military forcibly silenced political opposition, first through an aggressive campaign to suppress and eradicate leftists and neutralize the AL, and later through a soft form of authoritarian rule that incorporated and contained potential political opponents. The BNP emerged during the first part of this regime in the late 1970s. Industrialists and civilian and military bureaucratic elites along the lines of the old Pakistani elite reentered national politics, along with some of the religious right that had opposed national independence and collaborated with the Pakistanis during the 1971 war.

Multiparty Elections and the Ratcheting up of Political Competition, 1991 to 2007

In the democratic or multiparty period after 1991, voters showed a willingness to hold governments to account, ejecting incumbents whenever feasible. However, weak state institutions, weakly institutionalized political parties, and fundamentally clientelistic politics prevented democratic norms from taking root. The winner-takes-all form of rule also meant that with each election, the parties grew ever more willing to subvert due process to retain or capture power.

By 1990, the movement for democracy had gathered pace, and in a rare moment of unity, the AL, BNP, and civil society came together to oust the former General H. M. Ershad and his Jatiya Party from power. This movement marked the beginning of the long trajectory of confrontation that has brought polarization to its current level, as the AL and the BNP used electoral and extrainstitutional means to fight an increasingly divisive, no-holds-barred struggle for power. This process of political polarization originated in the democratic competition between the two parties, which were established as the main players in 1991 and which (until 2006) alternated in power.

In 1991, the BNP won Bangladesh's first free and fair multiparty election, securing a small share of the vote but a larger proportion of seats thanks to the first-past-the-post system. The BNP's victory came as a shock to the AL, which had assumed that the end of military rule would pave the way for it to take power. Indeed, at the time many observers saw the AL as the natural party of government. After its victory, the BNP formed a governing alliance with the Jamaat-e-Islami, an Islamist party that was comparatively moderate despite its history of opposing independence from Pakistan and the secular nationalism of the liberation struggle. In another rare moment of agreement, the main parties passed a constitutional amendment replacing the presidential system, inherited from the period of military rule, with the original parliamentary system. The BNP then sought to translate its incumbency into a second term in power by rigging the 1996 election. This elicited an election boycott by the AL, which had been using movement tactics to push for the prime minister, Begum Khaleda Zia, to resign and for elections to be held under a caretaker government since 1994. In the large and wide-ranging backlash against the BNP, even the ostensibly nonpolitical civil service and civil society organizations famously took a stand against its political maneuverings.[18]

In response to the 1996 election crisis, the 14th Constitutional Amendment was introduced to allow for a nonparty interim caretaker government to oversee the election and the political transition. This NPCG would consist of senior members of the judiciary and respected nonpartisan leaders of civil society and the business community. This interim regime presided over a second election in 1996, in which the AL emerged victorious. The electorate then ejected the AL in the 2001 election, and the BNP again came to power. During its term in office, the BNP then illustrated how well it had learned the rules of this political game by packing the upper echelons of the judiciary with its own candidates. The increasing rancor of politics amounted to what Harry Blair described as a "metastasizing pathology," with symptoms that included the criminalization of politics, a decline in human security, and significant disruption to economic and social life. As the 2006 election drew near, political violence erupted on the streets between AL and BNP supporters. There was also a sharp rise in extremist violence at this time, with a nationwide campaign of bombing led by an Islamic group that appeared to have at least the tacit support of the ruling BNP, keen to add "an active Islamic militant tone to the alliance they had built with the Jamaat from the 2001 election onward."[19]

The Extended Caretaker Regime and Its Aftermath, 2007 to the Present

The military intervention of 2007—though intended to temper political divisions—inadvertently gave rise to a new period of heightened polarization by upsetting the delicate balance of power between the AL and BNP. In response to rising violence and perceptions that the election commission was complicit in the BNP's effort to steal the 2006 election, a military-backed caretaker government took power in January 2007. It had the expressed aim of cleaning up Bangladeshi politics and of staying in power until it achieved this objective. What came to be known popularly as the "Minus Two" strategy was widely seen to be aimed at removing the "begums" or leaders of both parties, and it received the support of a broad cross-section of the social, economic, and civilian and military bureaucratic elites, as well as the international community. The caretaker government also launched a campaign over a two-year period to root out corruption by prosecuting politicians from both camps and reforming the political parties, judiciary, and election commission, including through the establishment of a new electronic voter registration system. The international community and aid donors appeared satisfied with the results of the reform, and elections were held in late 2008. The political reforms were incomplete, however, and while the BNP was greatly weakened by the imprisonment of its members and other forms of accountability for the crimes of its 2001–06 tenure, the AL was less badly affected and won the election with a resounding mandate.[20]

Since 2008, the AL has become an increasingly dominant force in Bangladeshi politics. It has maintained this dominance despite a series of security crises involving a revolt within the army, a campaign of terror against foreigners and secularists, and a major, organized, Islamist backlash against the conviction of war criminals from the Jamaat-e-Islami party. The constitutional amendment allowing for the creation of caretaker governments was removed in 2011, with the courts facing political pressure from the AL to support this constitutional revision.[21] In what may have been a major political miscalculation, but which more likely reflected the party's organizational weakness and lack of alternative political strategies, the BNP boycotted the 2014 election, which was contested only by the AL and a dissident section of the Jatiya Party. Unlike in 2006, when the international community had pushed the military into acting to prevent what was seen as an illegitimate or unopposed election, there was no such response in 2014, or at least, it was not effective in triggering military intervention. The AL has presided over a period of high economic growth and significant investments in social protection, human development, and infrastructure, yet it has also gained growing control over state institutions and civil society.[22]

The increasing dominance of the AL is likely to mean the continued weakening of the BNP and enable suppression of the symptoms of political polarization, such as political violence, extremist radicalization, and *hartals*. It seems unlikely, however, that a free and fair election will be held in the near future. The imprisonment of Begum Khaleda Zia in February 2018 on corruption charges, thereby preventing her from leading the BNP's election campaign, has more or less guaranteed that the AL will have the upper hand in political competition. At the same time, the AL government has been working to neutralize or incorporate the religious right within this new political settlement and has placed great emphasis on economic growth and development to shore up its legitimacy with the wider population. Such a settlement may well be a fragile one. In the absence of a wider, more strategic distribution of the benefits of power across the political elite, including protections from prosecution when out of power, the movement politics that are so ingrained in Bangladeshi political culture could easily destabilize it.

The December 2018 election returned the AL government with an overwhelming parliamentary majority and over 95 percent of the contested seats in parliament, in what has been widely acknowledged as a crudely rigged election. The BNP competed, but from a greatly weakened base, with many activists in prison or too intimidated to campaign or monitor polling booths. The media reported the worst excesses of the election campaign, but neither domestic nor international pressure was strong enough to seriously threaten the nullification of the election results. Within Bangladesh, a common view is that the AL may well have won a fair election, given the strength of the economy and weakness of the BNP. On this view, the extreme repression of the opposition witnessed in many constituencies reflects a political leadership unable to control the police and other administrative officials who have been fully incorporated within the party-state system.

Consequences

Political polarization in Bangladesh has had three principal ramifications: rising political violence, an increasing reliance on extrainstitutional strategies of political contestation such as parliamentary or election boycotts, and the politicization of key state and societal institutions.

The most overt adverse consequence of Bangladesh's political polarization since 1991 has been the high levels of political violence. Between 1991 and 2006, almost 5,000 incidents of political violence were recorded; between 2001 and 2006 alone, these incidents cost 1,501 lives and caused 38,690 injuries. Reflecting the intensification of polarization, in January 2015 alone, over 100 people were killed in political violence or extrajudicial killings, and over a thousand vehicles were firebombed during BNP-led protests against the 2014 election.[23]

With comparatively little space for meaningful opposition politics within the parliamentary system, such as parliamentary boycotts to assert opposition to government policy, political polarization has led both main parties to rely on the *hartal* or all-out strike as their main repertoire for political action when in opposition. The *hartal* emerged in the anticolonial movement and through the country's long history of antisystemic struggles has come to be institutionalized as an effective political tactic. Unlike a labor strike, the success of a *hartal* depends on the capacity of opposition party activists to disrupt economic and social life sufficiently long or frequently to force the ruling party into an accommodation of some kind— usually to give up power or yield on a particular policy, generally one of concern more to the opposition party than to the wider society. *Hartals* can be extremely violent and frequently cause loss of life, injury, and damage to public and private property. Episodes of *hartal* are thought to inflict high costs on education, livelihoods, and the economy. Although the anticolonial and democratic struggles generally drew wide social support, in the democratic period *hartals* have relied more on people's fear of violence if they attempt to break the strike. The capacity for disruption relies on threatened or actual violence against people, vehicles, and organizations that attempt to maintain normal patterns of life, and so depends ultimately on whether opposition party cadres are strong enough to control the streets.

In recent years, however, the success of *hartals*, measured in terms of their disruption of daily life, has declined significantly. The frequent calling of *hartals* by an enfeebled BNP since 2009 appears to have weakened their potency: in the past few years, most *hartals* have been ignored, and for most people, everyday life has continued as usual. Although the tactic has been used chiefly by the AL or BNP while in opposition, no doubt because their effectiveness depends on the ability to mobilize or threaten violence at scale, the past decade has also seen Islamist parties call strikes, though with limited success. Overall, the *hartal* appears to have had its day.

Alternative repertoires of political action are now called for but have yet to emerge.[24]

Finally, polarization has resulted in an all-out effort to deny the opposition space to compete politically. In addition to suppressing the BNP, the AL has also turned state institutions against the Jamaat-e-Islami. Jamaat leaders have been convicted of and hanged for their roles in war crimes in 1971, in what many observers view as a flawed legal process strongly influenced by partisan political considerations. There is, however, compelling evidence of complicity in such crimes, and capital punishment has enjoyed wide public support as part of a long overdue process of transitional justice. Successive oppositions have boycotted parliament or elections, aiming to render the country ungovernable until their demands are met. At the same time, political polarization has divided Bangladeshi society and led to the entrenchment of partisan identities.[25] It has been accompanied by strong pressure on civil society groups and the media to align with the ruling party and resulted in shrinking civic space.

In the febrile global context of Salafist Islamic ideology and mobilization, the effective closure of political space for moderate Islam has also helped pave the way for the rise of more extremist Islamism in national politics, most notably the Hefazat platform. Hefazat, which is a broad platform of Islamist groups rather than a political party, emerged first in 2011 in reaction to gender equality principles in the AL government's policy on women's development. Hefazat then burst onto the political scene with a massive demonstration in Dhaka in 2013, said to have drawn around half a million supporters. The demonstration voiced a number of extremist demands such as reversing policies and laws guaranteeing equal rights for women, removing protections for "blasphemous" speech and religious minorities, and prohibiting various "un-Islamic" symbols. Although the state crackdown on terrorism since the 2016 Holey Café attack in Dhaka appears to have halted or stalled the process of Islamist mobilization, it is generally believed to be a temporary or superficial peace. The broader process of ideological polarization appears to continue: in some Bangladeshi communities, a sharp rise in religiosity is apparent in the growing use of the outward symbols of Islam, such as the *niquab* and *hijab* for women and beards and Arabicized dress for men, yet in other communities there has been an opposite growth in Western lifestyles and behaviors.[26]

It is more complicated to assess the implications of political polarization for Bangladesh's economic and social development. The country's development success over the past thirty years has featured high growth rates and rapid human development progress. Although Bangladesh's political factions have differed on who should hold the reins of power, they have generally maintained a robust consensus on development policy. For the most part, the major parties agree on the model of economic growth and on broadly pro-poor and inclusive public service delivery, including efforts to reach women and the rural masses in particular. This elite consensus on development reflects a shared understanding of the existential threat faced by a Bangladeshi state that fails to secure the basics of development and has included a significant amount of space for political contenders to engage in economic activity. It has also generated a modest degree of competition over performance with respect to the delivery of basic public services.[27] During the more balanced competition of the 1990s, both parties strove to gain or retain office, with the periodic spells out of power ensuring that the parties needed to work hard to both win support and rig elections.

In the period of growing AL dominance since 2009, the government has been feeling pressures to earn performance legitimacy. It has enacted developmental policies on a significant scale and has widely publicized its achievements while clamping down on critics in civil society and the media in an effort to ensure that its message is sent and received. As a single party comes to dominate politics, the implications for Bangladesh's development progress need to be considered. Previously, competitive pressures on the ruling party controlled corruption to some extent and fostered inclusive public policies. In a period of closing political and civic space, it remains to be seen whether such achievements can be sustained.

Remedial Actions

A number of efforts to reduce polarization or limit its adverse effects have been attempted in Bangladesh. Arguably, these have had at best trivial impacts and at worst have institutionalized and deepened political divisions.

Civil society and the mass media have long lamented the visible aspects of polarization in the form of personalized hostility between the two party leaders, the AL's Sheikh Hasina and the BNP's Begum Khaleda Zia, arguing for more constructive means of political dialogue and competition. Many people in these sectors appear to believe the polarization owes to personal antagonisms between "the Two Ladies" (as they are sometimes derisively referred to in news media and journalistic analysis). Although no serious political analyst views polarization as the result of personalistic female competition, the notion appeared to inform the ill-fated "Minus Two" campaign to topple the heads of both major parties, out of the apparent belief that removing the heads would somehow reform their bodies.

Instead, both leaders survived the political purge of the 2007–08 period and retained—and in the case of the AL's Sheikh Hasina, strengthened—their dominant power over their parties. Their long-standing domination of these party apparatuses owes in part to their inherited status as respectively the daughter (Sheikh Hasina) and widow (Begum Khaleda Zia) of assassinated political leaders. Their mutual hostility, meanwhile, owes no doubt in part to the enduring psychological effects of the traumas both experienced in their deeply intertwined personal and political lives. Nevertheless, the view that the polarization of Bangladeshi politics owes to personal female competition is plainly inadequate political analysis and is as equally blinkered by a misogynistic view of the role of women in relation to political power.

In addition to these efforts to replace the dominant political leaders, another initiative has attempted to counter the duopoly of the AL and BNP by forming a new political party. However, this effort to start a new party, launched in 2007 by the Nobel Peace Prize–winning founder of the Grameen Bank, Muhammad Yunus, underlined the limited grasp of civil society actors on the realities of Bangladeshi politics. Yunus's ill-advised entry into politics was short-lived, and his example has no doubt reinforced the view among the political parties that civil society is antithetical to, rather than essential to, the functioning of democracy. In recent years, as the AL has consolidated power, new political formations have also emerged (albeit fleetingly and unsuccessfully) to contest the AL's dominance. Ahead of the December 2018 election, the former AL leader Kamal Hossain formed an electoral alliance with the BNP and Jamaat-e-Islami in an effort to ensure a competitive race, but large-scale vote rigging ensured that this initiative had little effect.

The single most important effort to address the adverse effects of political polarization is the institution of the neutral NPCG to oversee elections and political transitions. However, the unintended effects of this institution include a shared failure among political parties to learn to police their own behavior and a corresponding effort to capture the electoral process. The NPCG innovation drew on the experience of the transition to democracy in 1990 and was one of the long-standing demands of the AL in the run-up to the 1996 election. Nizam Ahmed notes that the NPCG was "Bangladesh's 'home-grown' plant," an innovation that emerged in the early democratic period when the incumbent BNP rigged a by-election and showed its willingness to use its incumbency advantage to stack the electoral odds in its own favor. As Ahmed writes:

> [The AL] argued that elections under party governments could not be held in a free and fair manner; hence the responsibility for overseeing the conduct of parliamentary elections should be entrusted to a non-party caretaker government. Initially, the BNP seriously opposed the proposal, but ultimately yielded to opposition pressure. The sixth Parliament, elected in February 1996 amidst an opposition boycott, amended the Constitution in March 1996, empowering the NPCG to exercise state power for a limited period of time (between the dissolution of parliament and the election of a new legislature) in order to ensure the holding of free, fair and impartial elections.[28]

As noted above, after its first outing, the NPCG worked precisely once, when the AL gave up power to the victorious BNP coalition in 2001. By 2006, the BNP had concluded that it needed to win the election at all costs and rigged the judicial institutions that were supposed to supply the leadership of the caretaker regime. This in turn prompted a return to military influence in politics, with the army backing the two-year caretaker regime in 2007 and 2008. In a new twist to an old tale, the international community supported military involvement in politics and appeared to take a collective view that elections in a polity so divided and dominated by a ruthless incumbent party were best delayed until politics could be made safe for multiparty elections. The United Nations Resident Representative is understood to have made it clear to military leaders that their lucrative peacekeeping role would be at risk should they support a one-sided election.

Despite broad international support for the interim regime, as well as the NPCG's redesign of institutions of accountability and political parties, this institution has delayed and perhaps fatally weakened the consolidation of Bangladeshi democracy in four ways. First, the NPCG was a technical and idealistic bureaucratic fix to what remains an essentially political matter. One of the major interventions of the donor community at this time was the introduction of a national voter database, a technological intervention on which the international community congratulated itself as the means of ensuring free and fair elections. Such efforts have proven inadequate to addressing the fundamentally political problem of the exercise of power. Second, the support this extended caretaker government enjoyed from civil society and the donor community has fueled hostility and suspicion toward these actors on the part of the ruling AL and may have paved the way for the shrinking of civic space in Bangladesh. Third, while much commentary on the NPCG has focused on its short-term success in managing changes of government, in the long term the NPCG institution weakened the institutions of the judiciary and the election commission. The NPCG itself undermined these institutions by taking on extraconstitutional powers during the extended interim regime of 2007–08. Finally, the reliance on an external institution to police elections enabled political parties to avoid the need to establish their own mechanisms of internal control and regulation of interparty relations or indeed to agree between them to abide by the rules of the game.

As the AL continues to consolidate its power, the BNP is fundamentally weakened, with its top leadership in jail or exile, and apparently lacks the capacity to unseat the government through a campaign of *hartals*. In the lead-up to the December 2018 election, few citizens or observers doubted that the AL would win. As theorized by Adrienne LeBas, given the present imbalance of power between the governing party and opposition, political polarization will most likely continue to undermine democratic institutions in Bangladesh. However, the concentration of power in the AL may itself become a unifying force for the opposition, as the increasingly authoritarian party appears to be alienating all but its core supporters. Mass protests in 2018 unleashed a fresh round of attacks on civil society and the student population, and the rigged election at the end of the year cemented the popular view that the AL government is if not authoritarian, then at least increasingly dominant over all aspects of politics and the state. These moves have been generally unpopular and have started to attract adverse international attention. It is possible that popular discontent about the growing concentration of AL power will serve to defuse, offset, or in other ways complicate the trajectory of political polarization. For the present, the victor of Bangladesh's long-running political contest may be generating not polarization, but an increasingly widely shared hostility to authoritarian rule.

NOTES

1. Rounaq Jahan, "The Parliament of Bangladesh: Representation and Accountability," *The Journal of Legislative Studies* 21, no. 2 (2015): 250–69. Harry Blair has argued that Bangladesh has passed the "two transitions" test of democratic consolidation suggested by Huntington, but as these transitions occurred under the aegis of a nonparty caretaker government, they cannot be treated as evidence of agreement on the political rules of the game. See Harry Blair, "Party Dysfunction and Homeostasis in Bangladesh: The Old Disorder Restored (or Not)," in *Politics and Governance in Bangladesh: Uncertain Landscapes*, ed. Ipshita Basu, Joe Devine, and Geof Wood (London: Routledge, 2017), 31–52.

2. Adeeba Aziz Khan, "Electoral Institutions in Bangladesh: A Study of Conflicts between the Formal and the Informal" (PhD diss., London: School of Oriental and African Studies, University of London, 2015).

3. Adrienne LeBas, "Can Polarization Be Positive? Conflict and Institutional Development in Africa," *American Behavioral Scientist* 62, no. 1 (2018): 59–74.

4. M. Moniruzzaman notes that the opposition boycotted parliament 43 percent of the time between 1991 and 2006. See M. Moniruzzaman, "Party Politics and Political Violence in Bangladesh: Issues, Manifestation and Consequences," *South Asian Survey* 16, no. 1 (2009): 81–99. The main BNP opposition boycotted the 2014 election and the tenth session of Parliament (2014 to 2019) in its entirety. On the significance of informal strategies in political culture, see Naomi Hossain, "The Significance of Unruly Politics in Bangladesh," in Basu, Devine, and Wood, *Politics and Governance in Bangladesh*, 157–81. On the "partyarchy" in Bangladesh, see Mirza Hassan and Sohela Nazneen, "Violence and the Breakdown of the Political Settlement: An Uncertain Future for Bangladesh?," *Conflict, Security & Development* 17, no. 3 (2017): 205–23.

5. Tahmina Rahman, "Party System Institutionalization and Pernicious Polarization in Bangladesh," *The ANNALS of the American Academy of Political and Social Science* 681, no. 1 (2019): 173–92.

6. Mushtaq H. Khan, "Bangladesh: Economic Growth in a Vulnerable LAO," in *In the Shadow of Violence: Politics, Economics and the Problems of Development*, ed. Douglass C. North, John Joseph Wallis, Steven B. Webb, and Barry R. Weingast (Cambridge, UK: Cambridge University Press, 2013), 24–69.

7. Naomi Hossain, *Elite Perceptions of Poverty in Bangladesh* (Dhaka: University Press Limited, 2005).

8. On a "'Middle-Class' Elite," see Naomi Hossain, *The Aid Lab: Understanding Bangladesh's Unexpected Success* (Oxford: Oxford University Press, 2017), 52; on the Awami League, see Shyamali Ghosh, *The Awami League, 1949–1971* (Dhaka: Academic Publishers, 1990); on Bangladesh as an "intermediate regime," see Rehman Sobhan and Muzaffer Ahmad, *Public Enterprise in an Intermediate Regime: A Study in the Political Economy of Bangladesh* (Dhaka: Bangladesh Institute of Development Studies, 1980).

9. For an account of polarization in Bangladesh that emphasizes how the International Crimes Tribunal inaugurated a new period of pernicious polarization, see Rahman, "Party System Institutionalization and Pernicious Polarization."

10. The standard source for discussions of the origins of Bengali Muslim identity is Rafiuddin Ahmed, *The Bengal Muslims, 1871–1906: A Quest for Identity* (New York: Oxford University Press, 1996). On the popular movement for capital punishment of Islamists convicted of war crimes, see Nadine S. Murshid, "The Shahbag Uprising," *Economic & Political Weekly* 48, no. 10 (2013): 13; and David Lewis, "The Paradoxes of Bangladesh's Shahbag Protests," *South Asia @ LSE* (blog), 2013 (http://blogs.lse.ac.uk/southasia/2013/03/21/the-paradoxes-of-bangladeshs-shahbag-protests/).

11. On the ideological differences between parties, see Moniruzzaman, "Party Politics and Political Violence in Bangladesh." On the schism between secularism and religiosity, see M. Rashiduzzaman, "The Liberals and the Religious Right in Bangladesh," *Asian Survey* 34, no. 11 (1994): 974–90.

12. See BRAC University and Institute of Governance Studies, *The State of Governance in Bangladesh, 2008: Confrontation, Competition, Accountability* (Dhaka: Institute of Governance Studies, BRAC University, 2009); and Hassan and Nazneen, "Violence and the Breakdown of the Political Settlement."

13. Harry Blair, "Party Overinstitutionalization, Contestation, and Democratic Degradation in Bangladesh," in *Routledge Handbook of South Asian Politics*, ed. Paul R. Brass (London: Routledge, 2010), 102.

14. Joya Chatterji, *Bengal Divided: Hindu Communalism and Partition, 1932–1947* (Cambridge, UK: Cambridge University Press, 2002); and Shelley Feldman, "Bengali State and Nation Making: Partition and Displacement Revisited," *International Social Science Journal* 55, no. 175 (2003): 111–21.

15. Craig Baxter, "Pakistan Votes—1970," *Asian Survey* 11, no. 3 (1971): 212. On the political effects of the Bhola cyclone, see Naomi Hossain, "The 1970 Bhola Cyclone, Nationalist Politics, and the Subsistence Crisis Contract in Bangladesh," *Disasters* 42, no. 1 (2018): 187–203.

16. On the U.S. "tilt," see Gary J. Bass, *The Blood Telegram: Nixon, Kissinger, and a Forgotten Genocide* (New York: Knopf, 2013). On the use of aid conditionality to prevent justice for war crimes, see Rehman Sobhan, "Politics of Food and Famine in Bangladesh," *Economic & Political Weekly* 14, no. 48 (1979): 1973–80.

17. For accounts of the political polarization of the period, see Talukder Maniruzzaman, "Bangladesh: An Unfinished Revolution?," *The Journal of Asian Studies* 34, no. 4 (1975): 891–911; and idem., *The Bangladesh Revolution and Its Aftermath*, 2nd ed. (Dhaka: University Press Limited, 1988). For an account of the attack on the left, see Lawrence Lifschultz and Kai Bird, *Bangladesh: The Unfinished Revolution* (London: Zed Books, 1979).

18. M. Rashiduzzaman, "Political Unrest and Democracy in Bangladesh," *Asian Survey* 37, no. 3 (1997): 254–68.

19. Blair, "Party Overinstitutionalization, Contestation, and Democratic Degradation in Bangladesh," 106.

20. Nizam Ahmed, "Party Politics under a Non-Party Caretaker Government in Bangladesh: The Fakhruddin Interregnum (2007–09)," *Commonwealth & Comparative Politics* 48, no. 1 (2010): 23–47.

21. Khan, "Electoral Institutions in Bangladesh."

22. Hassan and Nazneen, "Violence and the Breakdown of the Political Settlement."

23. For the figures until 2006, see Moniruzzaman, "Party Politics and Political Violence"; and Jalal Alamgir, "Political Violence as a Core Governance Challenge" (paper presented at Governance in Bangladesh: Retrospective and Future Prospects Conference, Institute of Governance Studies, BRAC University, Dhaka, Bangladesh, 2011). Figures for 2015 are from Hassan and Nazneen, "Violence and the Breakdown of the Political Settlement."

24. See United Nations Development Programme (UNDP), *Beyond Hartals: Towards Democratic Dialogue in Bangladesh* (Dhaka: UNDP, 2005); Bert Suykens and Aynul Islam, "Hartal as a Complex Political Performance: General Strikes and the Organisation of (Local) Power in Bangladesh," *Contributions to Indian Sociology* 47, no. 1 (2013): 61–83; and Hossain, "The Significance of Unruly Politics in Bangladesh."

25. BRAC University and Institute of Governance Studies, *The State of Governance in Bangladesh*, 2008, 14.

26. Martin Griffiths and Mubashar Hasan, "Playing with Fire: Islamism and Politics in Bangladesh," *Asian Journal of Political Science* 23, no. 2 (2015): 226–41.

27. Mirza Hassan, "Political Settlement Dynamics in a Limited-Access Order: The Case of Bangladesh," ESID Working Paper (Effective States and Inclusive Development Research Centre, 2013) (www.effective-states.org/wp-content/uploads/working_papers/final-pdfs/esid_wp_23_hassan.pdf); and Hassan and Nazneen, "Violence and the Breakdown of the Political Settlement."

28. Ahmed, "Party Politics under a Non-Party Caretaker Government in Bangladesh," 25. For a history of the NPCG, see also Nizam Ahmed, "Abolition or Reform? Non-Party Caretaker System and Government Succession in Bangladesh," *The Round Table* 100, no. 414 (2011): 303–21; and Khan, "Electoral Institutions in Bangladesh."

Part IV

STAYING CLEAR?

EIGHT

Polarization and Democratic Decline in Indonesia

EVE WARBURTON

Observers have long characterized Indonesia's political landscape as remarkably free of deep ideological fissures or entrenched social divisions. Indonesia's parties do not sort along traditional left-right lines, and sectarian identities have not been channeled into the party system in a contentious or exclusive way since the country democratized in the late 1990s. The most prominent cleavage in Indonesian politics is religious: Islamic parties pursue a larger role for Islam in the public sphere, whereas nationalist parties promote a pluralist vision for Indonesia's nation-state. However, scholars have argued that even this divide has few implications for political coalition-building, social cohesion, or policy formation. Instead, pragmatism and patronage motivate political actors to work together, regardless of their Islamic or pluralist orientation.[1] Dan Slater and Aries Arugay have even concluded that Indonesia is "one of the least polarized democracies in Asia, despite its practically bottomless raw material for polarizing conflict."[2]

Yet the tone of political analysis on Indonesia has undergone a perceptible shift in recent years. Observers talk about the "repolarization of post-Soeharto politics"[3] and "the return of ideological competition."[4] Three contentious political events motivated this shift: the 2014 presidential election; the 2017 election for governor of Jakarta, the nation's capital; and the 2019 presidential election. Each election was marked by an increasingly divisive brand of populist politics, whereby one side deployed an exclusivist and Islamist-themed campaign to undermine its more pluralist opponent. This populist turn has re-politicized an old ideological divide between pluralist and Islamist groups and produced a more polarized political atmosphere than at any other point in the post-Suharto period.[5]

What explains the timing and intensity of electoral polarization in Indonesia? This chapter puts forward three arguments about the sources of contemporary polarization. First, it emphasizes elite agency. Politicians on both sides of the divide consciously mobilized religiously charged and divisive rhetoric to attack their opponents. In doing so, opportunistic elites gave new form to otherwise latent and inchoate ideological divisions. Second, broader sociopolitical conditions were conducive to this kind of polarizing conflict.[6] The increasing personalization of Indonesian politics, general popular dissatisfaction with the political status quo, and the gradual Islamization of Indonesia's social and political life in the preceding decades made religiously-themed and populist campaigns particularly appealing. Finally, the incumbent government of President Joko Widodo (Jokowi), which is associated with Indonesia's pluralist political tradition, has used illiberal and repressive measures against what it views as politically threatening Islamist figures and organizations. Such actions have ultimately enflamed political conflict and widened the divide between each side.

But has polarization in Indonesia become *severe*? As this case study indicates, polarization reaches peaks in moments of intense electoral conflict, and in between election seasons tensions between pluralist and Islamist groups rarely surface. At the level of mass polarization, surveys show that Indonesians generally do not see their world in Manichean binaries or through the lens of the Islamic-pluralist divide. At the elite level, the party system remains largely scattered and fragmented, rather than polarized, and politicians running for the national legislature or in regional head elections generally seek support from a wide spectrum of voters, rather than from narrow, ideologically defined or identity-based constituencies. Political parties, religious organizations, and various social groups from across the ideological spectrum tend to compromise with and accommodate one another in pursuit of opportunities for patronage.

The Indonesian case demonstrates, however, that polarization—even if contained to moments of electoral competition—is an incremental process. Polarization is already eroding Indonesia's democratic institutions and damaging its social fabric. Exclusivist political rhetoric has entered the mainstream in recent years, targeting minorities and attacking the legitimacy of secular-pluralist politics. The government's illiberal approach risks further entrenching divisions and accelerating a decline in the quality of Indonesia's increasingly fragile democracy.

Roots

Indonesia's Islamic-pluralist cleavage has deep roots. In the years leading up to the country's independence in 1945, nationalist intellectuals and Muslim leaders were locked in fierce debate over the ideological basis of the new nation. Proponents of political Islam wanted sharia to be enshrined in the constitution, but secular nationalists sought a pluralist and secular state that did not favor one religion or group over another. The nationalists won that battle. The final constitution did not make reference to Islam but instead outlined a general "Belief in God" as one of the nation's five founding principles, known as the *Pancasila*.

In the years that followed, however, Indonesia's fledgling democracy became bogged down in an intractable conflict between the parties that represented these two divergent visions for the nation. During the period of parliamentary democracy (1950–59), two major Islamic parties—the modernist Masyumi party and the traditionalist Nahdlatul Ulama (NU)—as well as the secular-nationalist Indonesian Nationalist Party (Partai Nasional Indonesia; PNI) (established by Indonesia's first president, Sukarno) and the Communist Party (Partai Komunis Indonesia; PKI), dominated Indonesian politics. Each had cultivated strong connections to and represented the interests of a specific sociocultural constituency. The parties became increasingly extreme and unyielding in their demands, determined to have their own ideological priorities realized in the heated constitutional and regulatory debates taking place at this early stage of nation-building.[7] The result was political conflict, deadlock, and eventually the collapse of the democratic order.

Under the authoritarian rule of President Sukarno between 1959 and 1967, polarization intensified. As support for the PKI grew in the rural areas and the party built closer ties to the president, the Islamic parties and their constituents, together with the Army, became suspicious of a PKI-Sukarno alliance. These tensions culminated in the anticommunist purges of 1965–66 and the slaughter of between 500,000 and 1 million Indonesians suspected to have links to the PKI. The left was effectively wiped from the country's political landscape.

The polarizing ideological conflicts of the previous decades came to an abrupt end after 1967, when General Suharto took over in the wake of the massacres and established his authoritarian New Order government. He established a party, Golkar, as his own political vehicle and consolidated the remaining non-Islamic parties into the Indonesian Democracy Party (Partai Demokrasi Indonesia; PDI), while all Islamic parties were merged into the United Development Party (Partai Persatuan Pembangunan; PPP). The New Order was a "repressive developmentalist" regime that forbade opposition mobilization and controlled ideological debate.[8] Public discussion of SARA—an acronym for *suku* (ethnicity), *agama* (religion), *ras* (race), and *antargolongan* (intergroup social relations), as well as anything related to these potential flashpoint topics—was officially forbidden. Using a mixture of coercion and repression, Suharto's Golkar won every election for the next thirty-two years.

Only when Suharto resigned in 1998 in the wake of a devastating financial crisis and a popular democratic movement were political cleavages allowed full expression once more. However, since democratization, scholars have generally characterized Indonesia's politics as remarkably free of ideological division and identity-based conflict.[9] Severe communal and ethnic violence accompanied the democratic transition (from 1998 to roughly 2004), but in the years that followed most conflicts were peacefully resolved, and, as Edward Aspinall argues, "democratization . . . produced powerful new norms of compromise."[10] The number of political parties, both religious and secular, also exploded in this period. In general, though, their platforms were far more centrist, flexible, and accommodating than those of the parties that dominated Indonesian politics during the 1950s.[11]

In Indonesia's democratic transition, patronage served as a powerful incentive for compromise and cooperation. As Aspinall explains, "the tendency was to accommodate and absorb all major political forces, including those which, in other circumstances, might have challenged the new democratic dispensation. Patronage and corruption provided the oil to grease this arrangement."[12] Those potential democratic spoilers included military factions, ethnonationalist separatists in the regions, and Islamist forces. All of these groups were integrated into the new democracy, primarily (though not solely) through the offer of material opportunity. Thus, the post-Suharto polity evolved quickly into a patronage democracy, rather than a programmatic democracy of the sort found in many industrialized Western countries.

Even though patronage-based politics weakens democratic institutions and accountability, in Indonesia it has cut across identity-based cleavages. Parties have been willing to enter into governing coalitions with all sorts of other parties, regardless their ideological orientation, in pursuit of electoral victory and access to state resources.[13] Parties receive little public financing in Indonesia, and elections are immensely expensive. The collection and distribution of patronage therefore are essential to funding party activities, and this imperative motivates much of what political elites do during and between election seasons. This need for patronage encourages coalition-building and collaboration in pursuit of state resources, rather than polarization.[14]

The marked absence of polarization for much of the post-Suharto period was also a function of President Susilo Bambang Yudhoyono's (2004–14) personal approach to governing. Yudhoyono valued accommodation and stability above competition and conflict.[15] His leadership style was driven by a desire to contain social conflict by coopting spoilers and satisfying potential sources of opposition. As Edward Aspinall, Marcus Mietzner, and Dirk Tomsa argue:

> Yudhoyono viewed himself as leading a polity and a society characterised by deep divisions, and he believed that his most important role was to moderate these divisions by mediating between the conflicting forces and interests to which they gave rise.[16]

Under Yudhoyono, Indonesia's program of democratic reform stagnated, but these were also years of peace, stability, and a notable absence of polarizing political conflict. The presidential election in 2014 marked a sharp departure from the status quo.

Trajectory

Polarization entered the analytical lexicon of Indonesia observers in the wake of three contentious elections, in 2014, 2017, and 2019. All three were marked by competition between political figures who were remarkably distinct in terms of their style and whose political coalitions reflected the opposing sides of the old Islamist-pluralist divide described above. In each case, politicians mobilized religiously-themed narratives as part of a populist campaign style to cast their opponents as a threat to Islam, as an affront to Indonesia's national identity, and as an illegitimate "other."

2014: A Polarizing Presidential Election

Indonesia's 2014 presidential election presented voters with two starkly different populist choices: Jokowi and Prabowo Subianto. Populism is a form of mobilization in which a political figure seeks direct connection to voters, bypassing traditional party-voter linkages.[17] To do this, populists often frame themselves as political outsiders and appeal to the notion of a pure, common people who are exploited by a corrupt and illegitimate "other," like the political elite or a minority group.[18] Populism has an inherently divisive and Manichean quality, particularly when tied to an illiberal political agenda.

While Jokowi did not design or deploy a divisive antiestablishment campaign, he embodied a populist spirit.[19] As mayor of Solo and governor of Jakarta, Jokowi gained attention around the country for his regular interactions with ordinary Indonesians at markets, malls, and public events. He connected directly with voters in a way that was rare in the Indonesian context, and he attracted a legion of volunteers from outside of the party system who helped to canvass votes across the archipelago. For these reasons, Jokowi stood out as an alternative to the familiar cast of corrupt oligarchs, bureaucrats, and military elites who had long dominated national politics.

Jokowi's politics also had a secular orientation. Indeed, he was far more secular than the previous president, Yudhoyono. Though he was a practicing Muslim, Jokowi did not initially make Islam a prominent part of his political identity. He attracted support from moderate Muslims, minority communities, reformist civil society groups, and human rights organizations. Jokowi's political coalition also came to reflect the secular-pluralist ideological stream that had long animated Indonesian politics. Jokowi belonged to the PDI-P (Partai Demokrasi Indonesia Perjuangan; Indonesian Democratic Party of Struggle), the direct descendent of President Sukarno's PNI and historically Indonesia's most pluralist party. He also had the backing of other nominally secular parties, together with the more moderate Islamic party PKB (Partai Kebangkitan Bangsa; New Awakening Party), which was linked to NU.

Prabowo Subianto, on the other hand, espoused a divisive and illiberal brand of populism. A former general of the New Order period, he launched a "classic populist" campaign, in which he blamed the country's economic and political problems on greedy elites and nefarious foreign agents.[20] Those "foreign agents" went unnamed, but Prabowo's strategy was to dog-whistle at the country's wealthy ethnic Chinese minority, a community that has faced a long history of prejudice and discrimination. He presented a neoauthoritarian challenge to the status quo, promising to return Indonesia to the old 1945 constitution, which heavily favored executive power and had no place for direct presidential elections.

Prabowo identified Islam as a key point of difference between his coalition and Jokowi's. Although Prabowo was backed by two major secular parties—Gerindra, the party he established in 2008 as a vehicle for his presidential ambitions, and Golkar—his coalition also included four Islamic parties: the Prosperous Justice Party (Partai Keadilan Sejahtera; PKS), the National Mandate Party (Partai Amanat Nasional; PAN), the Crescent Star Party (Partai Bulan Bintang; PBB), and the aforementioned PPP. Prabowo was not a particularly pious Muslim, but he had a history of opportunistically collaborating with hardline Islamic groups during his time in the military, and this alliance with Islamist forces outside the party system played an important role in his presidential campaign.[21]

According to Marcus Mietzner, the Jokowi coalition's "main task . . . was to fend off accusations from the Prabowo camp that Jokowi's election would lead to the marginalization of Islam from the political arena."[22] Prabowo and his coalition tapped into fringe Islamist narratives about the risks posed by Christians, Indonesia's Chinese minority, and communists. They spread a harmful smear campaign as well, which claimed that Jokowi had Christian Chinese lineage and a communist past. Both social media networks and traditional media outlets were used to spread rumors, memes, and doctored photos attacking Jokowi's Islamic credentials.

Online applications, like Facebook, Twitter, and WhatsApp, facilitated the spread of religiously charged slurs and insults. As one analyst put it, "smear tactics are nothing new to Indonesia's rough-and-tumble politics . . . [but] technology has . . . made it easier to inflame and keep alive unsubstantiated rumours or outright lies."[23] That smear campaign against Jokowi helped Prabowo gain significant ground and come close to taking the presidency.

In the end Prabowo lost, albeit narrowly: Jokowi won 53 percent of the popular vote to Prabowo's 46 percent. Prabowo's political coalition fragmented after the election, with several parties moving over to Jokowi. Though Gerindra and PKS remained out of government and swore to oppose Jokowi's every move, overall politics appeared to be returning to a "normal" state of affairs in which parties and politicians put ideological differences to the side in order to enter government and access state resources.[24] Over the next two years, Prabowo retreated from national politics, Jokowi consolidated his power over national politics, and the fissures that were so prominent in 2014 began to mellow.

2016 and 2017: The Islamist Mobilizations

Toward the end of 2016, another polarizing election campaign split Indonesia's political landscape. Prabowo and his Islamist alliance were back, and this time they ran a more explicitly sectarian election campaign. Gerindra, PKS, and PAN—core parties from Prabowo's 2014 election coalition—nominated Anies Baswedan, a well-known Muslim academic, to run in Jakarta's gubernatorial election. Again, this coalition faced off against a more pluralist candidate, and this time the pluralist candidate was especially vulnerable to sectarian appeals. Basuki Tjahaja Purnama (Ahok), the incumbent governor and close Jokowi ally, was a double minority: Chinese Indonesian and Christian. Still, his approval ratings were above 80 percent leading into the election, and he remained the favorite.

Anies and Prabowo's coalition allied with Islamist organizations outside the party system, such as the Islamic Defenders Front (Front Pembela Islam; FPI) and its front man, Rizieq Shihab, who waged a religiously charged campaign that called upon Jakartans not to vote for a non-Muslim, citing a passage in the Qur'an. The campaign took a dramatic turn when Ahok misspoke and accused Islamic figures of misleading their followers about the contents of that passage. A doctored recording was spread through various social media networks, in which it sounded as though Ahok had insulted the Qur'an itself. In response, Islamist groups mobilized the largest street protests in Indonesia's modern history, demanding that Ahok be imprisoned on charges of blasphemy. The protestors targeted Jokowi as well, claiming that the president's closeness to a blasphemer was further proof that he was an enemy of the *ummah* (the Muslim community). In the days leading up to the election, that campaign message was spread through social media networks and taken to mosques and prayer groups around Jakarta where Islamic teachers instructed their followers not to vote for a *kafir* (unbeliever) and a blasphemer. This sectarian campaign delivered Anies a resounding victory. Ahok, who had been the favorite leading into this election, not only lost decisively but was also charged with blasphemy and imprisoned for two-and-a-half years.

The fact that Anies was by no means a hardline Islamist ideologue underscores the importance of elite agency in exacerbating polarization. Once considered a moderate Muslim figure, Anies had also been a high-profile member of Jokowi's campaign team and his cabinet until mid-2016. After being removed from his ministerial position in the Jokowi government, the ambitious Anies switched political allegiances and entered the race in Jakarta against Jokowi's ally. He opportunistically built ties with Islamist organizations and mobilized sectarian fears in order to defeat his Christian Chinese opponent.

The election was traumatizing for the country's Chinese and non-Muslim minorities. For many Jakartans in particular, the results were shocking, because they saw their city as a cultural melting pot where sectarian appeals would not work. Yet quick-count results indicated that religious identity was indeed a central driver of voting behavior. There appeared to be a striking divide between Muslim and non-Muslim voters: uniformly, Muslims were more likely to vote for Anies regardless of their other characteristics, such as income or education.[25] Non-Muslims, by contrast, overwhelmingly voted for Ahok.

In the wake of Ahok's loss, analysts debated what the longer-term re-
percussions would be for Indonesia's democracy. Some argued that the
street mobilizations were not indicative of Islamism's growing political
clout and suggested that Jakarta's elections were too distinct to change the
broader political map in a more permanent way.[26] After all, Ahok was a
double minority, and his style of politics was unusually confrontational and
polarizing. Others, however, underscored that sectarian campaign messages had resonated with large parts of the electorate. For example, surveys strongly suggested that the Islamist message mobilized by Anies' allies
had increased levels of intolerance among the public. In their important
study of this phenomenon, Marcus Mietzner, Burhanuddin Muhtadi, and
Rizka Halida use longitudinal survey data to demonstrate that, prior to
2017, intolerance toward non-Muslims was actually decreasing in Indonesia.[27] Yet in the wake of Jakarta's divisive elections, that trajectory reversed,
and more Indonesians expressed opposition to non-Muslims becoming a
regent, governor, or president. The authors conclude that polarizing cues
from political actors and their allies within Muslim organizations, prayer
groups, and mosques shifted public opinion not just in Jakarta, but even
nationally. Some analysts, therefore, argued that Anies' pact with Islamist
forces had proven an immensely successful political strategy and would
become a new blueprint for candidates seeking high office.

In the years that followed Ahok's loss and imprisonment, the coalition
of Islamic figures and hardline groups that brought him down fractured;
personal differences prevented them from forming a cohesive political
entity. Most of the candidates they backed in the 2018 regional elections,
for example, failed to win office in the country's most important provinces.
However, in the 2019 presidential election, Islamist forces regrouped
behind Prabowo Subianto.

2019: Polarization Deepens

Prabowo ran against Jokowi again in 2019. Initially, the ideological differences between their two coalitions appeared less stark than in the past. This
time, Jokowi's coalition included two conservative Islamic parties, PPP and
PBB. Jokowi also appointed Ma'ruf Amin, a prominent but conservative NU
kyai (Islamic scholar and teacher), as his vice-presidential candidate. Ma'ruf

was widely expected to insulate Jokowi from an Islamist-populist campaign and potentially attract support from Indonesia's more conservative Muslim voters. Prabowo, on the other hand, chose Sandiaga Uno as his running mate, a wealthy business tycoon with little religious clout.

Yet 2019 proved to be an even more divisive election year. This time, religious organizations and figures on both sides of the Islamist-pluralist cleavage crystallized into more cohesive blocs behind their chosen candidate and played a critical role in the campaign. For example, the mix of Islamist groups and political parties that had been instrumental in mobilizing against Ahok came together to back Prabowo. Some of these groups, such as FPI, had also been active in Prabowo's 2014 presidential bid. Back then they were tasked with grassroots intimidation and smear campaigns. But in 2019, FPI members and other hardline and Salafist organizations and preachers were given formal positions in Prabowo's campaign team and made speeches at his public events. The sectarian message from Prabowo's Islamist allies was the same as it was in 2014: that Jokowi and his party, PDI-P, were anti-Islam and closet communists. But this time that message was delivered by groups and individuals who were no longer on the fringes.

Jokowi's 2019 coalition again represented Indonesia's moderate Muslim constituency and its minority communities. He was backed by a mix of secular-nationalist parties and the NU-linked PKB. One critical difference from 2014, however, was that a far more unified and combative NU took center stage in the Jokowi campaign. Back in 2014, NU was split, with some of the organization's most prominent leaders openly backing Prabowo, while PKB and other factions within NU supported Jokowi. In 2019, Ma'ruf Amin's appointment as Jokowi's vice-presidential candidate galvanized support from NU's leadership, and both NU and PKB formed a solid bloc behind the president. Particularly in the NU heartland of East and Central Java—two provinces rich in votes—NU's sprawling network of Islamic boarding schools was mobilized to support the president.[28]

But the campaign message was not a conciliatory one; rather, it was a message of "us" versus "them." NU and PKB leadership propagated a kind of militant pluralism, which painted any Islamist group affiliated with Prabowo as a threat to Indonesia's national identity and the state's pluralist foundations. NU's leaders around the country were enlisted to convince the electorate that a Prabowo victory would open the door to an Islamic caliphate and the rise of radical Islamic groups such as Hizbut Tahrir Indonesia (HTI), a group that the Jokowi administration had recently banned.

The divisive campaign produced a far more polarized election result. Quick-count reports published soon after the polls closed indicated that Jokowi won the election with around 55 percent to Prabowo's 45 percent. This victory was largely a result of an increase in votes from the heavily populated parts of Central and East Java. In these NU strongholds on Java, and in areas dominated by non-Muslim minorities, such as the eastern provinces of Bali and North Sulawesi, Jokowi won a larger share of the vote than he had in 2014.[29] Indeed, a staggering 97 percent of non-Muslims voted for Jokowi, according to exit polls.[30] The Ahok crisis and Prabowo's Islamist alliance had clearly pushed minorities further into Jokowi's camp. In the provinces traditionally known as a base for conservative Islam, and where Prabowo had long maintained strong support, the challenger *increased* his vote share. The 2019 electoral map bore a striking resemblance to that of the 1950s—a time of deep political polarization along socioreligious lines.

While Jokowi won by a convincing margin, Prabowo refused to accept his defeat. In the weeks between election day and the electoral commission's formal announcement of the results, Prabowo told the public that the election had been rigged and that the government had stolen the election from the people. On May 21, the final results were announced: Jokowi had received 55.5 percent of the vote and Prabowo 44.5 percent, as all of the quick counts had indicated. But the next day, thousands of Prabowo loyalists still took to the streets in protest. While initially peaceful, these protests evolved into violent riots that killed six people and left hundreds injured. This was some of the worst election-related violence the country had seen since 1998. At the time of this chapter's writing in May 2019, precisely who or which groups were involved remained unclear, though reports were emerging that paid thugs had instigated the violence and that the entire episode had been orchestrated from above.[31] The public may never know the true circumstances of these riots. However, it is clear that Prabowo strategically cultivated a tense atmosphere by rejecting Jokowi's victory, mobilized his followers onto the streets, and encouraged them to challenge Indonesia's democratic institutions. The effect was to further divide Indonesia's national political landscape.

The Underlying Conditions

What explains Indonesia's recent shift from a country described as largely devoid of divisive ideological conflict to one marked by increasing political polarization? This section examines the social and political conditions that brought Indonesia to this new political moment. At the political level, the shift away from party-centered to more personalized forms of electoral politics, as well as increasing popular disillusionment with status quo government, created an environment ripe for populist mobilization. At the societal level, a context of growing Islamization enhanced the political currency of the sectarian narratives deployed by Prabowo's coalition and motivated Jokowi to seek his own Islamic allies and embrace their militant brand of religious pluralism.

Fertile Ground for Populist Politics

By 2014, Indonesia had become fertile ground for populist mobilization. Populist politicians tend to succeed when voters have become disconnected from traditional parties and dissatisfied with the status quo. In his comparative study of populism, for example, Paul Kenny argues that patronage democracies like Indonesia are especially vulnerable, because "populist mobilization thrives where ties between voters and non-populist parties do not exist or have decayed."[32] An erosion in voter-party linkages creates conditions conducive to a populist turn, because charismatic individuals at the national level can more easily bypass party machines and subnational party brokers and make direct appeals to the masses. Populists often do so by using an antisystem, antiparty, and Manichean set of political narratives and symbols. This is precisely what transpired in Indonesia.

Widespread disillusionment with the political establishment made the Indonesian public more receptive to the populist style that Jokowi embodied and that Prabowo cultivated. By the end of the Yudhoyono era, there was a general mood of dissatisfaction with the status quo government: limited progress had been made in the fight against corruption, there had been little improvement in infrastructure and general economic development, and Indonesia was suffering from growing income inequality.[33] The sort of anticorruption rhetoric that helped Yudhoyono win in 2004 now sounded disingenuous and had little traction with the electorate, because large numbers of government ministers and parliamentarians from all parties had been arrested for extortion and bribery over the course of his presidency.

Indeed, the public's trust in and loyalty toward political parties and parliament were strikingly low at the end of Yudhoyono's second term. In the years after the democratic transition, around 80 percent of Indonesians identified with a particular political party; by 2004 that figure had dropped to 55 percent, and by 2014 just 7 percent of Indonesians identified with a political party.[34] Yudhoyono's own approval ratings had been dwindling for years, dropping from 75 percent after his reelection in 2009 to just 30 percent in May 2013.[35] As Marcus Mietzner put it, "Yudhoyono became the embodiment of the complacent stagnation that commentators had identified in both the political and economic arenas."[36] Against this backdrop, Jokowi and Prabowo emerged and tapped into this "inchoate mood of disenfranchisement"—but their populist styles were different, and each appealed ideologically to different parts of Indonesian society.[37]

The Traction of Islamist Narratives

Why did Islamist-themed populism have particular appeal? Some observers draw a direct causal line between the exclusivist brand of identity politics that emerged in recent elections and the growing Islamization of Indonesia's social sphere. Indonesia has become a far more pious Muslim country over the past three decades.[38] There has been a well-documented growth in mosques, Islamic education, Islamic publishing, halal businesses, and sharia banks. More and more Muslims attend Friday prayers and participate with increasing regularity in prayer groups and religious ceremonies. They also consume their religion in other less traditional ways, like following online preachers, participating in new Islamic youth movements, and purchasing on-trend Muslim fashion labels.

As Indonesians have become more religious, they have also become more socially conservative. Some analysts see rising conservatism as an important precursor to more polarizing electoral conflicts. In her article on the "normalization of intolerance" in Indonesia, for example, the Asia Foundation's Sandra Hamid describes a "decades-long trend . . . towards exclusivism in the practice of religion in the private and public spheres."[39]

For Hamid, this social shift explains why an intolerant and divisive brand of populist politics has had such traction with the electorate since 2014. However, the data are inconclusive when it comes to this question of rising intolerance, which remains a subject of debate. Some surveys have painted a picture of an Islamic community that has gradually become less tolerant of religious difference and secular politics.[40] More recent studies, however, indicate that intolerant sentiments toward minorities actually *decreased* in the years leading up to the 2016 Islamist mobilizations.[41]

Opinion polls might be inconclusive, but conservative and Islamist groups did become more assertive and politically influential during President Yudhoyono's decade in power. Tim Lindsey and Helen Pausacker explain how after the democratic transition, post-Suharto governments grew more concerned with winning "support from newly assertive advocates of conservative legal Islamisation."[42] A corollary of Yudhoyono's moderating impulse was the inclusion of once marginal Islamic groups and ideologies into the political mainstream. Yudhoyono struck deals with the country's conservative and Islamist organizations and provided them with patronage and institutional support. Perhaps the most powerful example is how Yudhoyono promoted the political and legal authority of the conservative Majelis Ulama Indonesia (MUI), or the Council of Islamic Scholars. The MUI has issued fatwas against secularism, pluralism, and liberalism and declared minority Muslim sects, like the Ahmadis and Shia, as deviant. The Islamic cleric responsible for many of these fatwas, Ma'ruf Amin, was a close advisor to Yudhoyono as well. The Yudhoyono years were thus marked by a rise to prominence of conservative Muslim figures and a growing legal and political majoritarianism.[43]

It is important, however, not to conflate either social or political Islamization with polarization. During the Yudhoyono period, Islam *infused* the sociopolitical sphere rather than *polarized* it. Election campaigns at the local and national level were often thick with Islamic rhetoric and religious symbolism, but sectarian themes and polarizing appeals were rare. Yudhoyono placed a premium on stability, and his political coalitions were always broad and inclusive. He made sure to distribute patronage resources to groups, parties, and individuals across the ideological spectrum.

It was the rise of Jokowi, a secular pluralist from outside the predominant political class, that triggered an upsurge in divisive Islamist electoral agitation. Once in government, Jokowi and the chair of PDI-P, Megawati Soekarnoputri, distributed key political positions to secular nonparty technocrats, as well as to several retired generals of the New Order era who had been associated with the military's more secular-nationalist faction, including Luhut Panjaitan, Wiranto, and Hendropriyono. Conservative Islamic groups feared marginalization in a polity led by Jokowi and his more secular-pluralist coalition. Prabowo allied with this constituency, enflamed those fears, and framed Jokowi (and Ahok, too) as a threat to the prominent political place that Islam enjoyed during the Yudhoyono era. These dynamics confirm Murat Somer and Jennifer McCoy's proposition that polarization often emerges when "(objectively or subjectively) marginalized elites and societal groups coalesce into new formations and mobilize to achieve social, economic, and political-institutional changes in their own favor."[44]

Jokowi viewed the alliance between Prabowo and Islamic groups as a menacing political force, particularly after Ahok's loss. The president went to great lengths to Islamize his own image and insulate himself against religiously-themed attacks: he developed closer relations with Islamic organizations such as NU and Muhammadiyah, invested in new programs for Islamic boarding schools, and went on several Islamic pilgrimages. Importantly, parts of NU's leadership shared Jokowi's feeling of vulnerability. According to Greg Fealy, NU has long seen itself as "under growing threat from 'transnational' and 'fundamentalist' forms of [Islam], which it associates with Arabised and intolerant religious expression."[45] Fealy suggests that many within NU and PKB viewed a coalition with the president as an opportunity to access patronage resources and state funds and gain leverage over their own Islamist adversaries. Against this backdrop, the 2019 election was marked by immensely divisive rhetoric in which both sides claimed to be defending the "right" version of Indonesian Islam and in which the other side was framed as an existential threat. In doing so, they raised the stakes of electoral competition and enflamed political tensions.

Still Shallow?

It is now clear that political polarization has increased since 2014. But how severe is polarization along this Islamic-pluralist divide in Indonesia? Jennifer McCoy, Tahmina Rahman, and Murat Somer define severe polarization as a process in which a range of different and cross-cutting identities collapse into one identity-based cleavage. That cleavage is then channeled into the party system and defines a spectrum of political and social preferences, penetrates community organizations, and "reduces normal political and social relations into two unyielding hostile factions."[46] Judged against these criteria, polarization in Indonesia still appears relatively shallow and contingent. Several institutional and sociopolitical forces at work in Indonesia favor a more fluid and fragmented political landscape and mitigate polarization.

First, the Islamist-pluralist cleavage is not linked to a range of political preferences, like the red-blue divide in America or the red shirt–yellow shirt divide in Thailand.[47] For example, a survey of Indonesia's provincial parliamentarians conducted in early 2018 revealed little ideological distance between members of the various political parties on almost all issue-areas.[48] Generally, members of Islamic and pluralist parties, and the voters who support them, clustered around the center on a series of questions that explored left-right and traditional-progressive divides, as well as on a range of economic and political questions, indicating an impulse for centrism and moderation, rather than polarization. Unsurprisingly, when it came to questions about the role of religion in public life, this same survey revealed clear differences between the preferences of politicians and voters associated with Islamic parties and those affiliated with pluralist parties. But this is not evidence of *severe* polarization; it simply shows that the Islamic-pluralist cleavage is an important source of political competition within Indonesia's democratic system.

Second, this cleavage is neither unyielding nor inflexible. Despite several polarizing national election campaigns, political relations in Indonesia have not descended into an unyielding conflict between two hostile, warring factions. For example, the same survey of provincial parliamentarians showed that a majority of members of all political parties stated that they could work and form coalitions with any other party, despite ostensible ideological differences. Even the most ideologically distant parties, like the Islamist PKS and the secular-pluralist PDI-P, regularly form coalitions in regional elections around the country. And in legislative elections, party loyalty and ideological differences matter far less than personal connections and patronage distribution in determining voters' preferences.[49] At the national level, "promiscuous power sharing" between ideologically divergent parties and politicians remains the established norm in Indonesian politics.[50] It is driven by the pragmatic pursuit of patronage and is a key force for moderation within the Indonesian party system.

Another crucial factor that prevents severe polarization in Indonesia is the deep historical divisions within the Islamic political community itself. Even NU—long considered a bastion of tolerance and moderation—has its own internal ideological divisions, and its constituents are too diverse to place neatly on a spectrum between Islamist and pluralist. For example, Greg Fealy observes that "sectarian anti-Shia and anti-Ahmadiyah sentiment is deeply held in NU communities . . . [and] NU's leaders admit to hesitancy in responding to popular Islamist activism."[51] Its leadership takes a flexible, even opportunistic, approach to politics too, building alliances with parties and figures across the ideological spectrum. Further, exit polls after the 2019 presidential election suggested that many NU members (around 40 percent) voted for Prabowo over Jokowi. Rather than reflecting hard or stable identity-based groups, the Islamic-pluralist cleavage is often flexible and even inchoate, and many prominent religious figures and organizations do not fit neatly into one category or the other.

Finally, comparative scholars warn against discerning deep societal polarization by looking at party behavior, election results, or people's electoral preferences, because what appears to be a severe division within the population can be "a natural consequence of more polarized candidate choice."[52] As Morris Fiorina, Samuel Abrams, and Jeremy Pope argue, "voting decisions and political evaluations will appear more polarized when the positions candidates adopt and the actions elected officials take become more extreme."[53] In Indonesia, polarization may moderate when Prabowo and Jokowi fade from the frontline of national politics, and the electoral choices on offer become less differentiated.

Consequences

Even if polarization remains relatively shallow overall, these recent electoral conflicts have contributed to a perceptible decline in the quality of Indonesia's democracy. Most troublingly, President Jokowi's attempts to defuse and moderate polarizing conflict have in fact undermined core democratic institutions and norms.

Democratic Decline

Jokowi has eroded democracy by deploying illiberal tools to counter Islamist threats to his government.[54] For example, key leaders in the anti-Ahok demonstrations were targeted with trumped-up charges of treason, corruption, and the spreading of pornographic images. Jokowi then circumvented proper legal process to ban Hizbut Tahrir Indonesia, a radical Islamist group also involved in the anti-Ahok protests. In doing so he introduced a presidential regulation in lieu of a law that gave immense authority to the executive to ban groups it deemed to be "un-nationalist" or to have contravened the *Pancasila*. Rights activists and analysts called the new regulation a tool of repression and "a serious attack on legal protections of freedom of association."[55] Thomas Power even argues that, far more than any other post-Suharto government, the Jokowi administration has marshalled state resources and manipulated legal institutions for partisan purposes, in order to "tame" potential sources of opposition and to prevent political polarization.[56] Indeed, in the lead-up to election day in 2019, reports emerged that staff at state-owned enterprises, ministries, local government offices, and even private businesses were being compelled by their supervisors to vote for Jokowi and were banned from campaigning for Prabowo. The exploitation of incumbency in this way is unprecedented in post-Suharto Indonesia and arguably entrenches the divide between opposition forces, Islamist groups, and the pluralist coalition now in government.

The other crucial dimension of Jokowi's response has been cooptation and accommodation. Jokowi has sought to appease the more mainstream conservative Islamic elite and meet their demands for greater political influence and access to material resources. Jokowi channeled new patronage funds to Islamic organizations such as NU, Muhammadiyah, and the deeply conservative MUI in order to win their support. Ma'ruf Amin has been a key beneficiary of Jokowi's conservative pivot. Following the anti-Ahok protests, in which Ma'ruf's endorsement was crucial, Jokowi "began assiduously courting" the conservative cleric, providing him with access to the palace, new patronage resources, and eventually the offer of a vice-presidential nomination.[57]

These outcomes reflect Somer and McCoy's description of how polarization can erode democratic quality because, in an attempt to defend the status quo "against the 'undemocratic others,' people may begin to undertake actions or employ discourses that end up undermining democracy and advancing authoritarianism."[58] This is precisely the trend now emerging in Indonesia.

Rising Societal Tensions

Many Indonesians are also concerned about the damage that exclusivist and polarizing political campaigns have done to Indonesia's social fabric—even if those campaigns are temporary, and polarization remains relatively shallow. Since 2014, religiously-themed smear campaigns have become a more prominent feature of electoral discourse. Such campaigns can shift public opinion and create a new wedge between different groups within a society. The survey conducted by Mietzner, Muhtadi, and Halida found an uptick in political intolerance toward non-Muslims after the 2017 Jakarta elections. The authors argue that the mobilizations against Ahok "highlight that Indonesia's Muslim community (long viewed as inherently moderate) has become highly susceptible to exclusivist ideas."[59] As McCoy, Rahman, and Somer emphasize in their research, polarization is a process, not a static state, and elite actions can have deep and lasting effects on a community.[60]

Qualitative studies done in the wake of the 2014 and 2017 elections also suggest that people feel more divided than before. For some Indonesians, personal relationships changed in concrete ways after the 2014 elections. Sandra Hamid retells the experience of one Jokowi supporter:

> [A] woman reported that one side of her family refused to help in preparations for, and did not attend, a wedding because she had supported Joko Widodo, who was considered "not good for Muslims."[61]

Since 2014, and particularly after the sectarian mobilizations against Ahok, nongovernmental organizations such as The Asia Foundation, the Wahid Institute, Amnesty International, Human Rights Watch, and the Indonesian arm of the Washington-based National Democratic Institute have all documented an increase in divisive identity politics, hate speech, and prejudice toward more liberally oriented Muslims and toward religious, ethnic, and social minorities.[62] On many measures, Indonesia has not been reduced to a state of severe polarization, but attention to the lived experiences of many moderate Muslims and non-Muslim minorities can paint a different picture.

Remedial Actions

There are no straightforward solutions to polarization, particularly in a context where powerful political interests benefit from a more divided political landscape. Still, there are efforts under way in Indonesia, particularly since the sectarian campaign of 2016 and 2017, to try to manage the causes and consequences of polarization at the societal level. Prominent donors to civil society organizations such as the Wahid Institute, the National Democratic Institute, and The Asia Foundation—all groups with a long history of supporting programs for the consolidation of a liberal democracy in Indonesia—fund interfaith dialogues and support community initiatives that try to combat hate speech and religious extremism. New media personalities and smaller local nongovernmental organizations, such as Sabang Merauke and Masyarakat Anti Fitnah, have also received funding from international donors to expand their activities. These activities include sponsoring online social media channels that encourage religious tolerance, cultural awareness, and fact-based knowledge production and that are designed to generally cultivate a positive online discourse.

It is unlikely, however, that such efforts will have a measurable impact on political polarization unless there is genuine buy-in from Indonesia's political elite. Politicians and parties routinely assert their commitment to unity, peace, positive campaigning, truthfulness, and an end to divisive identity politics, but these rhetorical commitments have often proved disingenuous. Both Prabowo and Jokowi routinely called for an end to "fake news" and smear campaigns, yet both candidates had dedicated "cyber armies" that were tasked with generating social media messages that questioned their rival's personal piety and cast them as a threat to Indonesia's national identity.[63]

In sum, recent developments pose two challenges for Indonesian democracy. The first concerns the growing political clout of Islam and Islamic organizations in Indonesia's electoral politics. Jokowi's rise to power has brought the political implications of Islamization into sharp relief. In contemporary Indonesia, it is an electoral risk for a candidate to have a secular sensibility and a pluralist orientation or indeed to be a member of an ethnoreligious minority. Figures like Jokowi, and others at the regional level, have chosen to signal their support for conservative Islamic agendas rather than chance a religiously charged opposition campaign. Jokowi has appeased some of his conservative critics and sought allies from within their ranks. Ma'ruf Amin's ascendency to the vice presidency is a powerful illustration of this trend. The result is a narrowing of the space for secular politics and liberal ideas and a sustained drift toward a more majoritarian political and legal order.

The second concerns the threat to democratic institutions posed by growing polarization. While the level of societal polarization in Indonesia remains difficult to gauge, increasingly divisive campaign rhetoric, and recent electoral violence, will inevitably widen the divide between pluralist Muslim organizations and members of minority communities, on the one hand, and Islamist-oriented groups and political organizations, on the other. Another serious concern is how the incumbent administration treats the Islamist-linked opposition. Evidence from Jokowi's first term in office suggests that he and other elites in his government are willing to bend or erode democratic norms and institutions to contain perceived political threats. When incumbents abuse their power in this way, those alienated "others" are likely to feel more aggrieved, leading to deeper and more pernicious polarization.

Political polarization and Islamic majoritarianism might seem to be contradictory trends. But the increasingly prominent role of Islam in Indonesia's political sphere during the post-Suharto period has made old ideological divisions between pluralists and Islamists more politically relevant and more easily mobilized by opportunistic elites during moments of electoral competition. While President Yudhoyono's time in office was characterized by the inclusion and cooptation of competing interests on either side of this divide, the Jokowi era has been marked by populist mobilization, Islamist agitation, and deepening political polarization. Both trends, therefore, have brought Indonesia to this current moment of democratic decline.

NOTES

1. Dan Slater and Erica Simmons, "Coping by Colluding: Political Uncertainty and Promiscuous Powersharing in Indonesia and Bolivia," *Comparative Political Studies* 46, no. 11 (2012): 1366–93; Vedi R. Hadiz and Richard Robison, "The Political Economy of Oligarchy and the Reorganization of Power in Indonesia," *Indonesia* 96, no. 1 (2013): 35–57; and Edward Aspinall, "Democratization and Ethnic Politics in Indonesia: Nine Theses," *Journal of East Asian Studies* 11, no. 2 (2011): 289–319.

2. Dan Slater and Aries A. Arugay, "Polarizing Figures: Executive Power and Institutional Conflict in Asian Democracies," *American Behavioral Scientist* 62, no. 1 (2018): 104.

3. Marcus Mietzner, "Indonesia in 2014: Jokowi and the Repolarization of Post-Soeharto Politics," *Southeast Asian Affairs*, no. 1 (2015): 117–38.

4. Edward Aspinall, "Indonesia's Election and the Return of Ideological Competition," *New Mandala* (blog), April 22, 2019 (www.newmandala.org/indonesias-election-and-the-return-of-ideological-competition/).

5. Vedi R. Hadiz and Richard Robison, "Competing Populisms in Post-Authoritarian Indonesia," *International Political Science Review* 38, no. 4 (2017): 488–502; Edward Aspinall, "The New Nationalism in Indonesia," *Asia & the Pacific Policy Studies* 3, no. 1 (2015): 72–82; and Hadiz, "Indonesia's Year of Democratic Setbacks: Towards a New Phase of Deepening Illiberalism?," *Bulletin of Indonesian Economic Studies* 3, no. 3 (2017): 261–78.

6. Stephen P. Nicholson, "Polarizing Cues," *American Journal of Political Science* 56, no. 1 (2012): 52–66.

7. Masyumi represented modernist Muslims, who practiced a more puritan and doctrinal version of Islam. NU was—and remains—a mass organization for traditionalist Muslims known to hold a more flexible and tolerant interpretation of their faith. The secular PNI was led by urban intellectuals but had roots within the *abangan* community of Muslims, mostly on Java, who mixed their faith with syncretic beliefs and traditional cultural practices, and from non-Muslim communities as well. The PKI drew its support from *abangan* too, but mostly from among the rural peasantry.

8. Herb Feith, "Repressive-Developmentalist Regimes in Asia," *Alternatives: Global, Local, Political* 7, no. 4 (1981): 491–506.

9. Slater and Arugay, "Polarizing Figures."

10. Aspinall, "Democratization and Ethnic Politics," 289.

11. Marcus Mietzner, "Comparing Indonesia's Party Systems of the 1950s and the Post-Suharto Era: From Centrifugal to Centripetal Inter-Party Competition," *Journal of Southeast Asian Studies* 39, no. 3 (2008): 431–53.

12. Edward Aspinall, "Indonesia: The Irony of Success," *Journal of Democracy* 21, no. 2 (2010): 20–34.

13. Slater and Simmons, "Coping by Colluding;" Dan Slater, "Indonesia's Accountability Trap: Party Cartels and Presidential Power after Democratic Tran-

sition," *Indonesia* 78 (2004): 61–92; and Kuskridho Ambardi, "The Making of the Indonesian Multiparty System: A Cartelized Party System and Its Origin" (Ph.D. diss., The Ohio State University, 2008) (https://etd.ohiolink.edu/pg_10 ?0::NO:10:P10_ACCESSION_NUM:osu1211901025).

14. Marcus Mietzner, "Dysfunction by Design: Political Finance and Corruption in Indonesia," *Critical Asian Studies* 47, no. 4 (2015): 587–610.

15. Edward Aspinall, Marcus Mietzner, and Dirk Tomsa, eds., *The Yudhoyono Presidency: Indonesia's Decade of Stability and Stagnation* (Singapore: Institute of Southeast Asian Studies, 2015).

16. Ibid., 3.

17. Paul D. Kenny, *Populism and Patronage: Why Populists Win Elections in India, Asia, and Beyond* (New York: Oxford University Press, 2017).

18. Ronald Inglehart and Pippa Norris, "Trump, Brexit, and the Rise of Populism: Economic Have-Nots and Cultural Backlash," Harvard Kennedy School Faculty Working Paper Series, August 2016.

19. Marcus Mietzner, "Reinventing Asian Populism: Jokowi's Rise, Democracy, and Political Contestation in Indonesia," Policy Studies no. 72, East-West Center, 2015 (www.eastwestcenter.org/publications/reinventing-asian-populism-jokowis-rise-democracy-and-political-contestation-in).

20. Edward Aspinall, "Oligarchic Populism: Prabowo Subianto's Challenge to Indonesian Democracy," *Indonesia* 99 (2015): 1–28.

21. Mietzner, "Indonesia in 2014," 121.

22. Ibid.

23. Sam Bollier, "Voting in the 'World's Social Media Capital,'" *Al Jazeera*, July 2, 2014 (www.aljazeera.com/indepth/features/2014/07/voting-worlds-social-media-capital-2014725397392826.html).

24. Eve Warburton, "Indonesian Politics in 2016: Jokowi and the New Developmentalism," *Bulletin of Indonesian Economic Studies* 52, no. 3 (2016): 297–320; idem., "Inequality, Nationalism and Electoral Politics in Indonesia," *Southeast Asian Affairs* 2018, no. 1 (2018): 135–52.

25. Eve Warburton and Liam Gammon, "Class Dismissed? Economic Fairness and Identity Politics in Indonesia," *New Mandala* (blog), May 5, 2017 (www.newmandala.org/economic-injustice-identity-politics-indonesia/).

26. Greg Fealy, "Bigger than Ahok: Explaining the 2 December Mass Rally," *Indonesia at Melbourne* (blog), December 7, 2016 (https://indonesiaatmelbourne. unimelb.edu.au/bigger-than-ahok-explaining-jakartas-2-december-mass-rally/).

27. Marcus Mietzner, Burhanuddin Muhtadi, and Rizka Halida, "Entrepreneurs of Grievance: Drivers and Effects of Indonesia's Islamist Mobilization," *Bijdragen tot de taal, lan-en Volkenkunde* 174, no. 2–3 (2018): 159–87.

28. Azis Anwar Fachrudin, "Jokowi and NU: The View from the Pesantren," *New Mandala* (blog), April 11, 2019 (www.newmandala.org/jokowi-and-nu-the-view-from-the-pesantren/).

29. Indikator Politik Indonesia, "Laporan Quick Count: Pilpres dan pileg DPR

RI, 17 April 2019" [Quick count report: Presidential and national legislative election, 17 April 2019], April 24, 2019 (http://indikator.co.id/uploads/20190424182622. Laporan_QC_Pilpres_dan_Pileg_17_April_2019_Indikator.pdf).

30. Indikator Politik Indonesia, "2019 Election Exit Poll," April 17, 2019 (http://indikator.co.id/uploads/20190419215553.Exit_Poll_Pemilu_2019_Indikator.pdf).

31. Francis Chan and Wahyudi Soeriaatmadja, "Violence Was Coordinated: Jakarta Police," *Straits Times*, May 23, 2019 (www.straitstimes.com/asia/se-asia/violence-was-coordinated-jakarta-police).

32. Kenny, *Populism and Patronage*, 3.

33. Mietzner, "Reinventing Asian Populism"; and Hadiz and Robison, "Competing Populisms in Post-Authoritarian Indonesia."

34. Saiful Mujani, R. William Liddle, and Kuskridho Ambardi, *Voting Behaviour in Indonesia since Democratization: Critical Democrats* (Cambridge, UK: Cambridge University Press, 2018), 187–88. Likewise, trust in political parties has not improved: a 2018 poll found that only 0.3 percent of the population thought that political parties were trustworthy. Husein Abdulsalam, "Burhanuddin Muhtadi: Ideologi Parpol, Bukan Jokowi atau Oposisi, tapi Pancasil vs Islam" [Burhanuddin Muhtadi: Political party ideology, not Jokowi or opposition, but Pancasila vs Islam], *Tirto.id*, June 25, 2018 (https://tirto.id/ideologi-parpol-bukan-jokowi-atau-oposisi-tapi-pancasila-vs-islam-cMUB).

35. Mietzner, "Reinventing Asian Populism," 16.

36. Ibid.

37. Edward Aspinall, "The Surprising Democratic Behemoth: Indonesia in Comparative Asian Perspective," *The Journal of Asian Studies* 74, no. 4 (2015): 889.

38. Greg Fealy and Sally White, *Expressing Islam: Religious Life and Politics in Indonesia* (Singapore: Institute of Southeast Asian Studies, 2008).

39. Sandra Hamid, "Normalising Intolerance: Elections, Religion and Everyday Life in Indonesia," CILS Policy Paper (Centre for Indonesian Law, Islam and Society, 2018), 4 (https://law.unimelb.edu.au/centres/cilis/research/publications/cilis-policy-papers/normalising-intolerance-elections,-religion-and-everyday-life-in-indonesia).

Hamid offers a powerful account of the everyday experiences of Muslim and non-Muslim Indonesians who find their belief systems and lifestyles increasingly marginalized from the public sphere and under attack by proponents of a more conservative, puritan interpretation of Islam. Commercialization, Hamid argues, has played an important role in this shift: Television soap operas and online preachers compete for audiences and followers, and in response often simplify their religious messages into binaries—haram or halal, veiled modest women or loose immoral women, Muslim or non-Muslim, us or them. For example, Hamid documents stories of changed personal relations in villages on Java, whereby Muslim residents have slowly isolated themselves from their non-Muslim neighbors, conducting their community events separately for fear of engaging in haram activities. Many other stories in the media, in Hamid's report, and in this author's fieldwork have described the more widespread use of *kafir* ("unbeliever," used as a derogatory term) in social circles and on social media.

40. Greg Fealy, "The Politics of Religious Intolerance in Indonesia: Mainstream-Ism Trumps Extremism?" in *Religion, Law and Intolerance in Indonesia*, ed. Tim Lindsey and Helen Pausacker (New York: Routledge, 2016), 115–31.

41. Mietzner, Muhtadi, and Halida, "Entrepreneurs of Grievance."

42. Lindsey and Pausacker, *Religion, Law and Intolerance in Indonesia*, 4.

43. Hamid, "Normalising Intolerance: Elections, Religion and Everyday Life in Indonesia"; and Robin Bush, "Religious Politics and Minority Rights during the Yudhoyono Presidency," in Aspinall, Mietzner, and Tomsa, *The Yudhoyono Presidency*, 239–57.

44. Murat Somer and Jennifer McCoy, "Déjà Vu? Polarization and Endangered Democracies in the 21st Century," *American Behavioral Scientist* 62, no. 1 (2018): 4.

45. Greg Fealy, "Indonesia's Growing Islamic Divide," *The Straits Times*, May 3, 2019 (www.straitstimes.com/opinion/indonesias-growing-islamic-divide).

46. Jennifer McCoy, Tahmina Rahman, and Murat Somer, "Polarization and the Global Crisis of Democracy: Common Patterns, Dynamics, and Pernicious Consequences for Democratic Polities," *American Behavioral Scientist* 62, no. 1 (2018): 18.

47. See the following for a discussion of various methods for measuring polarization: Morris P. Fiorina, Samuel A. Abrams, and Jeremy C. Pope, "Polarization in the American Public: Misconceptions and Misreadings," *The Journal of Politics* 70, no. 2 (2008): 556–60; Lilliana Mason, "'I Disrespectfully Agree': The Differential Effects of Partisan Sorting on Social and Issue Polarization," *American Journal of Political Science* 59, no. 1 (2015): 128–45; and McCoy, Rahman, and Somer, "Polarization and the Global Crisis of Democracy."

48. Edward Aspinall and others, "Mapping the Indonesian Political Spectrum," *New Mandala* (blog), April 24, 2018 (www.newmandala.org/mapping-indonesian-political-spectrum/).

49. Edward Aspinall, "Indonesia's Election and the Return of Ideological Competition," *New Mandala* (blog), April 22, 2019 (www.newmandala.org/indonesias-election-and-the-return-of-ideological-competition/).

50. Slater and Simmons, "Coping by Colluding."

51. Greg Fealy, "Nahdlatul Ulama and the Politics Trap," *New Mandala* (blog), July 11, 2018 (www.newmandala.org/nahdlatul-ulama-politics-trap/).

52. Fiorina, Abrams, and Pope, "Polarization in the American Public," 556.

53. Ibid.

54. Marcus Mietzner offers a forensic account of Jokowi's response to the mobilizations: see Marcus Mietzner, "Fighting Illiberalism with Illiberalism: Islamist Populism and Democratic Deconsolidation in Indonesia" *Pacific Affairs* 91, no. 2 (2018): 261–82.

55. Usman Hamid and Liam Gammon, "Jokowi Forges a Tool of Repression," *New Mandala* (blog), July 13, 2017 (www.newmandala.org/jokowi-forges-tool -repression/).

56. Thomas Power, "Jokowi's Authoritarian Turn," *New Mandala* (blog), October 9, 2018 (www.newmandala.org/jokowis-authoritarian-turn/).

57. Greg Fealy, "Ma'ruf Amin: Jokowi's Islamic Defender or Deadweight?" *New Mandala* (blog), August 28, 2018 (www.newmandala.org/maruf-amin-jokowis -islamic-defender-deadweight/).

58. Somer and McCoy, 'Déjà Vu?" 4.

59. Mietzner, Muhtadi, and Halida, "Entrepreneurs of Grievance," 182.

60. McCoy, Rahman, and Somer, "Polarization and the Global Crisis of Democracy."

61. Hamid, "Normalising Intolerance."

62. See for example, Human Rights Watch, "Indonesia: Events of 2017" (www. hrw.org/world-report/2018/country-chapters/indonesia).

63. Ross Tapsell, "When They Go Low, We Go Lower: Will Fake News Decide Indonesia's Election Next Week?" *New York Times*, April 16, 2019 (www.nytimes. com/2019/04/16/opinion/indonesia-election-fake-news.html).

NINE

Brazil: When Political Oligarchies Limit Polarization but Fuel Populism

UMBERTO MIGNOZZETTI

MATIAS SPEKTOR

Brazil presents a significant puzzle for analysts of polarization. A cursory glance at contemporary Brazilian politics suggests that the country should be a clear-cut case of heightened polarization at both the mass and elite levels. In 2013, millions of Brazilians took to the streets in levels unseen since the country transitioned from authoritarian rule three decades earlier. Widespread citizen anger underpinned the ouster of President Dilma Rousseff in 2016. Her detractors accused her and her Workers' Party (Partido dos Trabalhadores; PT) of concocting a scheme of large-scale graft to rob public coffers, while her supporters denounced impeachment proponents as coup plotters set on kicking the left out of power. The country appeared to be "caught up in the sharpest and most polarizing political crisis in the young democracy's history."[1] Moreover, in 2018, the second round of Brazil's presidential election presented the country with two candidates representing opposing ends of the left-right political spectrum. In the process, traditional centrist parties that had been the hallmark of Brazil's democratic experience weakened. With the election of Jair Bolsonaro as president in October 2018, Brazilian politics became dominated by a figure who starkly divided public opinion. Brazil would seem to present a societal tableau prone to polarization as well. Brazil has long had extremely high levels of economic inequality, which in other Latin American countries such as Venezuela has been one of the foundation stones of harsh left-right polarization. Furthermore, Brazil has deep racial divisions along black-white lines that could also be a source of polarization, as is the case in Bolivia, with its divide between indigenous and non-indigenous parts of the society.

Yet for all the political turmoil, levels of ideological and partisan polarization in Brazil have been low when compared to polarization both in other countries and in Brazil's recent past. Neither the public nor representatives in Congress and their parties are divided into traditional left-right camps. The 2018 election caused levels of mass affective polarization—the extent to which people on one side of a political divide dislike people on the other—to skyrocket, yet this societal anger has not translated into rising partisanship to any great degree. It is not partisan polarization but rather rising antiestablishment sentiment that has driven Brazil's recent political upheaval.

Evidence suggests high levels of frustration among citizens with the ruling class. The October 2018 presidential election featured the highest level ever of null ballots, which doubled relative to the level in 2002 and reached 7.44 percent of the total vote. As Brazilians have taken to the streets in recent years, they have protested against a string of corruption scandals implicating politicians across the entire political spectrum. The eruption of spontaneous mass protests in 2013 was an antiestablishment, nonpartisan development. And since 2014, Brazilians have reacted with anger to revelations of a kickback scheme whereby large business conglomerates purchased political favors from both the left and right. The election of Jair Bolsonaro, a politician with three decades of experience in Congress who nonetheless campaigned as an ultraright outsider, demonstrated the widespread appeal of antiestablishment rhetoric. Having no support from any of the main parties and running a campaign primarily based on WhatsApp and other social media, he managed to make a credible commitment to radical change before the electorate. Brazil is a case where the relative absence of ideological and partisan polarization has coexisted with the rise of widespread antiestablishment sentiment.

Bolsonaro's presidency may inaugurate a new era of political polarization in the coming years, as the arrival to power in Venezuela of the populist Hugo Chávez in 1998 did over time. Yet polarization in Brazilian politics has, at least thus far, remained low in comparative perspective. Four sets of Brazilian political institutions—multiparty presidentialism, electoral rules, clientelism, and the weakness of oversight institutions—have tempered partisan polarization. These institutions have inhibited democratic accountability and reduced the importance of ideology and party programs, thereby limiting elements that typically fuel political polarization. At the same time, they have fostered collusion and corruption among the traditional parties, fueling disillusionment with the political status quo. Frustration with this system led many Brazilians to support a populist candidate who promised to overturn the existing system. In this respect, the most striking comparison to Brazil's 2018 election is the aforementioned 1998 victory of Hugo Chávez in Venezuela. Before Chávez rose to power, Venezuela's major establishment parties colluded to loot the state for resources. Thus, polarization between the two main parties was low, but their corrupt behavior fueled antiestablishment sentiment, especially when the Venezuelan economy began to decline. In the Venezuelan case, as in Brazil, oligarchic politics limited polarization but fueled populism.[2] This chapter assesses the consequences of this type of low-level polarization and discusses remedial actions to increase positive, democracy-enhancing polarization in Brazil.

Trajectory (I): Low Polarization and Endemic Corruption—Brazilian Democracy, 1985 to 2017

As Brazil transitioned to democracy in 1985 after two decades of authoritarian rule, expectations were high that universal suffrage would transform programmatic politics into the new game in town. Indeed, the introduction of majoritarian elections for mayors, governors, senators, and the president injected a hefty dose of programmatic politics into the system. As a result, elections became more defined by choices between the right and left. However, as the analysis that follows will indicate, Brazilian democracy featured several mechanisms inherited from the old authoritarian regime that militated against the rise of a clear programmatic divide. For one, the old authoritarian regime's tools of nondemocratic influence, such as vote-buying, widespread clientelism, and patronage, remained in use. The transition from authoritarian rule thus left mostly intact the powerbrokers of the old regime: the armed forces, old political dynasties, party bosses, rent-seekers around Brazil's large developmental state, business conglomerates, and civil servant unions. Brazil did gradually establish civilian control over the military, but the enduring influence of clientelistic practices meant that politics was more about capturing state resources than achieving ideological goals.

Furthermore, the rules of the new democratic game militated against polarization. Brazil has a multiparty presidential system in which the president's party typically does not manage to secure a parliamentary majority. In order to govern, Brazilian presidents therefore need to form a coalition with several other parties and are forced to dilute their original party platforms. In turn, parties in parliament throw their support behind the sitting president in exchange for targeted government funding (or pork, in the political sense of the term), cabinet positions, and opportunities for corruption in Brazil's sprawling developmental state. Here the role of party programs is secondary, not least because *deputados* (representatives) in the National Congress are elected through an open-list proportional representation system that severely reduces accountability to voters.

The Cardoso and Lula Presidencies, 1995 to 2010

The structure of legislative-executive relations in Brazil's democratic system thus militated against a stark programmatic divide. This dynamic is best seen in the successive tenures of Fernando Henrique Cardoso (and his center-right coalition) and Luiz Inácio Lula da Silva (and his center-left coalition) in the period between 1995 and 2010. For all their differences, in these years the two poles in Brazilian politics coalesced in the middle and produced numerous beneficial results such as financial stability, low inflation, conditional cash transfers, and minimum wage hikes above the inflation rate—all of which contributed to reducing Brazil's socioeconomic inequality. As Timothy Power has argued, convergence between the right and left during this period should be seen as an "implicit cross-party consensus."[3]

Yet this consensus relied fundamentally on a lack of programmatic politics and on rampant corruption. Both Cardoso and Lula built multiparty cabinets to secure a majority in the legislature, but rather than forming small, watertight winning coalitions in parliament, they built oversized coalitions with little ideological coherence. This was an insurance policy against defections and indiscipline, both of which are rampant and usually go unpunished in the Brazilian political system. The mechanisms for coalition-building included the distribution of ministerial posts and various lucrative positions in the state apparatus, pork, and opportunities for political corruption through bids and tenders for public contracts with large business conglomerates. As a result of this perverse mechanism at the heart of the executive's majority formation in the legislature, Brazil's reputation for corruption and transparency has been dismal, but polarization has been low.[4] President Lula's PT presided over rapid social inclusion supported by a global commodity boom, targeted social policies, and the government's activism to lift millions out of poverty. Lula managed to elect his anointed successor, Dilma Rousseff, in 2010.

The Rousseff Era, 2011 to 2016

Not long after her election, a combination of economic and political challenges overwhelmed Rousseff's presidency and rendered her deeply unpopular. On the economic front, Rousseff had to cope with the aftermath of the global financial crisis, the end of the commodity boom, and a shrinking economy. Between 2014 and 2016, Brazil experienced the worst recession in its history, with gross domestic product (GDP) per capita shrinking by 10 percent. Rousseff tried to stimulate Brazil's sagging economy by increasing public spending, but this policy only fueled a perverse cycle of fiscal deficits and failed to reverse rising unemployment. During her presidency, the deficit spiked from 2 percent of GDP in 2010 to 10 percent in 2015.

On the political front, two key developments—widespread protests in 2013 and an anticorruption investigation beginning in 2014—rocked Rousseff's presidency and signaled growing frustration with the political class as a whole. The 2013 protests originally began in opposition to a 10-cent increase in bus fares in the city of São Paulo, but before long they escalated into a broader national movement, the largest Brazil had seen in decades. Citizens swarmed the streets of cities across the country to denounce widespread corruption, police violence, growing economic inequality, and the low quality of public services amid the crushing expenses that the country had taken on as it prepared to host the 2014 World Cup and 2016 Summer Olympics. These demonstrations had a dramatic impact on Rousseff's popularity: her approval rating plummeted from 57 percent before the protests began to just 30 percent a month later. Yet more significantly, these protests showed growing frustration not just with Rousseff but with the Brazilian political class as a whole.

Outrage with the political establishment only intensified as an anticorruption investigation known as Operation Car Wash (Operação Lava Jato) began to reveal the systemic corruption at the heart of Brazilian politics. The investigation began in March 2014 as an investigation into allegations that Brazil's government-controlled oil company, Petrobras, had accepted bribes in exchange for awarding lucrative contracts. The investigation swiftly uncovered a pervasive pattern of corruption and unveiled that overpayments on contracts issued by the Brazilian government had been siphoned into a secret slush fund that funneled the money to political parties and well-connected business conglomerates. Billions of dollars in taxpayer money funded election campaigns illegally, while a broader scheme of corruption allowed private interests to purchase political favors in all three branches of government. Brazilian conglomerates and party officials involved in the scheme bribed officials in twelve other countries in Latin America and Africa and stashed their illegal funds in Europe and the United States.

The performance of the Lava Jato investigation has been remarkable. Since 2014, the task force has accused or sent to court or jail over 500 high-ranking politicians, bureaucrats, and businesspeople. Investigators discovered that politicians on both the left and right had received bribes and secret campaign-finance funds to the tune of some $10 billion. In the process, the task force has retrieved billions of dollars for Brazilian taxpayers. It has charged many prominent figures with numerous crimes, including corruption, money laundering, abuse of the international financial system, obstruction of justice, destruction of evidence, lying to prosecutors, and insider trading. The task force has indicted four former presidents, revealing crimes that go back decades and involve just about every major political party in the country. These revelations profoundly undermined public confidence not just in the ruling PT but in the entire political establishment.

Having never held elected office before, Rousseff struggled to manage her coalition in the face of these economic and political crises. When new corruption scandals broke, defections from the coalition picked up pace. In December 2015, the lower house of Brazil's National Congress formally accepted a petition to begin impeachment proceedings.

The run-up to Rousseff's impeachment certainly hardened group identities on the right and left. Each faction saw a marked rise in intragroup solidarity, with social media playing a role in structuring two opposing blocs for and against impeachment. Yet social media bubbles also made polarization appear more pervasive and severe than it actually was, in particular to wealthier Brazilians who are more likely to be active on platforms such as Facebook and Twitter. Data gathered for the 2014–18 period support this view: levels of polarization remained low, until affective polarization spiked around the 2018 presidential election. Furthermore, conflict over a polarizing leader does not in and of itself translate into deeper, lasting ideological polarization. The opposition to Rousseff succeeded in removing her from office but did not exclude her whole base of support from politics. There was no use of extrajudicial tactics, which would have paved the way for heightened polarization. Polarization over these episodes was temporary rather than lasting.

Thus, during the long months that the impeachment procedures lasted, there was a rise in polarization. Rousseff's embattled government sought to polarize politics and cast its opponents as right-wing conspirators to prevent its base from defecting. Factions working for the impeachment took advantage of widespread dissatisfaction with the government to come to power and implement policies that had not won popular support at the polls. Polarization again rose in early 2018 when the popular leader and former president Luiz Inácio Lula da Silva received a prison sentence over corruption charges. On social media, in particular, the months leading up to the judicial process that eventually sent Lula to jail made it appear as though Brazil was fractured between two opposing camps. After all, Lula was the most obvious candidate to represent a coalition of the center-left in the 2018 presidential election, and polls suggested he would easily win the contest. With the presidential election fast approaching, polarization spiked.

But divisions between the opposing blocs did not necessarily take root in the political outlooks of the population at large and foster societal polarization. One reason for this turn of events might be that the vast majority of the Brazilian electorate is politically disengaged and remained largely passive throughout the proceedings to impeach one president and imprison another. Also, the dominant platform for political mobilization among Brazilians is neither Facebook nor Twitter but WhatsApp—division and polarization online do not travel as easily through a private messaging system as they do through broader network- and connection-based social media platforms.[5] Moreover, party elites on both sides of the divide failed to tighten the bonds with their followers, and there is no indication that popular support for the anti-Rousseff, anti-Lula camp increased as a result of the impeachment. Brazilians generally were angry with their political class as a whole, and the split between contending right and left coalitions had little purchase with the population at large.

Thus, economic hardship, corruption scandals, rising levels of violence, and the lack of accountability of successive governments paved the way for the rise of antisystem candidates in the October 2018 elections, when Brazilians elected a new president, twenty-seven new governors, all the members of the lower chamber of Congress (513 representatives), and two-thirds of the Senate.

Trajectory (II): The Bolsonaro Era

On October 7, 2018, Jair Bolsonaro dominated the first round of Brazil's presidential election with an astounding 46 percent of the vote and carried dozens of candidates for state and national legislatures on his coattails. Two weeks later he sealed his victory against Fernando Haddad of the PT in a runoff that landed him a comfortable majority of ten million votes. Bolsonaro's rise to power left experts and pundits in shock. An obscure member of parliament whose extreme policy ideas and offensive style are outside Brazil's political mainstream ran a campaign that landed him in the driver's seat of one of the world's largest democracies. Many referred to his victory as representing a wave of radical extremism.

Yet Bolsonaro did not win the presidency thanks to a committed minority of zealots. For all his shocking rhetoric and actions, Bolsonaro managed to appeal to voters beyond his hardcore, right-wing base. Millions of voters who normally would have cast their ballots in favor of centrist candidates voted for him. Consider the results from the first round of the election in the state of São Paulo. Winning 53 percent of the vote, Bolsonaro dealt a humiliating defeat to the four-term governor of São Paulo and center-right presidential candidate Geraldo Alckmin, who ended up securing a mere 9.52 percent of the vote. Something similar happened to the centrist candidate Marina Silva. Back in 2014, she had won the first round of the election in states like Acre and the Federal District. In 2018, Bolsonaro took both states by wide margins (with 62 percent and 58 percent of the vote, respectively), and Silva ended up commanding only 1 percent of the total vote. Equally impressive was Bolsonaro's showing in the northeast, one of the country's most impoverished regions and the PT's core geographic base. Although the left-wing presidential candidate Fernando Haddad won eight out of the nine northeast states in the first round of the election, Bolsonaro outperformed him in the largest five capital cities in those states. Bolsonaro also received 52 percent of the vote in the state of Rio Grande do Sul, which four years earlier had given the left a clear victory in the first round.

The Roots of Bolsonaro's Appeal

Bolsonaro's success and his appeal beyond the extreme right resulted from the fact that this was an anger-driven, antiestablishment election. Data on mass affective polarization in 2018 suggest that anti-PT sentiment became a powerful force in the electorate, and Bolsonaro tapped into a wave of popular discontent.[6]

To begin, Bolsonaro's campaign resonated with an electorate that seems to support a more socially conservative set of policies than it has in the past. One driver of this shift is the rapid growth across Brazil of Pentecostalism, a form of evangelical Protestantism; Pentecostals now account for some 30 percent of the electorate. Issues of ethnicity, gender, and sexuality have come to the fore, with culture wars raging in ways that have not been typical of Brazil in the past. Bolsonaro gives salience to these issues through provocative comments about rape, LGBT (lesbian, gay, bisexual, and transgender) people, and indigenous Brazilians in ways that used to be unacceptable.

In addition, as has been the case in many other countries, populist candidates like Bolsonaro thrive on misinformation, fake news, and hearsay. The rise of misinformation is particularly worrying because it comes at a time when Brazil's traditional media organizations face significant financial constraints. The erstwhile influential media group Abril filed for bankruptcy in 2018, while other major national newspapers are either accumulating growing deficits or relying on sister companies to make ends meet. Media groups have also had a hard time adapting to online news and new technologies and seem to be developing a severe credibility problem. In the last few weeks of the 2018 presidential campaign, abuse and violence against journalists increased, and Bolsonaro has fueled anger against the press.

Yet most importantly, in an election year in which the dominant popular sentiment was anger at the political class, Bolsonaro rode a wave of discontent that had three core drivers. First, the wave began to crest as recent growth in unemployment created a backlash against affirmative action policies introduced by previous administrations. Second, an epidemic of violence has turned Brazil into one of the most dangerous countries in the world and given rise to widespread support for more stringent policing, at a time when memories of abuse during Brazil's 1964–85 dictatorship have faded among older voters and hold little meaning for voters who are too young to have any first-hand experience with authoritarianism. Bolsonaro has supported the use of torture against criminals, spoken favorably of extrajudicial killing squads, and told security forces they will receive protection under his watch if they use violence against criminals. Finally, as previously discussed, corruption scandals tarred political elites from across the political spectrum and fanned the flames of widespread discontent with the political establishment. Bolsonaro addressed these grievances by promising radical economic reform to curb unemployment and falling incomes, tougher policies on crime, and unquestioned support for the Lava Jato anticorruption probe.

Of all the candidates on offer, Bolsonaro was the only one to give the electorate clear signals of his commitment to change. He has considered radical steps, such as taking Brazil out of the United Nations Human Rights Council. On economic reform, he appointed as his economy minister a Chicago-trained economist who has promised a maximalist neoliberal agenda. This commitment to radical change appealed to a broad swath of voters frustrated with the political status quo. And in a country where support for political parties and democratic norms has fallen to historical lows, Bolsonaro cleverly tailored a message that appealed to the few institutions that still command popular respect: family, religion, and the armed forces.

Bolsonaro as a Potential Driver of Polarization

With Bolsonaro now in power, many observers fear that he might initiate a new form of polarizing populism. The logic here is that outsider politicians who run on antiestablishment platforms frequently violate democratic norms in ways that can be highly polarizing. Furthermore, political outsiders often champion and then adopt radical policies that divide public opinion. Finally, Bolsonaro has the potential to be polarizing given his use of social media, WhatsApp, and other outlets to rail against the political class. Already, as the data in the appendix show, levels of mass affective polarization in Brazil have spiked, more than tripling between 2014 and 2018. Indeed, in 2018 Brazil exhibited higher levels of mass affective polarization than Turkey in 2011 or any other country in the data provided by Alban Lauka, Jennifer McCoy, and Rengin Firat.[7]

But under what conditions precisely could Bolsonaro contribute to a sustained increase in polarization? First, if he were to elicit a uniformly hostile elite response, which paints him and his followers as backward, uneducated, and threatening to democracy, that elite discourse could further antagonize vast sections of Brazilian society that opted to vote him into office. Second, if Bolsonaro aggressively pursues controversial policies that would never pass under normal circumstances, he could aggravate divisions within society and create lasting polarization over his own legacy.

Yet it is unlikely that even a divisive figure like Bolsonaro will generate a serious move toward lasting polarization at a level that would cause a democratic crisis and collapse of the kind that Venezuela has experienced. In Brazilian politics, the name of the game is compromise, and existing rules will create strong incentives for members of parliament to cooperate with Bolsonaro to gain access to pork, patronage, and indeed opportunities for establishing close ties—legally and illegally—with private conglomerates. The more likely scenario is that Bolsonaro will govern with the support of key establishment parties. Indeed, the new Congress elected in October

2018 has shown that it is willing to work with Bolsonaro on several policy initiatives. To date, there is no evidence to suggest that he stands a chance of becoming dominant over other political groups, a development that would foment polarization. It is unlikely that cross-cutting cleavages recurring in Brazilian politics will lose their salience. Thus, the current spike in affective polarization does not seem likely at present to translate into an enduring partisan divide that could form the basis for severe polarization.

Brazil's Deeper Malaise: Antiestablishment Sentiment

Rather than being a cause of democratic backsliding through polarization, Bolsonaro may be a symptom of deeper problems facing Brazil's political regime, such as endemic corruption and a lack of democratic accountability. If the political system remains unreformed and Brazilian politics retain oligarchic features, then the gap may well expand between the political class running the country and the populace at large. This is where the real danger lies. The worry is not polarization between parties on the right and left, between government and opposition, or between the executive and any of the two other branches of government. Rather, the biggest threat facing Brazilian democracy today is a widening gap between the political establishment and the people. Given the rise of antiestablishment sentiment, some level of political polarization that sharpens programmatic choices for the country may be a positive counterweight to populist politics.

Growing disillusionment with the political status quo is particularly disturbing and should be cause for concern given how little support democracy enjoys among poorer Brazilians, who account for the vast majority of the electorate. According to Latinobarómetro, a large number of Brazilians are indifferent as to whether democracy or authoritarianism is preferable, and the percentage of Brazilians stating that "democracy is always preferable" is low. These survey results are consistent with the fact that most Brazilians mistrust a wide range of social and political institutions.[8]

Oligarchic Politics Limit Polarization

Severe polarization has not taken root in Brazil because the rules of the political game have privileged a specific type of oligarchic politics that runs counter to the core factors fueling polarization in democratic settings—ideological or programmatic differentiation between political parties, as well as the accountability of elected officials to voters. More specifically, four institutional arrangements help explain Brazil's relatively low levels of polarization over time.

First, Brazil's system of *multiparty presidentialism*, which combines a powerful presidency with a legislature filled with numerous small parties, creates incentives for presidents to form legislative coalitions based more on the distribution of material benefits than on shared ideological principles. Brazil features one of the most fragmented political party systems in the world; currently, over two dozen parties are represented in Congress. Since the return to elected civilian rule in 1985, the president's party has never controlled a majority and usually holds under 20 percent of the seats. Thus, in order to govern, Brazilian presidents cannot rely solely on their own party and must form legislative coalitions, often with parties that putatively have conflicting ideological positions. Brazil's constitution further undermines the potential for programmatic politics by giving the president significant power to distribute cabinet seats, budgets, and pork. These material benefits, not ideological principles, are usually the glue that binds legislative coalitions together. Presidents thus have several constitutional powers to obtain legislative support and govern effectively, but these tend to make representative institutions even more crippled.[9] Furthermore, as the Lava Jato investigation has revealed, the Brazilian president also provides his or her legislative coalition with opportunities for securing illegal funds to defray the cost of political campaigns. One way presidents can do so is by appointing party brokers to key positions in Brazil's sprawling state enterprises and regulatory agencies.[10] In spite of high fragmentation, the Brazilian party system has a great deal of party discipline. Yet this party discipline has significant negative consequences, as parties within the president's coalition can threaten to abandon the government on key votes in Congress, thereby vying for higher concessions before each relevant vote and turning legislation into a bidding war for their support.[11]

Second, Brazil's *electoral rules* reduce the potential for programmatic politics in several distinct ways. In Brazil's open-list proportional representation system, voters cast their ballots for individual politicians, rather than the parties on whose tickets these politicians run. The vast size of electoral districts—which are massive statewide territories populated by millions of voters and returning a large number of seats—results in low levels of accountability. Voters seldom meet or even get to know the views of their representatives in parliament.[12] With the focus on individual politicians rather than on parties, virtually no political party in Brazil is structured around class, race, or ethnic foundations to give it a distinctive programmatic identity. To be sure, the PT was unquestionably programmatic at its inception in the 1980s, but once it gained office at the municipal and state levels in the 1990s and secured the presidency in the 2000s, it evolved into yet another business-as-usual party. This state of affairs might be changing now with the rise of parties that are closely attached to various evangelical denominations and take a more clearly programmatic stance on issues of religion. Until now, however, this has not generated a political dynamic whereby religion becomes a significant polarizing force: the evangelical parties do make religion the bedrock of their program, but they are inclusive of various denominations, do not campaign on exclusionary programs, and have proven to be as willing to trade away programmatic demands for cabinet positions, pork, and opportunities for corruption as any other party in Brazil. Their religious identity is used to secure the votes necessary to elect representatives, which explains why few evangelical candidates running for majoritarian seats actually win these elections.

Another electoral rule mitigating against programmatic politics is that alliances among parties are unusually malleable. It is not uncommon for party leaders of opposing camps to grant their operators free rein to form coalitions at the local level that are at odds with party programs at the national level. This practice further undermines accountability to voters, who for the most part are kept in the dark as to the actual leanings of their representatives in Congress. Since coalitions are amorphous and change frequently, it is difficult for voters to punish any individual party for the failure of a particular coalition. This lack of electoral accountability creates a system whereby coalition members have little if any attachment to the success of the government's agenda. Whether the government succeeds or fails in implementing its program does not translate immediately into rewards or punishment for individual representatives and parties in the coalition.

Brazil's electoral rules also allow a variety of small, largely nonideological parties to proliferate. Given that Brazil until recently did not have an electoral threshold for parties to qualify for public funds, the National Congress now features over two dozen parties. The smaller parties often trade their seats with nonideological politicians, and once in parliament, they will trade votes for procurements, patronage, and the like. Not only do these practices result in low levels of accountability to voters, but it also may well be the case that in Brazil, as in other countries, such a system is particularly prone to capture by interest groups, a dynamic that helps fuel endemic corruption.[13]

Third, in the realm of *informal practices*, vote-buying, clientelism, and patronage remain pervasive and reduce the importance of programmatic divides between parties. In this context, party programs are less salient, because voters are primarily interested in receiving material benefits in exchange for their support. Voters are less likely to hold their parties to account for specific policy programs.

Finally, the *weakness of Brazilian oversight institutions* long allowed a culture of corruption to flourish. To be sure, as previously discussed, the Lava Jato investigation has led to indictments against scores of Brazilian politicians since 2014 and exposed the rot at the heart of the country's politics. But these figures would be significantly higher were it not for a law that grants Brazilian politicians special standing and protects them from prosecution. When charged with a crime, politicians can only be tried by the Supreme Court. This system effectively grants politicians immunity—in the past thirty years, the court has convicted only four sitting politicians. A third of the members of Congress today face criminal proceedings before the high court, for instance, but keep their posts because their cases never go to trial thanks to friendly Supreme Court justices whom they appoint. Crucial here is that since 2014, the political class and its associates in the courts have pushed for new legislation to curtail the powers of prosecutors and magistrates. They have also tried to free those who are serving terms in jail and to cap the ability of judges to imprison those already convicted. As Senator Romero Jucá mused in the run-up to Rousseff's impeachment, without knowing he was being recorded: "We have to stop this s--t. We have to change the government to be able to stop this bleeding, [working] with the Supreme Court, with everything we've got."[14]

Vice President Michel Temer took over in August 2016 to honor that pledge. Himself accused of numerous crimes, Temer was a stalwart of the old order, shielded from prosecution by his office. When Lava Jato prosecutors put forward a ten-point reform package to Congress supported by the signatures of more than two million citizens in a public petition, Temer's coalition in Congress killed it. Moreover, Electoral Court justices with ties to the government dismissed all evidence that in 2013 the Rousseff-Temer ticket violated campaign-finance laws. Temer's allies put forth numerous legislative proposals stripping prosecutors of investigative powers and making it easier for judges to dismiss evidence from plea bargains. Supreme Court justices close to Temer have also been reinterpreting the current law to try to remove parts of the investigation from the team based in the city of Curitiba and to give them to friendly judges elsewhere.

Meanwhile, representatives of the old political class have denounced Lava Jato for violating civil rights by limiting the leeway that defense lawyers used to have to keep clients out of prison. Prominent criminal lawyers and college professors in a similar vein have likened the plea bargains at the heart of Lava Jato to torture, and other maneuvers have included smear campaigns against judges and prosecutors. Lula's PT has also mobilized a vast network of left-wing allies in the United States, Europe, and Latin America to make the case in the international press that Lava Jato is a politically motivated plot by organized right-wing forces in Brazil—some have even claimed that the U.S. Central Intelligence Agency is involved in it—to bring down progressive change.

Lava Jato's biggest test yet will be the Bolsonaro administration. The new president has appointed Judge Sérgio Moro, who embodies the probe, as his justice minister overseeing anticorruption activities. But it remains to be seen whether Bolsonaro will side with Moro when push comes to shove and investigations threaten politicians in Bolsonaro's governing coalition.

The four factors above contribute to a situation in which Brazilian democracy remains subject to, in the words of Supreme Court justice Luís Roberto Barroso, an "oligarchic pact."[15] Oligarchic politics of this kind are best defined as political dynamics under democracy that oppose, make difficult, and retard meaningful popular participation in politics. As the comparative politics literature on democratic transitions emphasizes, Brazil's oligarchic establishment was dominant in the transition from authoritarian rule and in the system that resulted from it.[16] To the degree that Brazil has seen higher levels of popular unrest, rising frustration among the people with their representatives in Congress and the executive should not necessarily be seen as a threat to democracy, but as a symptom of a more fundamental crisis: the betrayal of democracy by the governing elites.[17]

None of the factors above can on its own explain the paucity of polarization in Brazil. Nor does this analysis claim to have mastered the precise causal chain linking the rules that govern the country's democracy to low levels of polarization. But any satisfactory answer as to why levels of polarization remain low in Brazil must grapple with these factors.

Consequences

U.S. and European analyses of political polarization usually highlight the negative, destructive potential of political polarization.[18] This is understandable, given the hollowing of the political center in many established northern democracies, as well as the increasing difficulty of achieving compromise and consensus, the rise of radical parties on the right and left in some European countries, and ultimately the rise of political exclusion and violence. But in Brazil, the problem is not too much polarization but too little of it: voters have a hard time differentiating between party programs.

Consider the presidential contest between Bolsonaro and Haddad in 2018. The former ran a campaign filled with angry denunciations of everything and everyone but thin on substance. To be sure, Bolsonaro presented himself as the candidate of "law and order," but he did not offer a detailed template for what his policies would be once in power. Haddad, in turn, did present a more left-leaning party manifesto for the first round of the vote, but he quickly ditched this program for a more centrist one in the run-off. Low polarization in this sense is a problem, as politicians rarely flesh out clear policy programs to which voters can hold them accountable. What the case of Brazil highlights is that there is a positive dimension to political polarization—that which is useful to strengthen the quality of democracy, an overlooked feature of the polarization debate in much of the existing literature.

The absence of polarized political conflict may be related to the dynamics of oligarchic politics. An oligarchic political system leaves little if any room for programmatic politics, favoring instead a political class that as a whole has no firm commitment to party programs because of the joint presence of formal institutions and informal practices that militate against accountability. Reduced polarization in the Brazilian context has coexisted with political parties that for the most part have no true programmatic identity and therefore struggle to mobilize the popular support needed to resist capture by particularistic interest groups.[19] When voters think that "all parties are the same" and that "all politicians are crooks," their disillusionment with the political status quo can fuel the rise of a Bolsonaro. In this context, higher degrees of polarization may encourage greater citizen engagement and programmatic politics, in which voters have a clear sense of their choices.

Remedial Actions

Brazilian politics would benefit from increased partisan polarization if such polarization could help improve the accountability of the political class to voters and encourage the development of stronger parties less prone to elite capture. Democratic politics are built on clashing ideas, dissenting opinions, and party-mediated conflict. Polarization, of a degree at least sufficient to distinguish parties along clear programmatic lines, can thus be a counterweight to oligarchic politics.

In recent years, initiatives to clean up Brazil's political system have focused on reducing the number of parties in the legislature, reforming campaign-finance laws to lower the cost of political campaigns, and barring candidates who have been convicted by Brazilian courts from running for office. But no progress was made toward what would be the most radical change of all, namely the adoption of either smaller district sizes or single-member districts. To make matters worse, recent reforms have actually increased the ability of parties to rely on public campaign funds, a measure that further reduces their accountability to voters. Moreover, the new rules banning private corporate donations to political campaigns lack the teeth necessary to curb the extensive use of backroom deals. And while the creation of a new performance barrier for entry into the legislature will indeed shrink the overall number of political parties, the reform redistributed the remaining seats not to the largest parties but to the smaller ones. As a result, the system will have a smaller number of parties but will remain fractious.

These existing initiatives, however, likely will not be able to counteract the effects of the numerous institutional arrangements that mitigate against partisan and ideological polarization. Practical measures to increase positive, democracy-enhancing polarization in Brazil would include reforms to reduce the number of political parties represented in parliament, encourage them to form ideologically coherent blocks, and give them a stake in the success of the government. The causes of antiestablishment feeling and low polarization lie in the rules that shape Brazil's political system. If these rules are not fundamentally altered, the system will maintain low levels of accountability of politicians to their voters.

Brazil needs profound reform in the realm of legislative-executive relations, the kind of transformation that requires replacing old rules and institutions with better ones. Unfortunately, there are no influential groups at this moment putting forth proposals for this type of reform. Most importantly, Brazilian members of Congress need to be made more accountable to the majority of the electorate rather than to specific interest groups seeking privileged treatment. Bolstering democratic accountability would require rewriting the electoral rules. The agenda for renewal would also entail a more independent judicial system, in which Supreme Court justices no longer act on behalf of their political patrons and are better equipped to resist pressure from the legislature and the presidential palace. But translating such an ambitious agenda into reality would demand long, sustained debate and painstaking institutional reengineering. It is not something that can be done overnight.

Appendix: Measurement Techniques

POLARIZATION DATA

This paper uses the polarization measurements proposed by Alban Lauka, Jennifer McCoy, and Rengin Firat.[20] See, as an example, figure 9-1, which displays the distribution of a theoretical population of 850 people, using a 0 to 10 left-right scale. The distribution on the left presents a non-polarized environment, where the ideological scores within the population are concentrated mostly in the center of the political spectrum. The dis-

Figure 9-1. **Theoretical Distributions**

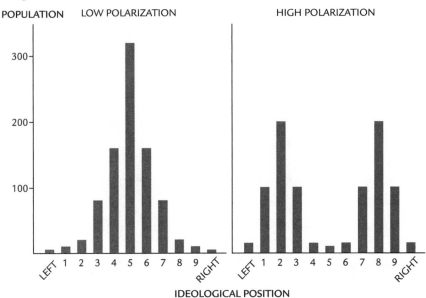

tribution on the right presents a bimodal, highly polarized environment, depicting a situation where liberals compose half of the population and conservatives compose the other half. The measurements here are tailored to capture these ideological positions.

Estimates of the polarization in the Brazilian population come from data from the Brazilian Electoral Study (ESEB), a survey by the Center for Studies on Public Opinion at the University of Campinas at the end of each presidential election. These data are supported by three waves of the Datafolha and IBOPE electoral polls and the self-reported ideological positions taken by Brazilian representatives, collected by Timothy Power and Cesar Zucco in their Brazilian Legislative Survey.[21] The figures below present three measures of polarization: Mass Affective Polarization (MAP), Mass Partisan Polarization (MPP), and Mass Ideological Polarization (MIP).

MAP considers the proportion of respondents that mostly like a given party versus the proportion of respondents that mostly dislike that same party. Figure 9-2 displays the results for the years for which data are currently available. Brazil's MAP was notably elevated in 2002, the first presidential election year ever to have seen a shift in poles, from Cardoso's center-right coalition to Da Silva's center-left one. Afterward, MAP stayed

Figure 9-2. Mass Affective Polarization in Brazil (2002–18)

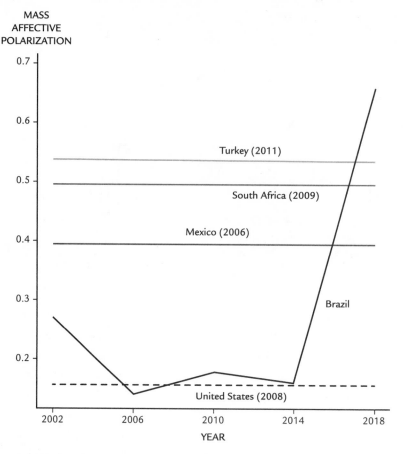

low until 2018. With the election that year, the anti-PT sentiment in Brazil pushed MAP up to 65 percent. The 2018 Brazil election represents the highest point for MAP across the data provided by Lauka, McCoy, and Firat. This finding is consistent with the abovementioned argument that Bolsonaro's election was mostly an emotional reaction against an establishment smeared by corruption scandals.

The second measure is MPP, which consists of the proportion of people that would definitely vote for a party multiplied by the proportion of people that would never vote for that same party. Figure 9-3 depicts the results between 2002 and 2018, showing that Brazilian voters do not hold strong or polarized opinions about parties. This finding reinforces the idea that party

Figure 9-3. Mass Partisan Polarization in Brazil (2002–18)

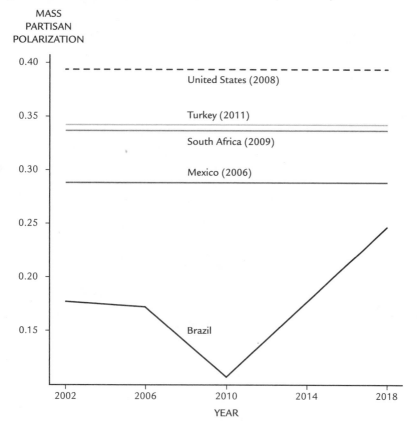

labels are by and large unimportant in the context of Brazilian politics, though party labels have become more important in recent years.[22]

The final measurement considers the traditional left and right self-reporting of ideological position, combining ESEB data with surveys from Datafolha (one for 2016 and two for 2017), and the Zucco and Power members of Congress self-reported ideological positioning, and considering Mass Ideological Polarization Spread (MIPs) and Extremes (MIPe). Figure 9-4 displays the results for the Brazilian Legislative Survey (Power and Zucco), and the ESEB population scores. The population scores are high for the ideological spread. Brazilians situate themselves between center-left and center-right poles, and they seem to have a more or less coherent perception of what their position on the ideological spectrum is and

Figure 9-4. Mass Ideological Polarization in Brazil (1990–2017)

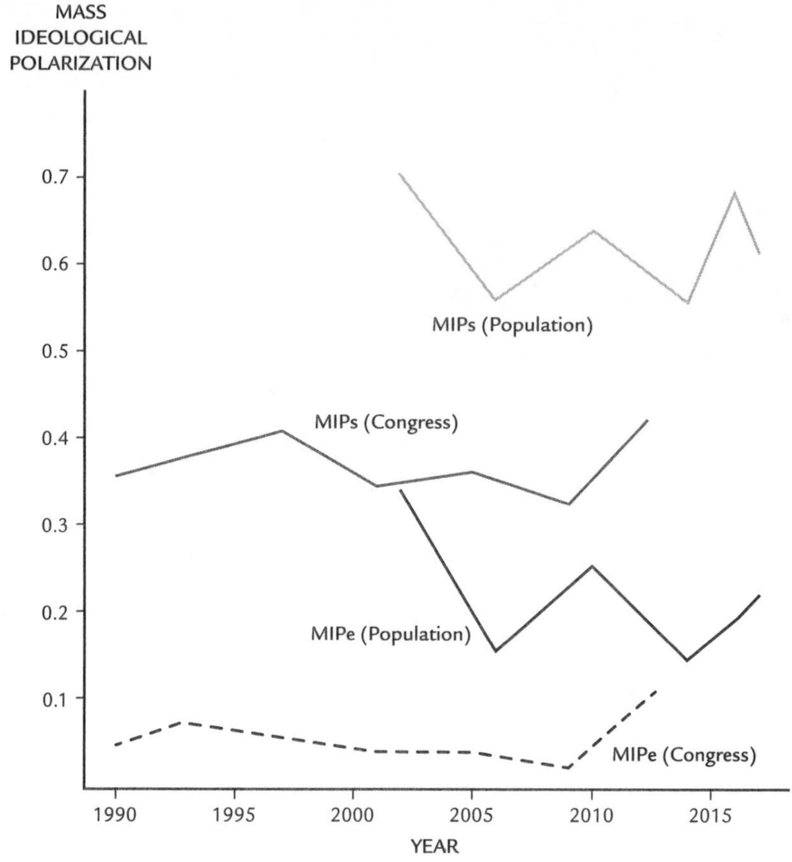

what their position implies. However, focusing on ideological extremes, the electorate presents a consistently lower level of ideological polarization. Both lines peaked in 2002—the first electoral pole shift under democratic rule—but the values are considerably lower than what would be expected in a polarized political environment.

Neither Brazilian governing elites nor the electorate are particularly polarized. Curiously, the Congress is less polarized than the population on both measures. Although Congress follows more closely hypothesized polarization peaks such as the 2013 protests or the impeachment of sitting president Dilma Rousseff in 2016, polarization is considerably less extreme than the (already low) polarization experienced by the population as a whole. In a system like Brazil's, politicians worry more about proximity to the executive as a way of securing the goods that they need to retain power (irrespective of what ideology that executive might espouse) than chasing votes on a robust ideological platform. Crucially, the 2013–14 mass protests and political crisis did not produce a detectable peak in polarization as might have been expected.

IDEOLOGY MEASUREMENTS

As discussed by Lauka, McCoy, and Firat, although polarization is an important cross-country feature, only a few measures are suited for survey data.

Mass Partisan Polarization

MPP is computed using the following formula:

$$MPP = \frac{\sum_{i=1}^{N} Sp_i \times Op_i}{N \times 0.25}$$

Where Sp_i is the proportion of supporters of i and Op_i is the proportion that opposes party i.

Mass Affective Polarization

MAP calculations are performed using the following formula:

$$MAP = \frac{\sum_{i=1}^{N} Lp_i \times Dp_i}{N \times 0.25}$$

Where Lp_i is the proportion that like party i and Dp_i is the proportion that dislike party i.

Mass Ideological Polarization

First, the spread is computed using a formula similar to the standard deviation:

$$MIPs = \sqrt{\frac{\sum_{i=1}^{K} (p_i - p)^2}{25 \times K}}$$

Where p_i is the ideological position, p is the average ideological position, and K is the number of survey respondents. And for the extremes:

$$MIPe = \frac{Lp \times Rp}{0.25}$$

Where Lp is the proportion on the extreme left and Rp is the proportion on the extreme right. For more on these measures, see Lauka, McCoy, and Firat.

NOTES

1. Peter R. Kingstone and Timothy J. Power, eds., *Democratic Brazil Divided* (Pittsburgh: University of Pittsburgh Press, 2017).

2. We thank Andrew O'Donohue for drawing our attention to this analogy.

3. Timothy J. Power, "Brazilian Democracy as a Late Bloomer: Reevaluating the Regime in the Cardoso-Lula Era," *Latin American Research Review* 45, Special Issue: Living in Actually Existing Democracies (2010): 218–47.

4. See data from Transparency International, "Corruption Perceptions Index," (www.transparency.org/cpi2018).

5. Juliano Spyer, *Social Media in Emergent Brazil* (London: UCL Press, 2017).

6. David Samuels and Cesar Zucco, *Partisans, Antipartisans, and Nonpartisans: Voting Behavior in Brazil* (New York: Cambridge University Press, 2018).

7. Alban Lauka, Jennifer McCoy, and Rengin B. Firat, "Mass Partisan Polarization: Measuring a Relational Concept," *American Behavioral Scientist* 62, no.1 (2018): 107–26.

8. José Alvaro Moises, *Os Brasileiros e a democracia* [Brazilians and democracy] (São Paulo: Ática, 1995); Alberto Carlos Almeida, "Core Values, Education and Democracy: An Empirical Tour of DaMatta's Brazil," in *Democratic Brazil Revisited*, ed. Peter R. Kingstone and Timothy J. Power (Pittsburgh: University of Pittsburgh Press, 2008), 233–56; and Corporación Latinobarómetro, "Informe 2008" [2008 Report] November 2008 (www.latinobarometro.org/docs/INFORME_LATINOBAROMETRO_2008.pdf).

9. Matthew Soberg Shugart and John M. Carey, *Presidents and Assemblies: Constitutional Design and Electoral Dynamics* (New York: Cambridge University Press, 1992); Argelina Cheibub Figueiredo and Fernando Limongi, *Executivo e legislativo na nova ordem constitucional* [Executive and legislature in the new constitutional order] (Rio de Janeiro: Editora FGV, 1999); Octavio Amorim Neto, Gary W. Cox, and Mathew D. McCubbins, "Agenda Power in Brazil's Câmara Dos Deputados, 1989–98," *World Politics* 55, no. 4 (2003): 550–78; and Bernardo Mueller and Carlos Pereira, "The Cost of Governing: Strategic Behavior in Brazil's Budgetary Process," *Anais do XXXI Encontro Nacional de Economia* [Proceedings of the 31st Brazilian Economics Meeting], February 1, 2003.

10. Frances Hagopian, *Traditional Politics and Regime Change in Brazil* (New York: Cambridge University Press, 1996); Marcos Otavio Bezerra, *Em nome das*

bases: Política, favor e dependência pessoal [On behalf of the "bases": Politics, favors, and personal dependence] (Rio de Janeiro: Relume Dumará, 1999); Barry Ames, *The Deadlock of Democracy in Brazil* (Ann Arbor: University of Michigan Press, 2002); Timothy J. Power and Matthew M. Taylor, eds., *Corruption and Democracy in Brazil: The Struggle for Accountability* (Notre Dame: University of Notre Dame Press, 2011); Wendy Hunter. *The Transformation of the Workers' Party in Brazil, 1989–2009* (New York: Cambridge University Press, 2010); Benjamin Goldfrank and Brian Wampler, "From Petista Way to Brazilian Way: How the PT Changes in the Road," *Revista Debates* 2, no. 2 (2008): 245–71; and Eduardo Mello and Matias Spektor, "Brazil: The Costs of Multiparty Presidentialism," *Journal of Democracy* 29, no. 2 (2018): 113–27.

11. Scott P. Mainwaring, *Rethinking Party Systems in the Third Wave of Democratization: The Case of Brazil* (Stanford, CA: Stanford University Press, 1999); Carlos Ranulfo Melo, *Retirando as cadeiras do lugar: Migração partidária na Câmara Dos Deputados (1985–2002)* [Musical chairs: Party migration within Brazil's Chamber of Deputies] (Belo Horizonte: Editora UFMG, 2004); David J. Samuels, "Pork Barreling Is Not Credit Claiming or Advertising: Campaign Finance and the Sources of the Personal Vote in Brazil," *The Journal of Politics* 64, no. 3 (2002): 845–63.

12. Large district size generates lower accountability owing to the number of seats in dispute. For instance, in the 2018 national elections, the state of São Paulo elected seventy representatives to Brazil's lower house. In theory, each representative should represent one-seventieth of the electorate, or around 472,000 voters. In reality, however, the top ten politicians out of the seventy represent only half the number of voters (or 236,000). The representative that came out at the bottom of the list received a mere 31,718 votes. To put these figures in perspective, if there were seventy equally populated districts, then someone elected with 31,718 thousand votes would represent only 6.7 percent of the voters in this district. Because the election thresholds are so low, open-list proportional representation in Brazil favors politicians representing small slices of the electorate, who often are prone to capture by special interest groups.

13. Ames, *The Deadlock of Democracy in Brazil*; Jana Kunicová and Susan Rose-Ackerman, "Electoral Rules and Constitutional Structures as Constraints on Corruption," *British Journal of Political Science* 35, no. 4 (2005): 573–606; Torsten Persson, Guido Tabellini, and Francesco Trebbi, "Electoral Rules and Corruption," *Journal of the European Economic Association* 1, no. 4 (2003): 958–89; and Eric C. C. Chang, "Electoral Incentives for Political Corruption under Open-List Proportional Representation," *Journal of Politics* 67, no. 3 (2005): 716–30.

14. Rubens Valente, "Em diálogos gravados, Jucá fala em pacto para deter avanço da Lava Jato" [In recorded dialogues, Jucá speaks of a pact to block Lava Jato], *Folha de S. Paulo*, May 23, 2016 (www1.folha.uol.com.br/poder/2016/05/1774018-em-dialogos-gravados-juca-fala-em-pacto-para-deter-avanco-da-lava-jato.shtml).

15. Tahiane Stochero, "Barroso diz que Brasil viveu 'pacto oligárquico' para saquear o estado" [Barroso says Brazil underwent 'oligarchic pact' to loot the state],

G1, April 2, 2018 (https://g1.globo.com/sp/sao-paulo/noticia/barroso-diz-que-brasil-viveu-pacto-oligarquico-para-saquear-o-estado.ghtml).

16. Hagopian, *Traditional Politics and Regime Change in Brazil*.

17. Yannis Stavrakakis, "Paradoxes of Polarization: Democracy's Inherent Division and the (Anti-) Populist Challenge," *American Behavioral Scientist* 62, no. 1 (2018): 43–58.

18. For an exception to the rule regarding the helpful impacts of polarization in some African countries, see Adrienne LeBas, "Can Polarization Be Positive? Conflict and Institutional Development in Africa," *American Behavioral Scientist* 62, no. 1 (2018): 59–74.

19. Ibid.

20. Lauka, McCoy, and Firat, "Mass Partisan Polarization: Measuring a Relational Concept."

21. Timothy Power and Cesar Zucco, "Brazilian Legislative Surveys (1990–2013)," https://hdl.handle.net/1902.1/14970, Harvard Dataverse, V5.

22. Marko Klasnja and Rocío Titiunik, "The Incumbency Curse: Weak Parties, Term Limits, and Unfulfilled Accountability," *American Political Science Review* 111, no. 1 (2017): 129–48; and Lucas M. Novaes, "Disloyal Brokers and Weak Parties," *American Journal of Political Science* 62, no. 1 (2018): 84–98.

Part V

CONCLUSION

TEN

Comparative Experiences and Insights

THOMAS CAROTHERS
ANDREW O'DONOHUE

As the case studies in this volume illustrate, political polarization is tearing at the seams of democracies throughout the world. Threatening new and old democracies alike, it has emerged as one of the core challenges that are causing political observers on multiple continents to question democracy's future. Understanding polarization deeply is thus a critical imperative. Doing so requires a combination of detailed studies of polarization within diverse national contexts and cross-cutting analyses that draw out comparative experiences and insights from specific cases. The previous chapters have sought to do the former. This concluding chapter aims to do the latter, focusing on the major issues regarding polarization that lie at the heart of this study, including root sources, trajectories, drivers, consequences, and remedies.

Roots

Following the analytic lead of Jennifer McCoy, Tahmina Rahman, and Murat Somer, this study defines severe polarization as involving not just a significant divergence of views and lack of common ground between two opposing political sides, but a division rooted in clashing social identities. The identity basis of the divide fuels the collapse of "the normal multiplicity of differences in the society" into a binary opposition, leading citizens to "increasingly perceive and describe politics and society in terms of 'Us' versus 'Them.'"[1] As noted in the volume's introduction, there is no bright line between cases of severe polarization and cases where significant polarization exists but falls short of that condition. Bangladesh presents a useful illustration. As Naomi Hossain shows in her chapter, Bangladesh has been experiencing acrimonious political competition between two opposing camps for decades. This competition has broken through the country's weak guardrails of democratic norms and institutions, leading to violence and considerable antidemocratic behavior on both sides. It is a case of significant and damaging polarization. Yet political contestation is primarily elite-centric, and the two sides are not divided at the mass level by deep-rooted differences relating to ethnicity, religion, or ideology. As such, intense and destructive though it is, by this volume's definition it falls short of severe polarization.

What kinds of identity divisions are forming the basis of severe polarization in democracies (or recently failed democracies) today? A look at the nine case studies, as well as other examples, highlights two crucial categories: ascriptive identity (an identity that one is usually born into) and ideological identity.

Ascriptive Identity

Two ascriptive characteristics—religion and ethnic or tribal identity—frequently constitute the basis of severe polarization. *Religious cleavages* are central in a number of cases across diverse regions. These divides can emerge between different branches of the same religion, or different religions altogether. Adrienne LeBas highlights Côte d'Ivoire as a significant case of such polarization, in which clashing sides defined along religious and regional lines have fought two civil wars since the turn of the century.[2] Alternatively, a society may be divided between a religious outlook on politics and society versus a more secular one. Turkey presents a vivid case of this latter type. There, the secularist and Islamist camps differ not only in their views on the role of religion in public life, but also in their attitudes toward gender relations and other critical social issues. India is another case, having experienced over the past forty years an intensified and increasingly politicized cleavage between a Hindu nationalist outlook and a more secular one. Egypt's attempt at pluralistic democracy after the fall of President Hosni Mubarak in 2011 dissolved quickly under the white heat of division between an Islamist camp led by the Muslim Brotherhood and the traditional political forces. Rising worries about democracy in Indonesia also concern a divide between a more Islamist and exclusivist conception of politics and a more pluralist one. Differences over the interpretation of Catholic values and their desired role in political life are a factor in Poland's current polarization.

Ethnic or tribal divides also underlie severe polarization in some contemporary democracies. Ethnic-based party life plays a significant role in many African countries, such as Benin, Ghana, Malawi, Niger, and Zambia, but it has generated a sustained binary divide in only a relatively small number of cases.[3] Kenya is an important example, puzzling though it is to many outsiders how two tribes that together represent only about 30 percent of the population can have played such a dominant role in Kenyan politics. In Latin America, Bolivia has been experiencing significant polarization based on ethnic and cultural identity. As Jean-Paul Faguet argues, in the mid-2000s, an accumulating series of political and economic developments resulted in "a tectonic shift that moved the axis of political competition" away from old left-right divisions to "contrasting cultural and ethnic identities," above all those relating to indigenous versus non-indigenous ethnic and linguistic identities.[4]

Ethnic divides are not uncommon in European politics but do not form the basis of sustained binary polarization in most cases. Where ethnic or linguistic divides play a role in contemporary European politics, they more frequently appear in the form of minority communities struggling in their relations with dominant ethnicities or languages, such as in Estonia, Latvia, Lithuania, Macedonia, Romania, Serbia, and Spain. Belgium is an exception to this pattern. Its political life in the second half of the twentieth century was strongly shaped by a profound binary division between Flemish and French speakers. Through a welter of power-sharing and decentralization arrangements, the country has been able to manage severe polarization, though it has endured spells of polarized political paralysis.

Ethnic divides also define Bosnian political life, though they have fostered tripartite rather than binary polarization.

Ideological Identity

It is sometimes assumed that ideological differences within democracies are less prone than ascriptive identities to form the basis of severe polarization. Compromise over ideological differences, like the ideal degree of government intervention in the economy, seems more feasible. Migration in and out of groups divided by ideology also seems more possible than between ascriptive groups divided by religion or ethnicity.

Yet ideological differences can be of such a severity and persistence that they end up forming the basis of two irreconcilable opposing camps with powerful identity characteristics. Ideological divides may focus primarily on economic issues, usually on the left-right spectrum defined by the poles of redistributive, statist economic approaches and strict neoliberalism. Alternately, they may be centered on clashing sociocultural outlooks, involving opposing progressive and conservative approaches to issues such as LGBT (lesbian, gay, bisexual, and transgender) rights, abortion, and immigration. They may also fuse both economic and sociocultural issues. When ideological differences harden into identity divides, belonging to one camp or the other becomes not just about *voting* a certain way or *preferring* certain specific policies, but also about *being* a certain type of person with particular social values and *belonging* to a certain group.

The United States is a notable example of this phenomenon. As Thomas Carothers chronicles in his chapter, first U.S. society, and then U.S. political life, have become harshly polarized since the 1960s between contending progressive and conservative visions of the society. Today, U.S. political commentators describe partisan differences in the country as having become "tribal." This characterization points out the crucial fact that the ideological divide in U.S. politics has become more profound than conventional partisan politics, to the point that ideology has become rooted in identity. Ascriptive identities fortify this ideological cleavage, with both race and religion playing significant roles in defining and sharpening the divide.

In Latin America, left-right divides, usually rooted in opposing approaches to basic economic and social policy, have at different times taken on this identity character and translated into severe polarization. Deep class divisions in societies marked by high levels of inequality and exclusion create fertile ground for powerful ideological differences. The rise of Peronism in Argentina is an archetypal case. Being a Peronist quickly came to be much more than simply a matter of party loyalty or policy preferences but instead a defining social identity. Similarly, after the victory of Hugo Chávez in Venezuela's 1998 presidential election, being a *chavista* or *anti-chavista* became a fundamental identity choice for Venezuelans, fusing ideological preferences with other cleavages along class and ethnic lines.[5] As Andreas Feldmann describes in his chapter, Colombia in the mid-twentieth century descended into a horrendous period of severe and violent polarization between Liberals and Conservatives. In recent years, Colombia has experienced a late echo of this polarization in the divide within the political elite over whether and how to make peace with a leftist insurgent group.

Aside from the United States, severe polarization based on ideology has been rare in wealthy Western democracies since the end of World War II. Ideological differences generally have not been extreme nor translated into irreconcilable identity-based blocs that deny each other's legitimacy. Great Britain in the 1980s experienced a sharper and wider ideological cleavage than most other European democracies, with the divide between Thatcherism and the left-leaning Labour Party of the era. Yet this polarization was contained within the framework of rule-bound political competition, and the ideological inflammation faded in the 1990s as Labour moved toward the center under Tony Blair and the post-Thatcher Conservative Party moderated.

In recent years, however, ideological divides within Europe have been intensifying and taking on strong identity features, especially as a result of gains by right-wing populist parties that reject many elements of the sociopolitical status quo. This populist trend creates a profound ideological fissure, but it also has a strong ethnic element, being driven in part by xenophobic attitudes regarding race and identity. This change is opening the door to severe polarization. In her chapter on Poland, Joanna Fomina charts the unexpected and rapid emergence of severe polarization in that country, defined by a fierce political battle between a right-wing populist party and centrist and center-left forces. Hungarian politics have also become intensely polarized: the dominant ruling party, Fidesz, has denied the legitimacy of its opponents and pursued divisive, scorched-earth political tactics, including rewriting electoral rules in its favor, undercutting judicial independence, and taking over a preponderance of the media.[6] French politics have been roiled in recent years by a deep divide between a right-wing populist party and other political actors. British politics in the past few years have experienced a sharp identity-based divide that is not built on the traditional left-right spectrum of British politics, with the Brexit vote and the resultant squabbles over the appropriate form of exit from the European Union (EU)—or indeed, whether the United Kingdom should leave the EU at all.

Roots, New and Old

The identity roots of severe polarization, whether based on ascriptive or ideological characteristics, are sometimes abiding features of the society in question. In the useful terminology employed by McCoy and Somer, they may arise from "formative rifts" that date to the emergence or re-formation of the nation-state.[7] For example, the divide in India between a Hindu nationalist vision of the country and a more secular, pluralist vision can be traced back to the origins of the Indian state. In Turkey, the cleavage between secularist and Islamist visions of the Turkish state and Turkish society is similarly long-standing.

In other cases, however, the divide underlying the country's polarization may be a relatively recent one or at least may not have seemed nearly as significant in past years. In Poland, for example, the emergence of a bitter divide between a conservative religious and nationalist vision for the country and a more progressive and secular vision caught many Poles by surprise. It surged to the fore when what seemed to be the primary formative rift of postcommunist politics, that between former communists and liberal democrats, faded away. Sometimes, the core divide underlying severe polarization is a complex mix of old and new fissures. The divide that emerged in the United States in the 1960s and 1970s and has hardened in subsequent decades drew on previous ideological, religious, and racial divides, yet it caused these different cleavages to overlap and compound one another in a way that had not occurred before.

Trajectories

The tactics of polarizing political actors and the substance of their agendas frequently play a significant role in shaping the trajectory of polarization, as do the responses of opposition forces. The ensuing cycle of actions and reactions often leads polarization to escalate at a startling pace.

Polarizing Actors and Programs

The analyses of the trajectories of polarization in this volume's case studies highlight the importance of political actors as drivers of the process. Often, severe polarization is the primary product of a political actor—a leader, a movement, or a political party—pursuing a political program that fundamentally challenges the status quo and is rooted in or draws on one side of an identity cleavage. The *tactics* of such challengers frequently contribute to polarization—whether they are confrontational methods, like threats or use of violence and the demonization of opponents, or violations of established democratic political norms. Yet more fundamentally, the political program tends to be severely polarizing because of its political *substance*—it seeks radical changes to the sociopolitical order that the other side of the identity cleavage ferociously opposes. Thus, increasing polarization in India directly tracks the rise of Hindu nationalism as a political force. The rapid acceleration of polarization in Turkey over the past two decades is closely associated with the rise of the Justice and Development Party (Adalet ve Kalkınma Partisi; AKP). The arrival to power in the late 1990s in Venezuela of a leader bent on a radical program of economic and political change brought polarization to a boil over the succeeding twenty years.

It is striking how great a role individual politicians play in such processes. Since the early 2000s, Narendra Modi in India, Jarosław Kaczyński in Poland, Thaksin Shinawatra in Thailand, Recep Tayyip Erdoğan in Turkey, and Hugo Chávez in Venezuela decisively intensified polarization in their countries not just by rooting their political programs in sociopolitical identity and employing specific polarizing tactics, but also by personally symbolizing the identity issues at stake. The broad concept of elite-driven polarization masks how closely associated the emergence of severe polarization often is with one particular political figure.[8]

Why polarizing challengers of the status quo emerge when they do depends upon a host of country-specific factors, from the occurrence of political and economic crises to the emergence of historically contingent polarizing leaders.[9] It is notable how frequently the discrediting of existing political parties—often as a result of economic crises or high-profile corruption scandals—opens the door to polarizing new political actors and dynamics. In Brazil, as Umberto Mignozzetti and Matias Spektor point out, the combination of a prolonged recession and a corruption scandal discredited the political elite and fueled the rise of a polarizing populist figure, Jair Bolsonaro. In Poland, the collapse of the center-left in the early 2000s set the stage for the current process of polarization. In Turkey, the 2001 financial crisis wiped out all the parties that had previously been in parliament and allowed Erdoğan and his newly formed party to win a legislative majority. Hungarian Prime Minister Viktor Orbán built his polarizing narrative about the need for a second revolution in Hungary out of the ashes of the 2008 financial crisis and the implosion of the country's main center-left party. Bolivia's divisive political realignment in the mid-2000s around the country's core ethnic cleavage followed from a crisis of performance and legitimacy facing the country's traditional parties.

Opposition and Reciprocity

The nature of the responses by opposition forces confronted with a polarizing political actor also bears significantly on the degree of polarization and democratic erosion that occurs.[10] Drawing on their comparative study, McCoy and Somer summarize the key strategic choices confronting the opposition as follows:

> Opposition political strategies thus include the basic decisions whether to reciprocate polarizing tactics or to try to depoliticize politics based on inclusive and unifying platforms, whether to compromise and share power with the incumbent or unite against the incumbent, and whether to use electoral and institutional accountability mechanisms (judicial rulings or impeachment proceedings) or extra-constitutional or nondemocratic efforts to constrain or remove the incumbent.[11]

The cases in this volume exemplify a wide range of opposition strategies, ranging from reciprocal and often antidemocratic confrontation by the secularist opposition in Turkey to high-road appeals to the better nature of the society by Poland's opposition in response to the ruling party's polarizing tactics.

The issue of reciprocity brings to the fore the fact that some cases of severe polarization are not clearly driven by one political actor or set of actors carrying out a polarizing program in polarizing ways. Instead, actors on both sides of a major divide may contribute significantly to polarization at different times, even though each side tends to view it as an asymmetric process in which they are trying to behave responsibly, while the other is not. The United States is a telling example in this regard. Both parties have moved significantly away from the political center in different ways over the past sixty years. Asked to identify key polarizing developments in American politics, a conservative analyst might highlight the civil rights movement, the antiwar movement and the presidential candidacy of George McGovern in 1972, and the embrace by Democrats of LGBT rights. In turn, a progressive analyst might point to the conservative rejection of the Equal Rights Amendment, the Contract with America led by Speaker of the House Newt Gingrich in the 1990s, and the rise of the conservative Tea Party movement. As the chapter herein on the United States indicates, even though many scholars argue that the Republican Party has been the primary driver of U.S. polarization over the past three decades, others highlight that the Democratic Party moved significantly away from the center in the 1960s and 1970s. Similarly, in Bangladesh, both of the main political camps have had spells in power and can be said to have contributed to polarization. In Kenya, polarization between the Kikuyu and Luo is also a two-sided story.

Time Frame

Severe polarization often emerges surprisingly quickly given how significantly it reshapes the political and social life of the country involved. It frequently unfolds and entrenches itself in an intense five- to ten-year period of polarizing change. In Poland, for example, political observers inside and outside the country were startled by the speed with which severe polarization set in after the 2010 Smoleńsk presidential plane crash, which shifted the country's political discourse in unexpected ways. Just years after Kenya gained independence in the 1960s, the pattern of polarization between opposing camps led by the Kikuyu and Luo took hold. Venezuela descended into devastating polarization quickly after Chávez's election in 1998. A deep division over Brexit gripped British politics and society with notable speed once the 2016 referendum was called and campaigning for it began. Of course, antecedents to severe polarization always exist; profound sociopolitical fissures do not come from nowhere. Yet the core process of severe polarization often produces a dizzying acceleration of political change, as actions and reactions feed on each other in a quickening spiral.

Although it is relatively rare for severe polarization to emerge gradually through a prolonged process, such cases do occur. In India, for instance, polarization has been coming to a boil since the resurgence of the Hindu right in the 1980s. In the United States, polarization is now more than a fifty-year story. But even in these cases of protracted polarization, there tend to be key periods of intensification. In the United States, for example, societal polarization accelerated between 1968 and 1974, while party politics underwent an especially rapid descent into polarization in the second half of the 1990s.

Additional Drivers

Trajectories of polarization are determined by more than the interplay between the underlying identity cleavages in a society and the tactics and programs of polarizing political actors. Numerous other factors may temper or exacerbate polarization. From the case studies, several stand out as especially consequential—certain elements of political system design, the strength and neutrality of key guardrail institutions, changes in the media landscape, and economic transformation.

Political System Design

Three core features of political system design are particularly important in creating strengths or vulnerabilities with regard to the emergence and impact of polarizing dynamics.

Electoral system design is one crucial area. First-past-the-post systems tend to create two-party systems. Although systematic research on the relationship between two-party systems and the emergence of severe polarization is lacking, it is not hard to see how a system that fosters a two-party landscape may dispose a country to severe polarization more than an electoral system that tends to encourage multiparty formations and coalition governments. In the United States, laments about polarization sometimes suggest a third party or a third-party presidential candidate as one possible remedy, yet the basic structure of the U.S. electoral system presents major obstacles for third parties' electoral success. In Bangladesh, Kenya, and India, first-past-the-post systems have similarly favored binary political formations and raised the stakes of political competition.

All the same, a multiparty landscape does not inoculate a country against severe binary polarization. Bolivia, Poland, Turkey, and Venezuela have all experienced severe polarization despite having multiparty systems.[12] Nevertheless, electoral systems that are more open to the formation of new parties and allow small parties a place in legislative representation seem more likely than first-past-the-post systems to avoid binary "us" versus "them" political divides. In Brazil and Indonesia, for instance, open-list proportional representation has tempered ideological polarization by allowing for the emergence of multiple smaller parties.

Another key design feature is the degree of *centralization of political power*. In societies with significant ethnic, regional, or religious cleavages, a high degree of centralization may exacerbate divisions by raising the stakes of political competition. Turkey, for instance, is a highly centralized unitary state, in which federal officials have amassed even greater authority after the 2017 constitutional amendments. As a result, issues such as Kurdish cultural rights, which might be more easily resolved at the local level, have become polarizing in national politics. In Kenya, despite efforts to create decentralized institutions in the 2010 Constitution, the concentration of power at the federal level—particularly in the hands of the president— has intensified political conflict. In contrast, federalism in India has helped keep at least some conflicts revolving around ethnicity, language, or other divisive identity issues from rising up to become threats to democracy at the national level.

Finally, in the realm of informal institutions, a somewhat counterintuitive finding suggests that *clientelism and corruption*—two decidedly antidemocratic practices—can help mitigate polarization at both the elite and mass levels. In Brazil and Indonesia, widespread clientelism undermines the basis for ideological or partisan polarization, since patronage plays a more important role in winning votes than do party programs. Similarly, endemic corruption in these two countries reduces the importance of partisan divides, as political parties collude, regardless of their ideological orientation, to access state resources. Yet in the long term, these informal institutions provide no guarantee against polarization: they frequently engender popular disillusionment with the political establishment and fuel the rise of populist leaders, who may themselves foster new and harsh political divisions.

Guardrail Institutions

Many different democratic norms and institutions can help limit polarization, or at least its antidemocratic consequences. These include many informal but crucial norms like a tradition of mutual respect and trust, a belief in the value of fair play in politics, acceptance of the legitimacy of the opposition, and an appreciation of moderation and compromise.[13] In terms of formal institutions, two stand out as particularly important: the rule of law and independent, impartial election administration.

Well-functioning, impartial legal institutions—above all the judiciary, but also prosecutors and police—are probably the single most important bulwark protecting democracies against the antidemocratic ravages of polarization. Such institutions keep intense competition among political actors within bounds, arbitrate their disputes fairly and nonviolently, and maintain a neutral ground of fact- and norm-based discourse in the face of polarizing narratives. Countries that make transitions from authoritarian rule to pluralistic political competition yet have only weakly developed rule-of-law institutions are highly vulnerable to the negative consequences of intense polarization.

With its significant history of politically compromised judicial and other legal institutions, Turkey in the 2000s demonstrated this problem. In 2007, major figures within the judiciary, military, and state bureaucracy opposed Erdoğan's candidacy for president on the grounds that he was a threat to secularism, and such interventions fueled Erdoğan's attacks on these institutions. In Bangladesh, the lack of strong, impartial legal institutions has created fertile ground for an escalating cycle of polarization since the 1990s. In contrast, the considerable strength of India's independent judiciary has been crucial to limiting the divisive pressures exerted by the surge of politicized Hindu nationalism in recent years. The prized rule-of-law tradition of Great Britain helped keep the intense partisan polarization of the 1980s from degenerating into violations of democratic norms by the major political actors. Legal institutions in the United States have also blunted the impact of severe polarization, though growing perceptions of the judiciary as a partisan rather than neutral actor are shrinking secure neutral ground on important political issues.

A second crucial bulwark is *strong, independent election administration*, which can help defeat impulses or efforts by political actors to bend electoral rules in their favor, cheat outright in electoral processes, or deny the legitimacy of an electoral defeat. India's strong tradition of capable, independent election administration has been a crucial guardrail keeping polarization within bounds despite significant pressures in recent decades. In contrast, election administration in Bangladesh was significantly compromised in the 1990s and 2000s by the fiercely assertive opposing political actors. In the United States, startlingly weak election administration (for a country with such a long tradition of democracy and sufficient wealth to fund up-to-date state capacity) has become an area of polarized contention and a missed opportunity for keeping polarizing actors within bounds.

Changes in the Media Landscape

Though media landscapes vary widely across democracies, certain common contemporary elements of media development can enable polarization. In the first place, social media and other new media technologies facilitate leaders' direct communication with their followers, allowing them to bypass traditional media that challenge false statements and raise hard questions. Such direct communication helps boost polarizing narratives that are based on systematic distortions of the truth. In addition, social media and other forms of digital information tend to magnify and multiply extreme viewpoints and make it easier for individuals to live within self-selected informational environments that screen out perspectives not consistent with their partisan views. Furthermore, social media and other forms of digital information are more vulnerable to disinformation and distortion coming from domestic political extremes or foreign powers. Polarizing agents are thus able to amplify extreme views more easily.

Economic Transformation

It might be expected that sustained economic growth would tend to lift citizens out of narrow identity-based political viewpoints, de-escalating competition between opposing political camps. Yet this volume's case studies challenge such an assumption. In Kenya, for example, significant economic growth over the past two decades has not pulled national politics away from the basic tribal divide that has festered since the 1960s. Gilbert Khadiagala notes that even as Kenyans have become wealthier, they have stayed attached to the patronage structures around competing tribal groups. In India, the rising middle class produced by the economic growth of the past twenty-plus years may in some ways have actually fueled polarization. As Niranjan Sahoo observes in his chapter, Indians moving into the middle class tend to live more in homogenous urban communities, increasing their attachment to exclusionary, polarizing narratives. It is notable that in Turkey, polarization intensified during years of significant economic growth, after the country began to recover from the 2001 financial crisis. And in Poland, severe polarization emerged in a context of considerable economic success. These case studies suggest that certain common mechanisms—such as urbanization in the Indian and Turkish cases—may mediate the connection between economic growth and polarization; further comparative research is necessary to parse this complex relationship.

Consequences

As noted in the introduction, some degree of political polarization can be positive, especially in new democracies trying to establish stable party systems with programmatically distinct parties. Yet intense polarization, both that which clearly falls in the category of severe polarization as well as lesser but still high degrees of polarization, damages democracy, often seriously.

Political Institutions

Polarization poses distinct risks for all institutions in a democracy. The most important damage tends to concentrate in the judiciary, legislature, executive, and political parties.

A near-constant casualty of polarization is *the judiciary*. Polarization frequently undermines public faith in the institution as a whole, as citizens come to see the courts as yet another theater of partisan politics. More seriously still, the opposing sides may seek to pack the courts with party loyalists or undermine the independence of the judiciary in other ways. In Poland, for example, the ruling Law and Justice Party has implemented various measures undercutting the independence of the courts, though in October 2018 the European Court of Justice ordered Poland to halt certain reforms overhauling the judiciary. One of Viktor Orbán's early major moves after becoming Hungarian prime minister in 2010 was weakening the independence of Hungarian courts. In Colombia, polarization is harming the credibility of the judiciary, as politicians on both the left and right denounce the institution as biased and politicized. U.S. president Donald Trump has repeatedly singled out for criticism specific judges whose decisions have checked some of his divisive acts, such as an early version of his executive order to limit the entry into the United States of people from selected Muslim-majority countries. Bolivian president Evo Morales has politicized the judiciary and undermined its independence to such an extent that Bolivia's top electoral court allowed him to run for a fourth term in office despite a constitutional ban and referendum against his doing so.

Polarization routinely weakens *lawmaking processes* by reducing cooperation across party lines. It can produce legislative gridlock and block governmental policymaking more generally, as is the case in the United States. Yet the severity of polarization-induced gridlock in the United States is unusual in comparative perspective. It results from the atypical design of the U.S. Congress as a legislative institution that requires bipartisanship for effective operation in many essential functions. In most democracies, legislatures are designed to be run by a ruling party or coalition. When polarization deepens, they become rubberstamp institutions that do not engage in meaningful deliberation or review and pass laws along strictly partisan lines. The quality of policymaking tends to decline, and the institution loses legitimacy in the eyes of those citizens who are not sympathetic to those in power. This has been the case in Bangladesh under the Awami League, in Hungary under Fidesz, in Poland under Law and Justice, and in Turkey under the AKP.

In presidential systems, polarization also tends to damage the office of *the presidency*, as the president comes to be seen not as the president of all citizens, but only of his followers. In Turkey, for instance, the constitution used to require the president to sever any party affiliation so that he or she could serve as a nonpartisan figure. Yet after Erdoğan's accession to the presidency in 2014, the office became increasingly partisan in practice, and after the 2017 constitutional referendum, the requirement that presidents be nonpartisan was formally removed. In the United States, President Donald Trump has brought a degree of partisan animus to the presidency that is without parallel in modern American history. The presidency has become a highly partisan institution in numerous other polarized environments, such as Kenya, Poland, and Venezuela.

Political parties tend to experience a generalized loss of credibility in intensely polarized environments. Citizens see politicians engaged in constant fighting, including over the most minor of issues, which fuels public alienation from formal politics. In addition, polarization often allows party leaders to suppress intraparty opposition by emphasizing the need to stick together against a common enemy. The resulting lack of deliberation within parties prevents them from being more accountable to and representative of their constituencies.

The negative consequences of polarization can also extend to a country's *foreign policy*. Shrinking common ground between the major parties can weaken the basis of consensual, mainstream foreign policies that have traditionally reflected a bipartisan consensus. In India, polarization has led to fierce partisan bickering over critical issues such as relations with Pakistan, terrorism, and internal insurgencies. In Poland, meanwhile, the ruling party's reforms to the judiciary have strained relations with the EU, while its polarizing interpretation of Polish history has produced fresh tensions with allies such as Germany and Ukraine.

Society

The negative effects of polarization often extend beyond the political realm, reverberating throughout the society. These consequences are particularly acute in cases of severe polarization, in which divisions have taken firm root at the mass level.

Diminished trust and tolerance across the polarized divide lead to a general decline in civility, and increasing discrimination, hatred, anger, and violence. The cases analyzed in this volume demonstrate that polarizing political rhetoric can cause a rapid rise in intolerance. In Indonesia, survey data show that the 2017 governor's race in Jakarta caused a significant uptick in intolerance toward non-Muslims. In Poland, public support for receiving refugees dropped by approximately 30 percentage points in less than two years, in large part because of the ruling party's anti-refugee rhetoric. Even in polities where the rule of law is comparatively robust, severe polarization can also contribute to violence against minority groups. Poland and the United States have both experienced an increase in hate crime reports over the past several years.

Severe polarization also produces a less cohesive society, and a less effective one in many ways, given the great importance of trust and cooperation in making societies work well. Levels of affective polarization—the extent to which people on one side of the partisan divide dislike people on the other—have become so high in many cases that citizens often feel they cannot peacefully coexist with persons loyal to the opposing side. In Turkey, for instance, three-quarters of the public reject the idea of doing business with someone who votes for the party from which they feel most distant. In severely polarized countries such as Poland, Turkey, and the United States, it is as if the opposing camps have come to inhabit disparate sociocultural worlds, in which they live in different neighborhoods, rely on different news sources, socialize in different circles, and watch different movies and television shows.

Finally, heightened polarization tends to divide civil society, which entrenches and magnifies polarization in the political realm. It reduces the number and importance of societal leaders and organizations that are seen as above politics and as sources of apolitical thinking and action. The absence of such leaders and groups works against problem-solving that requires broad social cooperation.

Overall Political System

Taken together, the political and societal effects of polarization are significant enough to have a determinative impact on the overall political direction of a democracy. Five different macro-level outcomes of severe or at least intense polarization can be identified, presented here in descending order of negativity.

CIVIL WAR   Civil wars frequently grow out of an armed uprising against an exclusionary political system by fighters representing a disfavored ethnic or religious group, secessionist region, or suppressed ideological cause. In such cases, high levels of social and political exclusion spur the rise of polarization, which undermines the possibility of a consensual solution to overcoming the exclusion, contributing to a breakdown in the competitive political process and to civil war. In Colombia, polarization between Liberals and Conservatives fueled years of violent civil conflict in the middle of the twentieth century. As Iraqi political actors struggled to establish a new political settlement in the years after the U.S.-led intervention to oust Saddam Hussein in 2003, intense polarization between Sunni and Shia helped generate several bouts of civil conflict. Polarization over competing definitions of national identity contributed to two civil wars in Côte d'Ivoire over the past twenty years. Sectarian polarizing trends in political life were clear factors in Lebanon's descent into civil war in 1975. In Nepal, the nascent democratic system of the early 1990s was not polarized in a binary fashion, but the separation of the left from the mainstream, and then the establishment of an armed Maoist insurgency, were the result of polarizing trend that pitted the left against the rest. In Turkey, rising polarization between Turkish and Kurdish nationalists since 2015 has caused an uptick in violence in the decades-old conflict between the state and the Kurdish insurgency in the southeast.

MILITARY INTERVENTION   Though military coups have become relatively rare in the post–Cold War period, in several democracies polarization has contributed to militaries' deciding to intervene, usually on behalf of one side or the other. These interventions rarely reduce political tensions and indeed may contribute to deeper polarization when the country resumes competitive elections. In Bangladesh, the military's intervention in 2007–08, though intended to temper polarization, exacerbated the problem by creating a dangerous imbalance of power between the two major parties. In Turkey, similarly, secularists within the military worked to oust an Islamist precursor to the AKP in 1997 but proved unable to prevent Islamists from winning elections just five years later. In Thailand, the military proved so unsuccessful at excluding one camp from politics after staging a coup in 2006 that it ended up staging another in 2014, leading to sustained authoritarian rule. In Egypt, acute polarization that erupted in the immediate aftermath of the fall of President Mubarak in 2011 resulted in a military coup and takeover of political life.

ILLIBERAL ONE-PARTY DOMINANCE In cases of binary polarization, the balance of power is sometimes lost, and one camp becomes so dominant and abuses state power to such an extent that the regime becomes competitive authoritarian or outright authoritarian.[14] This occurs when one of the contending sides goes down the road of violating democratic norms with the intent of seriously constraining political rivals and choking off any alternation in power. Turkey is an example where severe polarization has marked a descent into a competitive authoritarian system. In Bangladesh, polarization has similarly fueled violations of democratic norms and the ruling party's consolidation of power. In Kenya in the 1970s and 1980s, severe polarization led to full democratic breakdown. In Latin America, Bolivia, Nicaragua, and Venezuela all exhibit a pattern in recent years of polarization as a precursor to illiberal one-party dominance. In Europe, Hungary under Fidesz is an example.

MAJORITARIAN DRIFT Polarization can also lead to majoritarian drift. This outcome occurs when one political side championing an exclusive vision of national identity succeeds in pushing the other side to embrace certain elements of that vision. In such cases, majoritarian, often illiberal ideas gain broader acceptance across the political spectrum, and the major parties are unwilling or reluctant to defend democratic pluralism. Along these lines, the main opposition Congress Party in India has distanced itself from religious minorities and the issue of minority rights in its effort to defeat the Hindu nationalist BJP. In Indonesia as well, although polarization has been relatively shallow and episodic rather than severe, even the more secular parties have sought to appease and coopt conservative Islamists who are advancing illiberal views, resulting in a drift toward majoritarianism. This dynamic appears most common in countries where one ethnic, racial, or religious group forms an overwhelming majority of the electorate. Hindus represent over three-quarters of India's population, and Muslims almost 90 percent of Indonesia's.

DEMOCRATIC DYSFUNCTION Some highly polarized democracies avoid the various negative paths outlined above. They remain clearly democratic but become troubled democracies, beset by the myriad negative consequences described, from poor institutional performance to elevated levels of social conflict. Among the cases of severe polarization, the United States has exemplified such an outcome since the mid-1990s, becoming a democracy marked by significant areas of political dysfunction. Poland has as well since 2005, when the populist Law and Justice Party emerged as a major and highly divisive political force. Belgium, too, is a deeply divided society in which severe polarization has produced institutional paralysis and other serious governance problems. Although its polarization has not become severe according to this volume's criteria, Great Britain has become mired in dysfunctional political churning over Brexit. In Colombia, polarization over the 2016 Peace Accord threatens to ruin the prospects of lasting peace. A central question confronting these polities is whether divided, dysfunctional democracy can be maintained as a stable equilibrium or whether the sustained pressure on institutional guardrails and basic democratic norms will begin to undermine the system in more fundamental ways.

Although high levels of polarization are usually damaging to democracy, there is not a strict correlation between the severity of polarization and the amount of democratic erosion. Polarization in India, for example, has deeper roots in society than polarization in Bangladesh, yet India has remained significantly more democratic. The strength of a country's democratic guardrails, as well as other factors, condition the overall impact of polarization. Severe polarization may not lead to a democratic breakdown in a long-standing democracy like the United States, even as bounded, elite-level polarization proves fatal to weakly institutionalized democracies.

Furthermore, even though this volume's case studies demonstrate that polarization often has negative consequences for democracy, polarization may in some instances be fueled by marginalized groups demanding greater political voice and representation. In the United States, for instance, the civil rights movement brought to the fore divisive but necessary debates over racial equality. In such cases, polarization may be a sign that actors within a political system are attempting to deepen democratization. Polarization increased sharply in Turkey in the early 2000s, for example, precisely at a time when democracy had progressed further there than ever before. Continued polarization will almost certainly accompany efforts to challenge the hegemony of Turkey's ruling party and make politics more competitive.

Remedial Actions

The cases in this volume as well as other recent or current cases make clear how difficult it is for countries that have become severely polarized to find a path back to consensus. The translation of partisan views into entrenched social identities that become competing, irreconcilable world views—in which the opposing side is regarded as illegitimate and compromise as immoral—entrenches polarization in minds and hearts. As various social psychologists have analyzed in revealing detail, "tribal" thinking among competing groups in a society leads to the inability to process differing points of view and to accept contrary facts.[15] The accumulation of grievances resulting from polarizing actions and reactions creates deep wells of anger and unwillingness to look for common ground. The collapsing of multiple cross-cutting identity cleavages into one overarching identity divide creates a seductive psychological simplicity that is harmful to a positive broader sense of pluralism in a society. In both Kenya and the United States, the trajectory of severe polarization now spans more than fifty years. In Turkey and Venezuela, polarization is starting to be measured in decades, and it is hard to see a way to return to a broader political consensus within the political elite and the society more generally.

Of course, there are numerous examples of divided countries that have experienced civil war but then managed to achieve reconciliation of at least some type. This is usually not just a fraught process but also a protracted one. Americans are reminded of how long full reconciliation can take by the continuing clashes over issues tied to the American Civil War, which occurred more than 150 years ago. The Spanish Civil War of the 1930s colored Spanish politics and society for the remainder of the twentieth century. Nevertheless, it may be important to bring lessons from postconflict reconciliation experiences more directly into the realm of grappling with polarized democratic politics. A crucial difference of course is that most cases of severe polarization lack the kind of resolution that marks the end of civil war—either a formal truce and peace negotiation or the clear defeat of one side. They are instead much more characterized by stuck politics, stuck psychologies, and stuck societies.

Rather than thinking in terms of reversing or overcoming severe polarization, the most productive approach is to focus on managing and limiting the problem. In countries beset with severe polarization, varied actors are usually attempting at least some sorts of actions in this vein. Their different national contexts notwithstanding, these responses tend to fall into a common menu of remedial actions.

Dialogue and Bridging Efforts

In many polarized societies, civic actors, such as religious organizations, mediation groups, multiethnic or multipartisan civic groups, and universities, have launched initiatives to foster dialogue and greater understanding across the partisan divide. These are sometimes aimed at the elite level—at politicians, officials, and political parties—as is the case for example with efforts to encourage cooperation among parties in national legislatures. Such initiatives may also target society more broadly by teaching tolerance through civic education or facilitating conversations among citizens, representatives of different types of civic or community organizations, thought leaders, journalists, or others about polarizing local and national issues and how to foster greater national and local common ground.

Fully assessing the utility of such initiatives is difficult and beyond the scope of this volume. In certain cases, they clearly have helped ease societal tensions. For instance, regular interfaith dialogue has been able to check communal riots in Indian cities such as Hyderabad and Mumbai in recent years. However, these initiatives almost always face difficult challenges. They tend to be small in scale and to lack deep, sustained support from political elites. At the community level, they face the realities of deeply ingrained sociocultural and sociopolitical cleavages. In Colombia and Kenya, government agencies established to foster societal cohesion lost influence after the administration that created them fell from power. In Poland, politicians have been criticized for using dialogue events as opportunities to advance their own narrative rather than listen to the other side.

Institutional Reform

Given how various democratic design features can work for and against polarization, efforts to reduce polarization sometimes aim for relevant institutions reforms, especially relating to the electoral system and the degree of centralization of political power. In the United States, for instance, the push by some civic actors to spread the adoption of ranked-choice voting and the top-two primary system seeks to encourage political candidates and parties to move to the center. Measures to reverse gerrymandering and reform campaign finance laws may also mitigate certain drivers of polarization. In Brazil, by contrast, with the problem being less about partisan polarization and more about political parties' lack of accountability to voters, recent reforms have sought to reduce corporate influence in politics and the number of parties in the national legislature. Yet as the examples of the United States and Brazil show, such electoral reforms mostly have effects at the margin. The major electoral rules that shape the negative political outcomes—such as first-past-the-post elections for legislators in the United States and open-list proportional representation in Brazil—are deeply entrenched.

Reformers in some countries hope that devolving power to regional and local governments may help reduce polarization. Under the internationally-backed Government of National Unity, for instance, Kenya adopted a new constitution in 2010 that provided for greater decentralization. However, this formal institutional change had little effect in practice, because informal networks of corruption and patronage continued to concentrate power in the hands of federal officials. Belgium has decentralized significant areas of political authority as a way to lower the stakes for partisan political actors, yet it remains deeply divided.

Political Party Reform

Citizens in severely polarized democracies are usually frustrated by the fractious, combative behavior of the main political parties, and they often look for reforms that might make parties less conflict-driven and more productive political actors. Civic groups sometimes try to engage parties in dialogue processes, conciliation efforts, and reforms aimed at renovating stagnant party leadership. Yet party reform is stubbornly difficult. One or both of the main contending political sides often perceives electoral benefits in political antagonism toward the other side. Political party leaders fear looking weak if they participate in dialogue efforts. The bad blood of political divisions and tensions is usually concentrated in the parties and their leadership and is hard to overcome. Reform-minded party activists often are shut out of the main internal party power structures. It is noteworthy that in countries experiencing asymmetric polarization, such as Poland and Turkey, relatively few efforts explicitly seek to reform the political parties that are primarily responsible for rising polarization. In the United States, internal changes in the Republican Party of the past decade or two have mostly contributed to greater rather than lesser polarization.

Broader Political Action

Broader political action in the domains of individual leadership, opposition strategy, and governance structures can also help reduce polarization or at least ease its symptoms. Perhaps the most valuable but also the most elusive type of broader action is enlightened leadership that steps back from polarizing tactics and narratives. An important example is that of Ecuadorian president Lenín Moreno, who since taking power in 2017 has built consensus and strengthened democratic institutions—moving away from the divisive tactics of his predecessor, Rafael Correa, even though the two come from the same party. Prominent politicians can set important examples by exercising self-restraint and putting democratic values ahead of partisan goals. As the case studies in this volume demonstrate, however, it is a challenge to replace polarizing leaders with less divisive ones. Even a military intervention in Bangladesh did not succeed in changing the leadership of the two main political parties.

A second class of broader political action aims to disrupt the binary political divide through the establishment of alternative political parties that eschew polarizing narratives and illiberal values, to provide voters with a less polarizing option. Yet such efforts frequently underestimate how powerfully partisan attachments and strategic considerations discourage voters from switching over to newly formed parties. In Bangladesh, for instance, efforts to create a new party in 2007 that might present an alternative to the two main parties imploded within months. In Turkey, the formation of a new nationalist party in 2017 failed to draw voters away from President Erdoğan's base. Opposition leaders may also form broader coalitions that include a wide range of opposition voices in order to de-escalate a narrow partisan divide. Although this strategy helped the Congress Party and other opponents of the Hindu right win state-level victories in India in 2018, the Congress-led alliance suffered a humbling defeat in the 2019 general elections. An opposition alliance also failed to dislodge the ruling AKP in Turkey's 2018 elections, though opposition candidates fared notably better in the 2019 local elections.

Finally, countries may form governments of national unity to bridge partisan divides at times of crisis. After widespread violence following the 2007 presidential election, for instance, Kenya formed a Government of National Unity that temporarily eased polarization between the two dominant ethnic groups and enabled the passage of a new constitution. Such structures may be particularly useful in helping profoundly polarized societies such as Venezuela find a transition path toward competitive elections and political renovation.

Media Reform

Given the significant role of media in polarization, some remedial actions focus on mitigating the divisive impacts of social and traditional media. In the realm of social media, various initiatives have sought to combat disinformation, block extremist voices, and reduce the built-in tendency of some social media to amplify the extremes. Under intense public scrutiny, companies such as Facebook and Google have taken some steps in this domain to curb the spread of misinformation and reduce the partisan bubble effect of social media platforms. Yet governments have done relatively little to enact regulations that would mitigate the polarizing effects of online platforms.

Some news sites and organizations have responded to polarization by emphasizing substantive, unbiased reporting in contexts where it is becoming rare. In Poland, for instance, a recently created news site seeks to hold both government and opposition politicians at arm's length. In the United States, certain news sources have tried to find ways to expose their readers to alternative viewpoints that they otherwise might be disinclined to take in. In deeply polarized societies, however, many citizens simply do not want to hear or do not listen to unbiased or contrary viewpoints.

Military Intervention

An extreme measure is domestic military intervention to try to put a stop to the pattern of polarization and reset political life on a less polarized basis. The 2007 military intervention in Bangladesh is a prime example. In Thailand, the military also sought to restore national unity and establish a less polarized political system after the 2006 coup, though it clearly favored one side of the country's polarizing divide. As discussed previously, such interventions rarely temper polarization and may result in enduring military rule.

International Action

In some countries, international actors have the power to play a role in attempting to reduce polarization. This was the case in Bangladesh in the late 2000s, when international donors had to decide whether to support the military intervention. In Colombia, Pope Francis has attempted to mediate in recent years and offered to facilitate dialogue between supporters and opponents of the peace accord. In Kenya, the African Union led the mediation initiative that restored peace and created a national unity government after election violence in 2007. And in Poland, the EU has tried to put limits on the current government's efforts to politicize the judiciary.

Though international actors sometimes have an important role to play, their interventions can encounter problems. In highly polarized societies, international actors can be caught up in the partisan fray, as is the case in Poland, where the government has harshly criticized the EU. International interventions can also meet fierce partisan resistance and inadvertently fan the flames of polarization. In Kenya, two politicians indicted by the International Criminal Court used resistance to foreign interference as a key campaign issue and went on to win the 2013 elections. Additionally, as noted in the Bangladeshi and Kenyan cases, international interventions frequently focus on technical and bureaucratic fixes, such as improving the election administration, but rarely alter underlying political dynamics.

Local Research and Study

In countries where polarization has come on quickly and strongly, there is usually only a weak base of knowledge about the exact nature of the problem, its causes, and possible solutions. In Turkey, for example, the subject is not well developed in the domestic research community. The first extensive survey on Turkish polarization was not conducted until 2017. Developing local capacities for such research, and helping researchers inform political and public debates about the patterns and implications of polarization, can be useful. This is also true in countries that are not yet far down the path of polarization, such as Brazil and Indonesia, but where polarization shows worrying signs of increasing. Research that highlights comparative lessons can be essential to understanding the emergence and deepening of divisions that put the country along the path of polarization.

The Challenge Ahead

Taken together, these comparative insights paint a daunting picture of what can without exaggeration be called the global challenge of political polarization in democracies. The authors in this volume have found that almost all democracies have the potential to experience highly damaging polarization. Polarization can grow out of divisions that have existed for many decades but had not become inflamed until recently. These divisions can be of many different types, ranging from religion, ethnicity, and tribe to class and ideology. Polarization can emerge in societies that are commonly regarded as socioculturally homogenous, such as Poland, where 97 percent of the population identifies as ethnically Polish and 87 percent as Catholic. It thrives on identity conflicts in a world that seems to be gravitating ever more strongly toward identity politics. Once it emerges, it often moves fast. In countries as diverse as Kenya, Poland, the United Kingdom, and Venezuela, polarization intensified rapidly, often ratcheting up within a few years of a major event. Yet it is usually slow to recede. In India, Kenya, and the United States, polarization has endured and deepened over decades.

The analysis in this chapter of polarization's drivers points to reasons why this challenge may continue to grow in the coming years. The changes in media landscapes that contribute to polarization, such as the extraordinary fragmentation of public space and deep vulnerability of all types of information to manipulation, have become widespread. It is not clear that economic growth will do much to temper polarization; in some places, it may fuel polarization's rise. Other global trends, such as increased migration flows across borders and the growing transnational diffusion of authoritarian narratives and strategies, are also liable to drive the trend toward growing polarization. And while the consequences of polarization are punishing, they do not necessarily galvanize responsive action by those with the most power to reduce the problem. In key respects, polarization is a type of negative externality—those who play the most significant role in producing it, such as polarizing politicians, mostly benefit from it and bear little of the cost, while ordinary citizens suffer from the degradation of the rule of law, less effective policymaking, and diminished levels of governmental accountability.

Yet as these case studies have shown, polarized polities do respond with efforts to counteract or at least limit the problem. Much more needs to be done to examine which kinds of efforts to mitigate polarization are most effective and under what circumstances. Democracies can be saved by their own capacity for renovation and renewal. They will need to demonstrate this capacity in new and determined ways if they are to swim successfully against the swelling global current of political polarization.

NOTES

1. Jennifer McCoy, Tahmina Rahman, and Murat Somer, "Polarization and the Global Crisis of Democracy: Common Patterns, Dynamics, and Pernicious Consequences for Democratic Polities," *American Behavioral Scientist* 62, no. 1 (2018): 20.

2. Adrienne LeBas, "Can Polarization Be Positive? Conflict and Institutional Development in Africa," *American Behavioral Scientist* 62, no. 1 (2018): 59–74.

3. Matthias Basedau, Gero Erdmann, Jann Lay, and Alexander Stroh, "Ethnicity and Party Preference in Sub-Saharan Africa," *Democratization* 18, no. 2 (2011): 462–89.

4. Jean-Paul Faguet, "Latin America's Shifting Politics: The Lessons of Bolivia," *Journal of Democracy* 29, no. 4 (2018): 93.

5. María Pilar García-Guadilla and Ana Mallen, "Polarization, Participatory Democracy, and Democratic Erosion in Venezuela's Twenty-First Century Socialism," *The ANNALS of the American Academy of Political and Social Science* 681, no. 1 (2019): 62–77.

6. On polarization in the Hungarian case, see Federico Vegetti, "The Political Nature of Ideological Polarization: The Case of Hungary," *The ANNALS of the American Academy of Political and Social Science* 681, no. 1 (2019): 78–96.

7. Jennifer McCoy and Murat Somer, "Toward a Theory of Pernicious Polarization and How It Harms Democracies: Comparative Evidence and Possible Remedies," *The ANNALS of the American Academy of Political and Social Science* 681, no. 1 (2019): 234–71.

8. Dan Slater and Aries A. Arugay, "Polarizing Figures: Executive Power and Institutional Conflict in Asian Democracies," *American Behavioral Scientist* 62, no. 1 (2018): 92–106.

9. McCoy and Somer provide an insightful analysis of the types of grievances that can fuel the emergence of polarizing political actors or actions. See McCoy and Somer, "Toward a Theory of Pernicious Polarization," 240–42.

10. On the role of opposition strategies in mitigating democratic erosion, see Laura Gamboa, "Opposition at the Margins: Strategies against the Erosion of Democracy in Colombia and Venezuela," *Comparative Politics* 49, no. 4 (2017): 457–77.

11. McCoy and Somer, "Toward a Theory of Pernicious Polarization," 254–55.

12. McCoy and Somer suggest that proportional representation electoral systems may be vulnerable to severe polarization particularly when they "employ majoritarian-enhancing mechanisms," as is notably the case in Turkey. Ibid., 261.

13. Steven Levitsky and Daniel Ziblatt, *How Democracies Die* (New York: Crown, 2018).

14. Steven Levitsky and Lucan Way define competitive authoritarian regimes as hybrid "civilian regimes in which formal democratic institutions exist and are widely viewed as the primary means of gaining power, but in which incumbents'

abuse of the state place them at a significant advantage vis-à-vis their opponents." See Steven Levitsky and Lucan Way, *Competitive Authoritarianism: Hybrid Regimes after the Cold War* (New York: Cambridge University Press, 2010), 5.

15. Jonathan Haidt, *The Righteous Mind: Why Good People Are Divided by Politics and Religion* (New York: Pantheon Books, 2012).

Acknowledgments

The editors are indebted to Saskia Brechenmacher, Gareth Fowler, Janjira Sombatpoonsiri, Daniel Stid, Richard Youngs, and an anonymous reviewer for their valuable input and help along the way. We are also grateful to Bill Finan and all of his colleagues at the Brookings Institution Press for their effective work in bringing the book to life. Vital support for this book came from the Robert Bosch Stiftung—special thanks to Sandra Breka and Henry Alt-Haaker there. Valuable additional support came from the Australian Department of Foreign Affairs and Trade, the UK Department for International Development, and the William and Flora Hewlett Foundation.

Contributors

SENEM AYDIN-DÜZGİT is associate professor of international relations at Sabancı University, Istanbul, as well as a senior scholar and research and academic affairs coordinator at the Istanbul Policy Center. She was previously a Jean Monnet Chair of EU Political and Administrative Studies in the Department of International Relations at Istanbul Bilgi University. She holds a Ph.D. from Vrije Universiteit Brussel, an M.Sc. from the London School of Economics and Political Science, and a B.A. from Boğaziçi University. Her main research interests include European foreign policy, Turkish foreign policy, discourse studies, and identity politics. Her recent books include *Is Turkey De-Europeanising?* (Routledge, 2017) and *Turkey and the European Union* (Palgrave, 2015), both co-authored.

THOMAS CAROTHERS is senior vice president for studies at the Carnegie Endowment for International Peace and director of the Endowment's Democracy, Conflict, and Governance Program. A leading authority on international support for democracy, human rights, governance, the rule of law, and civil society, he is the author of numerous books, reports, and articles on these topics. He has worked on democracy assistance projects for many organizations and carried out extensive field research on aid efforts around the world. He previously worked as a lawyer at the U.S. Department of State and in private practice. He has a J.D. from Harvard

Law School, an M.Sc. in international relations from the London School of Economics and Political Science, and a B.A. from Harvard University.

ANDREAS E. FELDMANN is associate professor in the Latin American and Latino Studies Program and Department of Political Science at the University of Illinois at Chicago. He earned his Ph.D. in political science at the University of Notre Dame, and his research interests include forced migration, political violence and terrorism, human rights, and foreign policy, with a focus on Latin America. He is the co-editor of *New Migration Patterns in the Americas* (Palgrave, 2019) and has published in journals such as *International Affairs, Latin American Politics and Society,* and *Third World Quarterly.* He has worked as a consultant with the International Development Research Centre, the United Nations High Commissioner for Refugees, and the Special Rapporteur on Migrant Workers and Members of Their Families of the Inter-American Commission of Human Rights.

JOANNA FOMINA is assistant professor at the Institute of Philosophy and Sociology of the Polish Academy of Sciences, Warsaw. She earned a master's in English from Jagiellonian University, Krakow; a master's in British studies from Humboldt University, Berlin; and her Ph.D. in sociology from the Polish Academy of Sciences. She worked as a migration expert at the OSCE Office for Democratic Institutions and Human Rights and also coordinated the Europe Without Barriers international coalition of NGOs working toward EU visa liberalization for the Eastern Partnership countries. Her academic interests include EU integration, migration and migrant integration policies, Euroskepticism and populism, and democratization in Central and Eastern Europe.

NAOMI HOSSAIN is a senior research fellow in the Power and Popular Politics Cluster at the Institute of Development Studies at the University of Sussex. She earned her doctorate at the University of Sussex studying elites and poverty in Bangladesh, an M.Sc. in social anthropology from the London School of Economics and Political Science, and a B.A. from the University of Oxford. Her work in political sociology specializes in the governance and contentious politics of public service delivery, food security, and gender equality. She has published widely on the political economy of development, education and social protection, women's empowerment, the social and political effects of food crises, and the implications of closing civic space for development.

GILBERT M. KHADIAGALA is the Jan Smuts Professor of International Relations and director of the African Centre for the Study of the United States at the University of Witwatersrand, Johannesburg. He holds a doctorate in international studies from the Johns Hopkins University School of Advanced International Studies. He has taught comparative politics and international relations in Kenya, Canada, and the United States. He specializes in African international relations, conflict management and resolution, African regional and sub-regional institutions, and comparative political institutions. He has written widely on the mediation of African conflicts, Kenyan politics, and governance and leadership in Africa.

UMBERTO MIGNOZZETTI is assistant professor of the School of Social Sciences at Fundação Getulio Vargas, São Paulo. He holds a Ph.D. from the University of São Paulo and is a Ph.D. candidate in the Wilf Family Department of Politics at New York University, where he was a recipient of a MacCracken Doctoral Fellowship. His work concentrates on the fields of comparative political economy and international politics and investigates how collective action problems affect incentives, welfare, and the design of institutions. His current research studies how electoral systems and competition affect corruption, how legislature size influences welfare in Brazilian municipalities, and how international institutions contribute to the deterrence of rogue states.

ANDREW O'DONOHUE is a research fellow at the Istanbul Policy Center and was a 2018–19 James C. Gaither Junior Fellow in the Democracy, Conflict, and Governance Program at the Carnegie Endowment for International Peace. He received his B.A. in social studies from Harvard University. He has conducted research on civil–military relations in Chile, Thailand, and Turkey and on the effect of autocratic constitutions on democratic survival.

NIRANJAN SAHOO is a senior fellow with the Governance and Politics Initiative at the Observer Research Foundation in New Delhi. He earned his Ph.D. in political science from the University of Hyderabad. He was a recipient of an Asia Fellowship at the Ford Foundation, as well as a Sir Ratan Tata Fellowship. At the Observer Research Foundation, he contributes to and anchors studies on democracy, human rights, federalism, electoral reforms (particularly those related to political funding), and cross-cutting issues of exclusion, insurgencies, affirmative action, and inclusion. He is currently working on his third book, *Exclusion and Insurgencies in India*, as well as a co-authored monograph on "Funding India's Democracy."

MATIAS SPEKTOR is associate professor of international relations and chair of the School of International Relations at Fundação Getulio Vargas, São Paulo. He received his doctorate in international relations as well as an M.Sc. in the politics of Latin America from the University of Oxford. He served as Rio Branco Chair in International Relations at King's College London and was a visiting fellow with the London School of Economics and Political Science, the Council on Foreign Relations, and the Wilson Center. His research focuses on strategic choice and domestic politics in foreign policy, nuclear latency in global order, and the sources of and solutions to political corruption. He comments regularly on Brazilian politics and foreign affairs in his weekly column with *Folha de S. Paulo* and in other outlets such as the *New York Times* and *Financial Times*.

EVE WARBURTON received her Ph.D. from the Department of Political and Social Change at Australian National University's Coral Bell School of Asia Pacific Affairs. She is currently a postdoctoral research fellow at the National University of Singapore's Asia Research Institute. She received an M.A. from Columbia University and a B.A. from the University of Sydney. She has previously worked at the Sydney Southeast Asia Center at the University of Sydney and the Earth Institute at Columbia University. Her doctoral research examined the politics of policy change in Indonesia's natural resource sectors, while her broader research interests include Southeast Asian politics, with a particular focus on Indonesia, natural resources, nationalism, inequality, and identity politics.

Index

Abortion, 67, 68, 83, 137, 260

Abramowitz, Alan, 77–78

Abrams, Samuel, 218

Accountability: in Bangladesh, 195; in Brazil, 230, 231, 235, 239–42, 245–46, 279; consequences of polarization and, 284; credibility of political parties and, 272; in Indonesia, 205; in Kenya, 57; as opposition strategy, 264; in Poland, 11, 140, 143; in United States, 78

Advani, Lal Krishna, 99, 100

Affective polarization: in Brazil, 229, 234, 238–39, 247, 248; as component of severe polarization, 7; in Poland, 127; social cohesion and, 273; in Turkey, 27–28; in United States, 84

Afghanistan War, 75

Africa: democratization in, 38; ethnic-based political parties in, 259; ethnic polarization as product of postcolonial states, 43; increase of polarization in, 3. *See also specific countries*

African Union, 49, 282

Ahmed, Nizam, 194

Ahok (Basuki Tjahaja Purnama), 208–10, 216, 219, 220

AKP. *See* Justice and Development Party

AL. *See* Awami League

Alevis, 20–21, 26

American Gridlock (Thurber and Yoshinaka), 77

Amin, Ma'ruf, 210–11, 215, 219, 220

Anies Basweden, 208–09

Antiestablishment sentiment: in Brazil, 229–30, 236, 238–39; in Indonesia, 206; in Poland, 133, 135

Arab Spring (2011), 2–3

Argentina, ideological differences in, 261

Arugay, Aries, 201

Ascriptive identity, 258–59

276; democratic decline in, 219–20; drivers of polarization in, 268; electoral system in, 212, 267; Islamization of society in, 11, 214; overview of polarization in, 2, 8, 259; remedial actions in, 221–22; roots of polarization in, 203–05; severity of polarization in, 216–18; societal tensions in, 220–21; trajectory of polarization in, 206–12; underlying conditions in, 213–16

Inequality, 261; in Brazil, 229, 231; in Colombia, 155, 166; in Indonesia, 213–14; in Kenya, 10, 41–42

Informal institutions, 267–68; in Brazil, 242, 245; in Kenya, 52, 279–80

Institutional integrity: in Bangladesh, 178, 180, 186, 190–91, 195; in Brazil, 230, 233, 239, 242–43; in Colombia, 168; consequences of polarization and, 271–72; in Great Britain, 269; in India, 94, 112–13, 269; in Kenya, 46, 47, 57; to mitigate polarization, 268–69; in Poland, 141, 144; in Turkey, 18, 31, 33; in United States, 78–79, 82–83, 269. *See also specific institutions*

Institutional reform, 279–80

International Criminal Court (ICC), 50–51, 60, 283

International Monetary Fund (IMF), 21

International remedial actions, 282–83

Intolerance: combating through civic dialogue, 278; as consequence of polarization, 273; in India, 94, 98, 107–09; in Indonesia, 210, 213–14, 220–21; polarization and, 2. *See also* Hate crimes and speech

Iraq War, 75, 274

Ireland, lack of polarization in, 4

Islam: Babri Masjid mosque, India, 99–100, 103, 104, 106; in Bangladesh, 182–83; Council of Islamic Scholars (Majelis Ulama Indonesia), 215; divisions in, 20–21, 26, 218, 274; extremism in Bangladesh, 187, 191; hate crimes against Muslims, 108; interfaith marriages and, 108; partition of India and, 97; personal laws in India and, 97–98, 100; polarization and, 2–3, 11; political marginalization in India, 109; political participation in Bangladesh, 191; political participation in Indonesia, 214–15, 221–22; religious discrimination and, 101. *See also* Indonesia; Turkey

Jaffrelot, Christophe, 104

Japan, lack of polarization in, 4

Jews and Judaism, 137–38, 142

Johnson, Lyndon, 70, 71–72, 86

Joko Widodo, 202, 206–16, 218–22

Journalists. *See* Media

Jubilee Alliance, 51–54

Jucá, Romero, 242

Judicial activism, 114–15